A LIFE ON THE PEDALS

A LIFE ON THE PEDALS

Pedro Delgardo

with
Julián Redondo

A LIFE ON THE PEDALS

English edition first published in 2019 by:

Mousehold Press
6, Constitution Opening
Norwich
NR3 4BD

www.mousehold-press.co.uk

Originally published in Spain by El País y Aguilar

under the title *A golpe de pedal*

ISBN 978-1-874739-87-6

Printed by Page Bros., Norwich

CONTENTS

To my wife, Ludi, who has supported and helped me always.

Foreword

I believe that the reason for my friendship with Pedro could well be due to the fact that we like the same things, but we don't hanker after the same things.

This is a book that Pedro simply felt he had to write; he has always been a man to challenge himself, and that could well be the reason behind his success. He was never a conformist. Nor was he ever embittered when he lost; and he knew full well how to enjoy it when he won. Perhaps that is because his life has been full of light and shade, of the deeply felt contrasts between joy and suffering which make you sense happiness and pain more clearly. From a distance Pedro Delgado is an impressive character; close up he is a fascinating one.

"Excuse me, Madam, do you know where the football field is?" Perico in his Banesto shorts and jersey, still damp with sweat after the time trial, had wound down the window of the passenger seat. The lady, wheeling a baby in a push-chair, was looking at Pedro as if the Apostle St James had appeared before her, on horseback.

"Yes, yes," she stammered. "It's near here. Straight on and it's on the right."

That was the year when he won his last Vuelta a España. The time trial ended in Medina del Campo and it seemed that Fede Echave – the rider from the BH team – was going to win it, but suddenly Perico came into the finish and pulverised all the previous times, including Fede Echave's. He won the time trial and clinched the Vuelta, although the next day, on the Navacerrada, Parra and Omar Hernández made it a nail-biting ending.

I remember that from Medina del Campo we went to Ávila, where the next stage was starting. We had a *rendez-vous* on the football field with Paco Lucas, the pilot of the helicopter that was going to take us there. The square in Medina had been teeming with people, thousands crowding around Perico. He got into the Cadena Ser car and 'El Botas' (chief driver for the broadcasting channel covering the Vuelta) set off slowly, but there was such a multitude surrounding the vehicle it was impossible to get anywhere. Never have I seen so many people all around just one person. It was such an extraordinary human mass hanging on to the car that I felt afraid, and the police couldn't cope. I still don't know how, but in a matter of minutes El Botas got us out of there. We found ourselves on the outskirts of the town and saw that lady going past with her baby, possibly the only person there who hadn't gone to see Perico. "I'm hardly going to get a glimpse of him, so far off," she must have thought. Then, all of a sudden there he was in front of her, just half a metre away, with the car window wound down and asking how to get to the football field, with that child-like smile of his with his two top teeth showing.

One thing I always admired in Pedro was his serenity in moments of stress. "How do you do it?" I often asked him. He used to answer me with a smile, like somebody who has a magic formula he doesn't want to divulge. "With tranquility."

"Bugger your tranquility," I said to him, one night in Luxembourg, lying on the bed after the Prologue time trial in the Tour.

Pedro has that magic dust that makes a man shine even in his disasters, because people still love him even when he doesn't win.

I have seen people going crazy at his victories and weep after his defeats, but I have never seen people indifferent to Pedro Delgado. I am sure that you won't be either with this book, these pages, this story.

José Ramón de la Morena Pozuelo

Julián Redondo is a distinguished sports journalist, specialising in football and and cycling. He is President of the Spanish Association of the Sports Press.

José Ramón de la Morena Pozuelo is a radio journalist who has for many years been the director and presenter of the most popular sports programme on Spanish radio.

Chapter 1

Where is Cándido?

'Young people are like plants: by their first fruits we can see what we can expect in the future.'

Democrates

'Hey, Pedro, we're going to Segovia tomorrow to get the contract signed and to bring you a jersey and shorts. Where can we meet?' That was Moncho Moliner down the other end of the telephone.

'I don't know. Wherever you'd like.'

'Well if you don't have anywhere in mind, we could meet in Cándido's place. Is that alright by you?'

'Very good.'

'We'll meet at Cándido's then?'

'Yes, alright, but, this Cándido – where is it?'

'What do you mean – this Cándido, where is it? You're from Segovia, aren't you?'

'Yes, Sir. All my life.'

'And you don't know where Cándido's is?'

'Umm, no. No, Sir. I don't know.'

'You've never been to eat there?'

'No, Sir, never.'

Young Pedro hadn't the slightest idea what Cándido was all about, nor what it meant for Segovia.

"I lived in a totally different world; it had nothing to do with eating in restaurants. My father was a lorry-driver and he worked hard to support his family of four children: Marisa, Victoria, Julio and me. I knew that Segovia was known for its Aqueduct, for the Alcázar, for the Cathedral. But as for Cándido?"

'Well, then, don't you go to bars?'

'No, I don't go to bars. I don't like them.'

"I was just one more kid from the Segovia cycling school and I'd won a couple of small races. Now and again we would go to race in Salamanca, Ávila, Íscar – races between schools. The most important was the Segovia Provincial Championship, which takes place at the beginning of October. I remember that day a blue car arrived from Valladolid with a roof rack carrying bicycles, a man with a fat belly, and everybody saying, 'Oh, they've turned up, and they're going to beat us in the race'."

It was in 1974, the evening before the festival of Pilar. The autumn in Segovia was fairly mild, without that cold wind, the 'biruji'. It was still enjoyable to race, away from the stifling heat of the Castilian summer, and not yet into that dry cold which freezes even the stones. There was nothing particular about the day that struck Moncho Moliner, the driver of that blue car.

"He had a team in the Juvenile class which was full of the best cyclists in Castile and León. The season was coming to an end and I knew that in Segovia there would be a race for Juveniles; so I got hold of three of my friends and we went to take part in it. It was a club race; there were no prizes."

Before the start, Carlos Melero, a professional who was riding for the Teka team at that time, and the best cyclist Segovia had produced, advised Moliner to keep his eye on one of their cadets. 'I have a lad who is really special,' he told him. And he left it at that.

The race involved three or four laps of the circuit of the Pieta, and after a number of attacks, Moliner's boys were out in front with just one other. 'We attacked him left, right and centre,' Moliner recalled. 'One by one and again and again, and still we couldn't drop him. These were three of my very best lads, and they were three years older than him as well.'

This time David could not beat Goliath, and, as expected, it was the boys from Valladolid who won. But the youngster had made a big impression on Moncho; the only problem was trying to get near the lad afterwards, surrounded, as he was, by his friends, who were irate at their tactics and how the race had panned out. 'I wanted to have a word with the lad and Melero tried to get me through to him, but his supporters were calling me a bully, and it was only by a miracle they didn't scratch my eyes out. 'Oh, yes, you can beat him that way – three against one,' they were saying to me. I thought maybe it wasn't the right moment to speak to him. Eventually, when tempers had calmed down a bit, we did have a word and agreed on a later date to meet and draw up a contract.'

* * *

'It was one day in January 1975,' recalls José Miguel Ortega, the journalist from Spanish National Radio. 'My friend, Moncho Moliner asked me to go with him to Segovia for the signing of a contract with a juvenile cyclist – the same lad we had seen, a few months before, fighting like a young lion. Moncho thought the best way to deal with a rival was to sign him up. And there he appeared, the 15-year-old Pedro Delgado, while we waited for him in the entrance to the Mesón de Cándido.'

Many years later, and especially throughout the whole of 1989, Pedro's punctuality was the subject of a great deal of conversation. It is a failing of his which he has no intention of doing anything about. Being on time never was his strength and that particular day was just another indication of it.

Signing for Moliner would be just fantastic. His was one of the best juvenile teams around at that time and it wasn't everybody who got that opportunity. Pedro, however, was pondering over it: "I'm a very rational kind of person; I don't get carried away." And he walked slowly, lost in thought. Without fully realising it, he was walking towards the first day of his future. He did not know how the story would end and he was trying to remember every detail of how it had begun, three months earlier…

"The truth is that I had never planned to take cycling that seriously. For me, it was a week-end hobby, and not even week-ends, because we hardly ever raced. But that was alright; I didn't have any objections to that; I'd always liked sport. I used to run, play basket-ball, hand-ball, volley-ball, everything. I wasn't particularly moved one way or the other by the offer; all things considered, it seemed a perfectly natural thing to do. But my father had intervened: 'My son can join you, provided that he is able to carry on with his studies.' That was his only condition. Once that was accepted, the meeting was agreed."

Pedrito, as he was known at home, was a good, well-behaved little boy, the sort who never so much as broke a plate (unlike his younger brother, Julio, who was the unruly one). He was quiet and did as he was told; and as a youngster he was sensible, without being dull. For that reason he thought about his future, remembering that only a short time ago he hadn't even owned a bicycle.

"José Luis – what a really nice bloke he was. It was he who lent me his bike – me and everybody else in our gang. He was the only one in our neighbourhood who had a bike. I learned to ride on that when I was ten or eleven. My first efforts were somewhat eventful: I don't know quite why, but I crashed into some trees. As the years went by, other kids were getting their own bikes and they used to go off to the river to swim, leaving me on my own and full of envy. I wanted a bike, and I finally got one, thanks to my brother. He was more determined than me and he suggested that I help him with his paper-round, taking *El Adelantado de Segovia* around to its subscribers. First of all we saved, then I convinced Julio that we should buy a street bike, an ordinary little thing that cost us two thousand, five hundred pesetas."

Little by little, without him realising it, cycling was getting into his blood.

"I met a boy at school who was in the Youth cycling club and was winning races. When I went to his house, he had cups and trophies. That was something I hadn't seen before, and for a kid of 13, like me, something to envy. I carried on saving up some money, a bit at a time and I bought a racing bike, or what you might call a racing bike – it was made of steel, but it did have drop handlebars and front and rear dérailleurs. It cost five thousand pesetas, or rather four thousand, five hundred for cash payment. Although I had a good first ride, I did manage to fall off before I got home."

All these things were constantly whirling round in his head on that journey from home to Cándido's, where they had decided to have the meeting. It was barely a five-minute walk but he stopped every three paces.

"I had so looked forward to that day, but they had taken so long to telephone me that I thought they had forgotten about me. Although I wasn't all that worried."

'He doesn't spend time in bars; that's good, very good in fact,' Moliner remarked to José Ortega, while he continued to look at his watch. Like any self-respecting director, he was pleased by young Pedro's reply, although at first he believed he was pulling his leg.

And while the ideas were buzzing round in the head of that hopeful youngster, Ortega and Moliner, frozen stiff by the January cold, were asking themselves other questions in the doorway of Cándido.

'Listen, José, the only feature I can remember about the lad after the hectic end of that race in October is his very pronounced Adam's apple.'

'Don't worry, Moncho. We'll look carefully at every fifteen-year-old we see, and if one of them stands out because of his Adam's apple we'll lasso him.'

It was as cold as charity and after the two men from Valladolid had been standing around for twenty minutes, young Pedro arrived.

'He was smiling broadly,' Moliner remembers, 'but that physical feature which we'd been looking for most was hardly noticeable. His inactivity during the winter months had put a kilo or more on him and, as far as we could see, his distinctive Adam's apple – the only immediate clue as to his identity – was no longer obvious. We told him about that; he smiled again and that little incident made us forget our irritation at the long wait.'

The agreement was verbal and Pedro received his first Moliner jersey and shorts.

"It made me so excited. In the first races I'd taken part in, I'd worn a tee-shirt and track suit bottoms. Of course, I didn't look a bit like a cyclist. Now, with a cycling jersey and shorts, I felt I really looked the part."

Even more so because he was joining a team with a real structure. "I began to see that it was all very serious. I would be going to Valladolid, they told me. This was to get to know the people, and to see a bit more of the world. I had never been away from home by myself before. I had been to Madrid a few times, always with my parents, who took us there every year on the 25th of October, the Feast of San Frutos, the patron saint of Segovia. That day some eighty per-cent of Segovians would be there, shopping in El Corte Inglés. I have memories of the Calle de Preciados and of spending hours and hours going up and down on the moving staircases, which for a provincial boy was a marvellous entertainment.

"On my first journey from Segovia to Valladolid I realised I was scared. It seemed to be much more than going to New York or Australia, because I was all by myself, on the coach, and I felt full of anxiety. After all, I was just a kid."

But he was so pleased with himself that he didn't even worry too much about the bad moments when, on Sundays, returning in the train from Valladolid, the ticket inspector would put a thousand and one obstacles in his way because he wanted to carry his bicycle on a day when they didn't connect the goods-waggon to the train.

Moncho Moliner used to gather his pupils together in the La Farola bar. They had their breakfast there, lunch and their evening meal. They slept in a flat of his very close by.

"It was a flat full of beds where we slept and where we had some really good times. There were eight or nine of us. One of the rooms had a double bed and there were fights to occupy it. It was almost the exclusive property of the older boys."

Just before he turned 16, Pedro was discovering some important aspects of cycling, like team meetings, travelling to and from races, and other fundamentals: team mates and proper races. Every week-end he was growing into this wonderful sport; little by little it was revealing its secrets to him, and its customs, like shaving your legs. "That's something which comes and you don't know when, like the first time you shave your face. As I didn't have hair on my legs I didn't have to think about shaving them. The 18-year-olds, they did; they needed to. At first I thought – as did many others – that it would bring you good luck because some shaved themselves and the very next day

16

they won the race. 'Ah, so that's the secret: you have to shave your legs in order to win!'

"I don't even remember the first time I used the razor, but what I haven't forgotten is the bloody mess I made of myself. And it was necessary, for the sake of neatness; and in those days, it was even said to be necessary because of aerodynamics. The swimmers used to shave their head so as to slide through the water more easily. Hairs produce turbulence and eddies, and without them you move that much better through the air. And it's an advantage when you have a massage. Benefits all round!"

He was the youngest in the squad, almost a Cadet among the tall Juveniles and, unlike De La Fuente, Cabrero or Machín, who devoted themselves entirely to cycling, he continued studying. And he had to bury himself in his books, in case it didn't work out and he would have to finish with the bicycle. Moncho Moliner promised Julio, Pedro's father, that if the boy didn't pass his courses he would do something about it. And he did. 'In 1976 he failed French and I told him, "Look, if you don't pass the re-take in September I'm not taking you to the Montjuic hill-climb." I took out the aeroplane tickets, one with his name on it, and showed it to him, and he didn't pass, so I left him behind. In his place I took the weakest member of the team.'

He wasn't a bad student, but he was definitely a better cyclist. He always stood out because he climbed so well, and at first because he used to attack at every opportunity.

"We were a great team in '76. I don't know how many races we went to that season; what I certainly do remember is that we won all except one. That was when it was snatched away from us, in Segovia. Cabrera, De La Fuente, Machín, Camarillo and I always used to get away together. It was a joy. I would attack from the drop of the starter's flag, always on the climbs, and even if the circuit was flat. I remember in my first Cadet races I used to be out in front from beginning to end. I used to corner flat out and so I won three times. Obviously in the Juveniles the races were longer, and there I suffered some monumental *pájaras**. The

---

* *pájara* - that sudden, unexpected loss of strength that comes usually from dehydration or lack of food. In English cycling parlance – the 'bonk'.

team's tactic was attack, attack, attack, mercilessly. If it didn't work first time, it worked second time. There was no notion of having to spread our effort, and I could end up, as they say, being hit by the man with the hammer."

Learning, learning and gaining experience, that is what it was about. And Pedro Delgado, as thin as a rake at 16 years old, was making real progress through this effort. He paid attention to everything and everybody and immediately assimilated every detail. Whatever he learned came naturally and the rituals of cycling were just a matter of professionalism. A jersey is a jersey and shorts are shorts and they are worn with nothing underneath.

Clothing, feeding and cycling – and a very remarkable kind of cycling it was in the mid-70s in which Moncho Moliner played a distinguished role. He had a passion for the sport and he made sure that his riders lacked for nothing.

"He used to say, 'You have to eat; you have to eat a lot.' I don't understand how I ended up getting such *pájaras* with the amount I was eating, more than a professional. In the morning, almost as soon as you're out of bed, a two-egg French omelette with ham, a beautiful steak, boiled rice and, as it was breakfast time there were some who took coffee with milk, and biscuits, too. That for a 16 or 17 year-old. All that, two and a half or three hours before the race. I don't know how we were able to push the pedals round. And it didn't stop there. Because I was getting those *pájaras*, I carried a lot of food in my pockets, but it didn't make any difference: the sudden weaknesses still kept coming. What was happening to me? I asked. What was happening was that I was eating at the wrong time."

He was eating when he didn't have any appetite, and it was making his stomach heave: the smell of an omelette at seven in the morning; the aroma of a steak; the smoke from the kitchen that drifted into the dining room. But, he was doing all this in order to be a cyclist, in spite of the fact that he had not even planned to join the professional ranks. Leaving home on Fridays, travelling over the weekend, racing some 70 or 80 kilometres, winning or not winning, eating against his will, looking lost

18

through feeling weak – all that was an extraordinary way to enjoy yourself; it also included plenty of room for suffering, which was yet another stimulus.

"Yes, you suffer; you begin to do that as a Juvenile. You learn how to put up with it and to tolerate a bit more pain in your legs. When an opponent takes your wheel, you suffer; when he drops you from his wheel, you suffer; then a streak of courage rises up in you, an emotional, psychological charge that drives you beyond yourself, to stop that man from getting away from you. And in that way, everyday, when you learn to put up with a bit more, and a little bit more, you are teaching your body what it is to cope with difficulties on a bicycle and to carry on coping with them."

Cycling is a risk-laden sport; it is emotional, agonising, riveting, hazardous and merciless. How quickly it sorts out the weakest or the least talented, and reveals them. A football team is made up of eleven players – some to score goals, some to prevent them and others to supply the ball. In a basketball team some are there to pick up the rebounds, some to shoot baskets, others to help, and they are all on a par. In a cycling team, however, even in a team of 16-year-olds, there are already those who are the water-carriers, aware of their limitations and the fact that they are never going to become stars. Delgado never so much as realised any of that.

"I was in a really top team, to the extent that in some races we would end up getting three of us Moliners in a sprint finish. Among the three it would be a matter of deciding who would win. From the beginning I learned that so and so would win today because the race was in his home town so he had to win; tomorrow it would be someone else; and your turn would come round very soon after that. Or they used to say to you:
'Let's see now, how many races have you won?'
'Er, one,'
'And you, how many?'
'Well, three.'
'Right then, the one who's only won one, let him win.'
"As well as being team mates, we were friends. The prizes

were always shared out equally. I learned the discipline that first I had to attack from the very start, even if it meant exhausting myself, so that a team mate could win. I understood that. And to me it seemed peculiar how other directors or other riders would reproach each other, even though they were in the same team: 'You abandoned, so you're not getting paid.' 'And you're only getting paid a half because you didn't do anything.' But I was lucky with my team."

He was indeed fortunate. He did his stint as a water carrier, but only briefly and he never had to confront the fundamental question that confronts anyone who aspires to become a professional cyclist. The question is simple: will I ever be more than a *domestique*? If, face to face with the evidence, the honest answer is no, the solution is simple: 'Either I give it up, because I'm not good enough, or I learn to suffer more, much more, and carry on.'

That was not the case with Pedro. From when he was little he was a winner, the *sine qua non* for total commitment. And he got down to it because he was going to be a cyclist. He kept away from the flatterers and ignored those who told him he was 'born to be a champion' or that he was a 'rough diamond'. Little Pedrito was on the way to becoming Pedro.

At home they didn't ask him for a penny. It was all for him.

"In 1976 or 1977 I was getting 500 or 1,000 pesetas, depending on which week-end. Very often it was money that was used for replacing parts on the bike."

And he was competing nearly every week-end, almost like a professional, although he didn't earn a salary from cycling until 1980. That year he rode as an amateur for the Asturian team Gaylo-Vangüard for 15,000 or 20,000 pesetas a month.

"We were without a team because the previous year, Moncho had pulled out all the stops and achieved his dream of having a team in every category. From the youngest in the Cadets, via the Juvenile and the amateurs up to the top rank of the professionals. For his relatively small business that entailed a huge economic investment and, in the process, he incurred some hefty debts. The result was that the following year he was forced to liquidate all his teams. Some of us, myself included, wanted to keep it going; we tried to find a sponsor but that turned out to be impossible. Some moved on to become professionals. I had offers, but I didn't dare make the jump, because first of all I wanted to get my military service done. So, together with a couple of others, I went to the amateur team Gaylo."

He was now twenty years old; he had seen something of the world, but he had yet to discoverer his true vocation.

Chapter 2

The Tour

*'Do not reproach the genius for his frequent losses, his great
mistakes; they imply vast horizons and great results.'*

Pythagoras

The journalist, Luis Gómez, once explained how he came to
report his first Tour de France, and how he immediately became
addicted to the race.

Certain apparently inexplicable events become somewhat
less impressive when the truth is known. Half way through
July 1983, and against every prediction, a handful of Spanish
cyclists set about making history in the Tour. So it was that
one fine day Arroyo and Delgado finished first and second
in the mountain time trial on the Puy de Dôme and found
themselves just a stone's throw away from leading the
General Classification. The news astonished Spain; in fact,
it was only broadcast with a certain amount of difficulty
because, amongst other things, Spanish TV limited its
coverage of the Tour to a few brief images on the News, and
the number of special reporters barely numbered more than
the fingers of one hand (and that's no exaggeration). The
daily newspaper *El País* had sent nobody there to cover the
race so, when the good news came in from France, they had
to reassess this as a matter of some urgency.

Saturday evening, and a decision has to be made. That's to
say, a staff reporter has to be sent to the Tour, and the need
for haste cuts down the options to the bare minimum. There
were only two people working in the Sports section at that
time of the day. So it's you or me; heads of tails? But no coin
was tossed; the fact is one of us was the boss and the other
(me) was the odd job man.

Hired car, a bit of money, a road map, a few clothes stuffed into a sports bag and … off to the Tour. The man making that journey was an inexperienced sports journalist, who knew nothing about cycling (that's often the way it is) and who, in his whole life, had interviewed just one cyclist. All I could remember about the race was that Bahamontes and Ocaña had won it, that Anquetil and Poulidor were French and that Merckx was pretty well invincible.

And so I arrived at the Tour, at Saint Etienne to be precise. I looked for the hotel where Reynolds were staying and asked for Señor Echávarri, their Director, whom I didn't have the pleasure of meeting. It began badly because I was dealt with by a gentleman who seemed to be from Reynolds. At least that's what I deduced from the logo on his shirt. In fact, he turned out not to be; he was simply a Spanish fan with far too much knowledge of cycling and whom I also didn't have the pleasure of getting to know.

'Now, you've come to the Tour?'

'Yes, I've just arrived.'

'But I don't know you. You're not a cycling journalist.'

'No, I'm not.'

'So, how do you have the nerve to write about the Tour if you don't know about cycling? How come *El País* sends someone who is not an expert?'

'A journalist has to know how to write about anything.'

'The Tour de France is not anything.'

I'll spare you the end of the conversation, but it's not difficult to imagine how the indignation of my interrogator increased. My first contact with the Tour did not bode well

The following day my colleagues came to my assistance. I had no accreditation and they offered me a seat in one of their cars – the Spanish contingent was limited to two cars, a Peugeot 205 and a Talbot Horizon, if my memory serves me correctly. I hung on to the strap of the back seat and experienced my first live Tour stage, ending on Alpe d'Huez. We climbed flat out, descended with the brake pads sending out smoke signals and they deposited me at the finish line. 'Thank you; you are very kind.'

I spoke very little that day; it was as much as I could do to see the corners.

Finally, hours later, I asked for an interview with Pedro Delgado, and another with Ángel Arroyo. Everything went well. Delgado was the first cyclist I'd ever really met, for which reason I have to confess that, quite obviously, I don't count myself among the numerous journalists who, later on and as if they were dealing with a sudden virus, used to compete for the honour of having been 'the man who really discovered Delgado.' Me, yes, I discovered Delgado! ... Delgado and the Tour and cycling.

Some years have now gone by since that journey and in that time I have only ever missed one Tour. I can't help it. Whatever I'm doing, wherever I am, every year I need to get my fix of the Tour. I became Delgado-dependent and later on I couldn't be anything other than hooked; I became an Indurain-junkie. I must confess it: for years now I have been a Tour-addict.

Luis Gómez

P.S. I suspect that someone might try to offer a revised version of my landing at the Tour. A business of skirts, about which my colleagues – from whom I learned a lot about the Tour and with whom enjoyed myself greatly – don't forgive me. I deny everything.

* * *

Luis Gómez discovered the Tour, as well as Perico and cycling in 1983; I (Julián Redondo) had turned up at the Vuelta in 1980 in almost the same way, without having the slightest notion of what it was that people used to call the 'multicoloured serpent'; I was luckier than him – at least I think I was – in that I made my particular discovery of the *Grande Boucle* in 1984, in the company of Joan Manuel Serrat, that great singer-songwriter from Barcelona. The advantage that Luis had over me and thousands of other companions in that blessed profession of journalism, was of a very different kind. His première in France – yes, in a hired car and half-way through the race – happened just as he narrated it, except that he hid one vital piece of information: he was accompanied by a 'blonde' – a description not without some measure of envy on the part of the astonished colleagues who had adopted him. Furthermore, he didn't have the courtesy to introduce her, thereby giving rise to all manner of gossip.

'Look at him,' said those who had come to his assistance. 'Only just arrived and already he's picked up a blonde. He's some fast mover!'

The blonde followed a route parallel to the stages of the Tour in the hired car, and in the afternoons met up with Luis in the Press Room. Her entrance provoked a general silence, followed by irrepressible whispering – 'and I haven't even had time to put a comb through my hair,' murmured the young, and the not so young, whose Tours had always left them deprived of female company. Only at the end of the Tour, and only after putting up with some decidedly frosty comments and looks, did Luis Gómez introduce the blonde: 'This is Luz, my wife; these are some friends of mine.'

*   *   *

Under the guidance of José Miguel Echávarri, at that time Director of Reynolds, and after he'd completed his military service, and served his time as an amateur, Pedro Delgado joined the professional ranks. He was increasingly convinced that he had a good chance of making the grade, but didn't want to close the door on other options. Above all, he needed to mature as a rider, because for him it was never going to be enough just to turn up at the signing-on desk, scribble a signature, and pedal off. He yearned for the sweet taste of victory, although he never imagined that was to be found in France – on the other side of the Pyrenees, there where the Common Market was an established reality while in Spain it still hadn't moved beyond the bounds of the hypothetical.

Reynolds would later acquire a mythical status, but at that time they were just one more Spanish team 'without any serious ambition'. They passed through customs with an abundance of naive hopes, some chorizos from Pamplona, cheeses, ham and a couple of cartons of Rioja. All of this was so they could celebrate the festival of San Fermín on 7th July.

Then, during the race, which was nothing less than the Tour itself, there was something else to toast, as Pedro recalls: "After climbing to second place on General Classification, which I did on Alpe d'Huez, there was a rest day and, furthermore, a press conference. Eddy Merckx, Jacques Anquetil and other important names of cycling were there. Although I've never been a hero worshipper, I had familiarised myself with the men who had been the greats in this race. That was one thing I'd learned the previous year, 1982, when I turned professional."

What were they doing there, these sacred cows, in one of the many hotels, (and not the most hospitable, either) on Alpe d'Huez, on the rest day, hanging about, waiting for some Spanish cyclists? Someone had drawn their attention to an unknown rider from Segovia who had a recent victory in the Tour of Aragón to boast of – a little fact they hadn't picked up on. Pedro again:

"I, on the other hand, although I'd been told that Merckx and Anquetil had a high regard for me, just wanted to get out of there. The telephone was ringing constantly in my room, and all I wanted was to get away by myself, and go for a ride on Alpe d'Huez at my leisure."

And off he went in his tracksuit, three or four kilometres further uphill, so as to think about everything that was happening to him and these most recent events.

Back in the hotel, meanwhile, the Spanish journalists who'd been appointed to cover the Tour were still confused, or rather, surprised by Pedro's reaction at the beginning of the press conference. 'Look,' he had said, 'before going any further, I want to tell you that all of us in the Reynolds team are thoroughly annoyed by the way you are treating us.' One of the journalists who was there, José Luis Benito Urraburu, can still hardly believe it when he thinks back on that incident: 'He was only 23 years old, in just his second year as a professional. "Good God!" we thought. "What a nerve this kid's got".'

There was some history to this discontent. It was not the first time it had happened, as Pedro recalls:.

"Before the Bagnères de Luchon stage in the Pyrenees, I was pretty well anonymous. Until then I hadn't been pestered by any reporters. I do remember that among us riders in Reynolds a feeling of resentment had grown up against the Spanish press. In France we were getting hardly any Spanish newspapers, but the few we did read, which some fans had passed on to us, hadn't left us feeling very pleased. It wasn't that we were doing spectacularly well, but we weren't doing that badly, either. During Stage 3, which finished in Roubaix, we rode all the stretches of *pavé* and I lost nine minutes; Ángel Arroyo, however, escaped, only to fall just as he came into the velodrome with Marc Gómez. In the Spanish press a very curious expression appeared: 'As expected, nothing was seen of the Spanish riders.' All that sort of thing hurts you."

The first clash between Delgado and the journalists happened after he'd finished second on the tenth stage into Bagnères de Luchon on 11 July.

"I'd finished second on the stage, so that was a real piece of news; the special correspondents came to interview me and we had our first set-to. Very serious, and very sure of myself, I fired the first shot.
'Well, what about today, then?'
'Hombre, congratulations. You were second. You almost won.'
'Yes, and what now?'
'Well, nothing, except that we want to interview you.'
'Fine. Well, if I've got to speak to someone, I will only speak to one of you – I'll speak to Chico Pérez;* he's the only one of you who's on our side – and I'll speak to nobody else.'
'Why? What's the problem?'
'It's because of what you write.'
'Well, isn't it true that Laguía, Gorospe and Vilamajó took the first opportunity to go back home?'
'Sure, but what else were they to do? They couldn't continue.'
'Well, that's your opinion.'
"In short, it was a real confrontation. I was very sure of myself,

---

* Chico Pérez, the best-known and most distinguished cycling journalist in Spain during the 1980s.

but I didn't want the disagreement to get out of hand. I only intended to register my complaint. I suppose it was a sign of my strong character."

None of those journalists imagined that, a little later, young Pedro would be ready for them again. He could be short tempered, although he knew how to apologise, when necessary.

At the top of Alpe d'Huez, where the mountain merged with the peerless blue of the sky, Delgado, oblivious to the disturbance which his earlier remarks had caused, continued, with barely concealed delight, to relive his descent of the Peyresourde and the effect it had produced. From then onwards the French called him *Le Fou des Pyrénées* – 'The Madman of the Pyrenees' – because of his demonstration of courage and extreme risk-taking when he was chasing Robert Millar*, whom he almost caught.

"I copied the oval position which later on Graeme Obree popularised when he beat the hour record. Millar had taken half a minute out of me by the summit of the Peyresourde, and as I couldn't turn the pedals any faster I settled my head in the position of a Russian I'd seen during my amateur days. At the finish, when I crossed the line, I was hot on his heels. If only the stage had been a few kilometres longer … It was my first flash of popularity in France."

The images of Delgado descending with his head over the handlebar and his forehead scraping against the front wheel went round the world. He suddenly was no longer an unknown. Who would ever have told José Miguel Echávarri that, when he'd decided to take his team to the Tour.

"They said we were barmy. 'Riding the Tour de France! Whoever had that daft idea?' In the years beforehand, Spanish participation had been an epic failure. A good result was managing to get a top-ten placing on some stage or other; an exceptional performance was not to give in to the toughness of the route; and success was to finish the race.

---

* In 2017 Robert Millar made public his gender transition and change of name to Philippa York. We will use her original name throughout this book, since all the relevant events recalled here took place in that first phase of her life, riding as Robert Millar, among the elite of the professional peloton.

"Echávarri said to us, 'For me, this is incredible. I've been Director for a number of years and they've always looked down their noses at us.' Most of all, men like Peter Post, the Director of Ti Raleigh. He never spoke to anybody, but the day when Ángel Arroyo won the mountain hill-climb on the Puy de Dôme and I was second, he came over to congratulate us – we happened to be staying in the same hotel. He was pleasantly surprised at how well we Spaniards were doing, and especially the two climbers who were totally unknown on the international stage.

"The Alpe d'Huez climb, where I felt in stupendous form, gave a huge boost to my confidence. Even though Van Impe and Fignon stayed with me, I was going like a motorbike. That's when I first thought that the Tour was a race that I could win. That victory I'd had in the amateur Aragón-Béarn, a stage race for amateurs in the Pyrenees, and the fear of going beyond the frontier had been left far behind. So, too, had the snide remarks of almost all the riders and Spanish directors: 'What the hell do you think you're doing here in France?' When they first said it, we'd almost admitted they were right."

When, for example, the Reynolds' Director told his riders that his intention was to take them to the Tour, some of the older ones in the team asked not to be included; they did not want to be in the team. Bernard Hinault was not going to be there – he had problems with his knees after winning the Vuelta – so the race was wide open. Even so, it produced a real dread among those who didn't feel up to it, who thought they weren't fit enough, or didn't have enough spirit even to be seen on television.

"I remember we were saying it would be an adventure. José Miguel wanted to take full advantage of Ángel Arroyo who was riding really well; he had a lot of confidence in the Spanish riders going to the Tour and he needed to demonstrate it.

"My debut was just amazing. What with the stories some of the veterans told me, I didn't really know what was going on. What happened, in fact, was that they made all the team presentations and then a little while later gave the signal for the neutralised start. One moment I'm there, relaxed, taking a drink or picking up some fruit, a typical courtesy of the Tour. Then, suddenly they're off, and in all that chaos of cars, and people speaking French, I scarcely knew what was happening, until Arroyo and I realised that it had actually started. We took off going flat out."

The beginning of a stage in the Tour, just like in the Vuelta or the Giro, is a real stampede. First the vehicles that go in front of the peloton set off, carefully, so they don't knock over any scatterbrain who might be confusing them with the remains of the publicity caravan. It seems to be all shouting, rushing about, with car horns blaring, sirens wailing – apparently a monumental confusion, but it's perfectly orderly because generally everyone knows exactly where they should be. Then come the cyclists.

"I set off fast with Ángel Arroyo, and I'm saying to him, 'Look, they've already started.' We speed up and in the first corner, to the right, chasing hard, we come face to face with a crash – two or three riders down. Oh, no! What a way to begin: falling in the neutralised zone. And the peloton flying. Just when we are on the point of getting back on, another bend, another fall – three or four more riders down. My God, what is this? The speed was crazy.

"If this is the neutralised zone, what's it going to be like when the race gets going properly? Suddenly we realised that we'd passed through the neutralised section. The race really had started, and I was going at a thousand kilometres an hour. A thousand an hour, then bang – a little third or fourth category climb and another three or four riders on the tarmac. I looked at Arroyo, he looked at me, and we say to each other, 'This is worse than ever they told us.' Our encounter with the Tour was truly savage, far more barbarous than we had imagined."

The Tour is a many-headed dragon that goes way beyond anything you might previously have imagined, that is until you manage to tame it, or better still, until with the passing of years you become part of it. There is no discord when you are an appendix to the monster; the symbiosis is almost perfect when, with patience and over a glass of beer you finally get to know the French, who are so self-centred they sometimes even surprise themselves. A good example of that happened to Delgado and Arroyo on the eve of the Puy de Dôme hill-climb.

"I had raced very little in France: I rode the Aragón–Béarn just a couple of times, and the Tour de l'Avenir in 1979. In the hotels, being Spanish meant receiving pretty poor service. Echávarri, who knew the score, hired Francis Lafargue as the team's public relations officer, so he'd have fewer difficulties with the language and would feel more supported."

Lafargue began as an interpreter and ended up becoming a personal organiser for José Miguel, for Miguel Indurain and on occasions for Pedro as well. Because Francis managed things so easily on his home soil, Delgado and Arroyo went off with him on the eve of the Puy de Dôme stage to reconnoitre the climb.

"We had dinner early, as always in France. Around about nine we had finished and Francis drove us up to show us a bit of the route of the stage. It didn't surprise us to see it was full of people who were camping there to watch the time trial, since on race day itself they wouldn't let anybody go up. That was normal in the Tour. Three kilometres from the summit, the hardest stretch of all, we find the road closed by the French police. Francis gets out of the car and speaks to the *gendarmes*. 'We are riders from the Tour,' he informs them. We are carrying our passports which are all in order, and there is no barrier to stop us going on. The situation becomes very amusing. At first we felt a little as if we owned France; we were from the Tour, the cyclists, the heroes of the next day."

"'No. No, you cannot pass,' says the *gendarme*. After offering every conceivable explanation, Francis insists, in his perfect French, and not forgetting his *s'il vous plait*.

'You see, we are from the Tour. This is the Reynolds team car. This is Ángel Arroyo and Pedro Delgado. They will be riding tomorrow and they need to study this stretch of the route, *s'il vous plait*.'

'Nobody goes beyond here. We have our orders.'

'You see how it is; we don't go any further,' Francis turned and said to us. 'If a *gendarme* has orders from his superior, not even a resurrected Napoleon could make him redress matters. If he's that single-minded, that's the end of it.'

"But the funniest part of it was still to come; it was his reaction the moment we were back in the car. In perfectly clear and intelligible Spanish, but with a French accent, the Reynolds' Public Relations Officer expounded on his theme: 'These bloody French assholes who won't let us go up the Puy de Dôme! They just have to be French!'

"Arroyo and I looked at each other and we split our sides hearing such an outburst. It was so Spanish that he must have picked it up from us. After being with us for a couple of weeks he'd listened to so many protests against the French that he'd assimilated them like he was just another Spaniard."

However, going through this business of the Tour, day after day, and getting themselves known changed the way the Spaniards were treated.

"We were no longer discriminated against in the hotels, nor in the peloton. Riding the Aragón–Béarn I definitely remember how we were humiliated. On one occasion they didn't want us to eat in the place where we were lodged before a race; it was my amateur début in France. We were in a hotel along with two other teams – French teams. Several times we asked to be served. 'Yes, in a moment,' they'd say. Then nothing. We watched how the members of the two French teams were being served, but for us it was, 'Yes, in a moment'. We sat and watched as they finished their meal, got up from the table and left. And we hadn't even started. It was a very unpleasant experience. And we never did get our meal. Now, it's not like that at all. The treatment we get in France is wonderful.

"And the same in the peloton. If there was a fall, it was always the 'little Spaniards' who were to blame. We were the ones responsible even though we hadn't been anywhere near it. Everything bad that happened in the race – crashes, punctures, jamming on the brakes – any mistake whatsoever was because of us Spaniards. Then, because of Arroyo's good result – he finished second overall – and mine, it was no longer the Spaniards who got the blame. It became the Colombians: they were the ones who were at fault!"

After the initial shock, and the inevitable period of getting acclimatised, which lasted no longer than getting to the Peyresourde, or at most, to the summit of the Puy de Dôme, the Tour of 1983 was a real breakthrough for Spanish cycling. The much-feared Tour, for which we'd had such misgivings, ceased to be the ogre's cave and, in time, it became the promised land. However, its conquest undoubtedly required a substantial human investment.

Chapter 3

Pájaras

*'On the question of abstinence it is advisable to adopt the
middle way: if our body is very fat we cannot carry it,
and if it is very thin it cannot carry us.'*

Saint Francis de Sales

"I have always said that the first Tour I should have won was the
1983 Tour. Why didn't I? Because just as I have been known for
my lapses of concentration, I have also been notorious for ending
up with some monumental *pájaras*."

Pájaras – bad days, black days which more than once left him
on the edge of a technical knock-out, formed gaping setbacks
in Pedro Delgado's climb towards the top. In 1983, in the Tour
itself, he was struck by the first of these.

"It came as a complete surprise on the day after the rest day.
It's so often said that the rest day can backfire, so you really
need to be on your guard. Afterwards I was told that I should
have ridden the bike a bit more that day, but as far as that was
concerned my conscience was clear: I trained in the morning and
rode the bike again in the afternoon."

It was the 20th of July, very warm and with several mountain
cols up ahead – ideal for a rider like Pedro. He drew strength
from the sun, whereas others were drained by it. Sean Kelly, for
example: the first thing he used to do every morning, as soon as
he woke up, was to open the hotel window and look at the sky.
If it was cloudy or raining he was happy; if the sunlight dazzled
him and he heard the song of the cicadas he just wanted to turn
round and go back to bed. Delgado, however, was the very
opposite; he was driven by solar energy. So, with everything
in his favour and ready to attack Fignon, who had inherited
the yellow jersey after Pascal Simon had abandoned with a

34

broken shoulder blade, he took the starting line brimming with confidence.

"During long, mountain stages we eat food that's easily digestible. The Director and the team's support staff try to make sure the rider is kept well fed, but without his system having to spend too long digesting it. We'd brought from Spain some of those little bottles of mushy food, which they give to people with certain kinds of illnesses; they contain lots of proteins and hydrates and things like that. We picked up a load from the Navarra hospital's pharmacy and carried them with us in the team bus.

"The stage started in Bourg d'Oisans, the village on the lower slopes of the Alpe d'Huez, and headed towards Morzine. Fignon's Renault team were working very hard throughout that stage: 247 kilometres and it seemed it would never end. After the dreaded Glandon and the Madeleine, they were feeling it and we still had the Aravis, Colombière and Joux Plane to climb. I, on the other hand, felt fine and was planning how I was going to attack. One after another, Fignon's team mates were getting dropped, until only Marc Madiot was left, but he was finding it difficult to control the race. Arroyo and I were riding well together and rubbing our hands with delight at how the stage was panning out.

"The last climb of the day was the Joux Plane, a col that has always held good memories for me, ever since I won there in the Tour de l'Avenir, the *etapa reina* of that edition. Now, full of strength, and with my confidence sky high, I was telling myself, 'I'm going to crush little Fignon; I'm going to nail him.' We arrived at the feeding station; it was quick because we were riding very strongly. I ate plenty, knowing that in the last part of the stage I wouldn't be able to, and I remembered the *pájaras* I'd had when I was young through not eating adequately.

"One of the things I swallowed was the contents of one of those little bottles we'd brought from Spain, something that's supposed to give you instant energy replacement. I downed it in two long swigs because the Col de Aravis was rising up immediately in front of us. A few kilometres further on and I noticed that my stomach felt full, very full, blown up. I began to feel uncomfortable. Not in my legs – they felt tremendous. – and as far as the race was concerned, I was still thinking about putting the frighteners on my rivals. But that heavy feeling in my stomach didn't ease. I called José Miguel Echávarri and asked him for an indigestion tablet. He gave me a couple, but they had no effect; I felt just the same. I carried on with the knot in my stomach, feeling worse with every turn of the pedals. We called the race doctor and he gave me another couple of pills.

"We get on to the Colombière and I can't follow the Fignon group. I know my legs are good, but I feel my stomach coming up into my mouth; I want to vomit but I can't, and nor can I cope with the speed of the others. In the end I suffered a *pájara* because I couldn't eat again that day. I am convinced, in spite of the fact that I lost 25 minutes, which was a huge disappointment, that it was not a bad day from a sporting point of view, but that the cause was that blasted food."

A *pájara* in cycling is a sudden, sharp drop in physical capacity which prevents the rider from following the speed of the race. Its aetiology lies in a lack of food or in making an intense effort.

"But I still wasn't making an intense effort. The next day, which was the Morzine-Avoriaz hill-climb, I couldn't help but feel the effects. I'd lost 25 minutes on what had been a hard stage, and inevitably my spirit was low. I'd planned to take the yellow jersey that day: I'd had it within my grasp and I'd let it slip. Even so, I still finished sixth in the hill-climb, ahead of Fignon. Although I felt demoralised, physically I was still going really well.

"Later we confirmed what had happened to me, because it also happened to Arroyo on Alpe d'Huez; Hernández Ubeda and another of our riders also suffered identical problems. Then we knew for sure it was those little bottles, because while Manu Arrieta, one of our masseurs, was preparing our food bags in Morzine he decided to open one. It was extremely dry; he tried it and it was awful; it tasted disgusting. The content of some of them had gone off, as a result of the high temperatures we encountered during that Tour, and as the fridge in the team bus was too small for so many bottles, we had been carrying them in the luggage compartment at normal temperature for three weeks. We came to the conclusion that Arroyo and I lost that Tour because of those little bottles."

Pedro won't have it that a *pájara* was the cause of that bad day, but a real *pájara* is what gripped him in the 1985 Vuelta a España.

"I got the leadership on the Lagos de Covadonga stage, taking it from a very young Miguel Indurain. The following day was another mountain stage which ended on Alto Campoo. I felt full of strength, and with all the confidence that typically comes from having done something important in the Tour, I was thinking that the most difficult part was conquered. In my mind I was putting more time into my rivals. I was riding fluently and climbing easily, and after going over the Puerto de Carmona, we arrived at the feeding station. I took some food and, as in the Tour of 1983, felt my stomach was blown up. I didn't know what had caused it, nerves perhaps. The fact is that when we got to the lower slopes of Alto Campoo, on a gentle rise, I began to feel bad; I had nothing left; I was riding on empty. I lost contact with the main group and it was thanks to Jokin Mújika that I only conceded 3–49. I dropped to eleventh overall. Fortunately for the team, however, Pello Ruiz Cabestany was there to take over the leader's jersey."

A question mark still remains over the origin of this collapse in the 1985 Vuelta, but there have been *pájaras* in his life which cannot be excused by euphemisms. Racing in the Youth section, one day he would get one and another day he wouldn't. His first Director, Ramón Chamorro Moliner, cannot forget the one he suffered on the Puerto de Clavijo riding in La Rioja: 'It was a race for youths and second-category amateurs. We went to Logroño and young Pedro arrived there with a big reputation. He was a major figure in the Youth ranks. I told him before the start to take it easy. "When the whistle blows," I told him, "You just settle in. Full stop. Let Hernández Úbeda and De la Peña take the initiative; they are already amateurs." So what did he do? He did the exact opposite. He heard the whistle, stamped on the pedal and he was off. Úbeda caught up with him, then De la Peña. They had some nine or ten minutes over the rest but in the final stretch of the race, in the middle of the climb, little Pedro had the mother and father of all *pájaras*. I said to him, "Attack now. Be brave! You see? That's the way you'll learn." He gave it a go, but with the *pájara* and everything... Finally Ubeda won.'

As he was still studying, Delgado only did a little training, so it occurred to him that when he was taking part in a race he would go like a rocket the moment he got on his bike.

"I attacked on the flat; I didn't wait for the climbs; I attacked on any terrain. I would make a number of really big efforts, with the result that I ate at all the wrong times and – of course – I ended up with a *pájara*."

José Luis de Santos, who was a team mate of his at Banesto, used to double up with laughter every time he remembered what happened to Pedro at the pre-season training camp in Estepona in 1992. 'How he went when he saw a crisp packet in the road. He threw himself on it, looking for whatever might be left inside it, as if he'd never eaten in his life. All he got was the husks from some sunflower seeds.'

"As a rule," Pedro insists, "out of the ten days at the training camp, two would be devoted to a long-distance ride. My training, on the other hand, has always been a bit slower, more individualised; when the others did a ride of 200-kilometres or thereabouts, I would do somewhat less. The normal thing was to go through the hills around Ronda; we'd ride out towards Algeciras and at a certain point we'd turn to the right and make a lap that would take us through Ronda, then San Pedro de Alcántara and back to Estepona again. I carried that map in my head, and when we had covered a good part of it, rather than getting into the car, I'd take a right turn that shortened the route. I went with José Luis, who comes from the same place as me."

The first mistake was that in looking for a shortcut they had to drop down a pretty long mountain descent. At the bottom they asked a fellow on a donkey for the main road. He told them that the road was good for Estepona.

"After ten kilometres of climbing, it seemed like it was never going to end.
'José Luis, do you know I haven't got any food with me and I

haven't eaten anything. Have you got anything with you?

'Yes, a bit of cake.'

'Well, come on then. Let's eat it. Right now I'm famished'.

"We polished off that mouthful, but had nothing left for later. We carried on climbing the hill, pedalling rather more slowly.

"We arrived at a summit and I thought that now there would be the descent into Estepona, but in a few kilometres we were climbing again. It was not that it was particularly steep, but it was so long. It went on for ever.

'José Luis, listen. I've got a terrible *pájara*.'

'If you want, we'll stop and call a taxi.'

'No, hombre, no. We'll hang on. Estepona can't be very far away. The only thing is, no cars have gone past.'

'And we haven't seen anybody. Nor any villages.'

Pedro's hunger was getting worse. His companion didn't have that problem because he'd eaten.

'José Luis, how are you doing?'

'Not bad. I'm going OK.'

'Well. I've got a terrible *pájara*. It's like I'm climbing up a wall. We should have stopped in the village back there and got a taxi.'

'Listen, if you want we'll stop for a while.'

'No, no. If we stop it'll only be worse. Let's carry on. We'll come across a car soon enough and we can get it to stop and see what we can do'."

That's how things were when Pedro thought he'd seen the answer to all his problems. "I saw there was a packet of potato crisps lying in the middle of the road. I jumped off the bicycle to get it. I picked it up and what do you think I found? It was full of the shells of pipa seeds. I nearly died I was so disgusted, and José Luis, he died. He died laughing.

'I've never seen you like that,' he said. 'I'll have something to tell my grandchildren. I've never seen you in that state.'

"In the end we did reach the top of the puerto, dropped down the other side and just about made it back to the hotel in Estepona. What a *pájara*. And I only managed it because José Luis was pushing me. When we turned up at the hotel, the rest of the team were already there, and that was after riding fifty kilometres more. I could have eaten a whole cow as soon as I arrived."

Pedro's eating habits, once he'd turned professional, were very different from those morning beanfeasts he enjoyed as a youth. Altogether more rational, modern, more of the nineties, and more constrained. Yet he found that sporting directors, experts in race strategy, and erudite on cycling, didn't always share the same views on the matter of diet. There was often a good deal of confusion, and some quite arbitrary tastes.

"On this whole matter of food, I have always been very much struck by certain – let's call them – obsessions that different people in cycling have. One masseur in the Orbea team, Nicolás, better known as Nico, was anti-orange juice. I had some terrible fights with him. Always, before starting breakfast, I felt like a good glass of freshly-squeezed orange juice. Well, what a fuss he kicked up; he said that orange juice was terrible for the stomach, that it would disagree with us. It got to the point where if ever he saw an orange on the table he would remove it."

The opinions of Rafael Carrasco, at one time Director of Kelme, also became well known. "This man could never look at a tuna and olive salad. If any of the team's personnel allowed it, he would run the risk of a real bollocking. I'm no lover of olives, but I can't imagine what problems a sportsman is going to get from a few olives or a bit of tuna. But it gets worse. Javier Mínguez, who was Director of Amaya, and Faustino Rupérez from Kas were bitterly opposed to croissants. They just wouldn't permit them on the breakfast table. They said they were disastrous. And then the facetious joking that went on when, as often happened, the teams found themselves in the same hotel. Some stuffed themselves on croissants and then went on to win the stage – how they ragged the riders in the teams of Mínguez or Rupérez. So, when the directors weren't looking, the croissants were passed round under the table."

Miguel Moreno, also had his particular food fads and Pedro discovered one of them. "It was during the Vuelta a España of 1989 and he was Director of Zahor. One morning he saw me eating muesli. He didn't make a big issue of it because I wasn't in his team, but, since we've always got on well, he did, shall we say, give me a ticking off. 'What do you think you're doing, eating muesli?' he said. 'All it does is give you wind; it's just air and it doesn't nourish anything. You won't get anywhere with that stuff. Look at my riders – they're eating rice, meat…'

'Miguel, last year I won the Tour de France in spite of the muesli.'

'That was pure luck; you couldn't have eaten it every day.'

'I stuffed myself on it!'

"Then his riders told me that if a packet of cereals appeared on the table the masseurs would be hauled over the coals. Like I say, obsessions."

Muesli with yogurt or with orange juice, cooked ham, soft cheese, an omelette or fried eggs, ham, white rice or pasta – that's usually the cyclist's typical breakfast, finishing up with a coffee with milk and with toast and jam, plus anything else that's left. Croissants, perhaps? Dinner is substantial: salad or vegetables, pasta for carbohydrates – energy, the rider's fuel, and grilled meat or fish. But, be careful: something has to be clarified..

"Grilled fish, provided we are in Spain, but elsewhere, both in Italy and in France, fish is usually baked in the oven, which is then not the same at all. All this is washed down with a glass of red wine – always to be recommended. When we travel abroad, whether it be to France, Italy, Holland or Belgium the masseurs are responsible for bringing a couple of cases of Spanish wine. Abroad, you often have no idea what they're giving you."

And in the musette, water, mineral salts, sweet little fruit tarts, energy tablets, ham, cheese or jam sandwiches with nuts and figs. And when the weather is cold, or hot, take care: "Our nursemaids, the masseurs, prepare bidons of hot tea sweetened with honey and sometimes with a drop of cognac if the day is particularly cold. Some also believe they have a remedy against the heat. In 1981, when I was doing my Military Service, Eusebio Unzue, my Director, gave me something to combat the stifling heat during the Vuelta a Murcia. It was incredibly hot and there was nothing that would slake your thirst. But he gave me something before the Cresta del Gallo so I'd be able to face the final kilometres of the stage. It tasted strange. I don't know if it was cold beer laced with champagne; it didn't taste too bad, but on the descent from the col I fell – perhaps my reflexes were starting to slow."

During his time at PDM, the Catalan gin distiller, MG, became a co-sponsor of the team. They put on the market little bottles called 'Gin-Lemon', and 'Gin-Orange'. Needless to say, these were always available, cold, from the team bus fridge, especially for Pedro's team mate, the Swiss rider, Stefan Mutter, who took a real fancy to them. "When it's really hot, riders try to hydrate themselves one way or another. I would get hold of a bottle of water or a Coca-Cola, but Stefan discovered Gin-Lemon, and as soon as the stage was finished he'd head towards the refrigerator, straight as a die, and knock one back in a couple of swigs, get a bit tipsy and turn up very merry at the hotel."

Drink, food, and what about sex? Is that taboo? No, that's something different. "Everybody has his own opinion about those pleasures, just like they do about certain kinds of food. There are some directors who are opposed to wives and girl friends appearing at races; there are others who wouldn't refuse them entry when they drop by the hotels so long as they maintained some modesty; and there are others who don't want to see them at all. And then there are those who don't allow their riders to remain alone with their wives and girl friends; they place a chaperon in the room so they don't succumb to temptation."

The Italian sprinter Mario Cipollini used to claim that if he made love two or three times on the eve of a very important stage, then got through a couple of bars of chocolate to counteract his inevitable feeling of relaxation, he'd win the following day. The Pole, Zenon Jaskula, when he heard that, came back with the pointed question: 'Oh, yes? And how many Tours have you won?' To which Cipollini replied, 'And you, how many have you won with your six months of abstinence?'

Geographically closer, although more distant in time, Federico Bahamontes had his own formula: 'one month before the Vuelta and two months before the Tour – no sex with the wife.' Put those two together and what it amounts to is that Fede spent five months devoid of love-making.

"It's said that making love has very little effect on your physical performance; I'd go further: I believe, as do many doctors, that it does more good than harm. A cyclist accumulates a lot of tension in his body during the course of a race, and meeting up with his wife or girl friend gives him a feeling of relaxation. An hour or two with her helps him recover and leaves him mentally refreshed. And if there is also a sexual relationship, well there's no reason why it should reduce his power. At worst the rider is under a lot of stress and it is very possible that the wife or girl friend can help to relieve that. The Vuelta, like the Giro and the Tour are all three weeks of racing, plus the days beforehand when the team is getting together. Things should be left to happen as they will, and not trigger awkward situations, either for the rider or the director.

"To sum it up, I'd say sex, yes, but in moderation; whatever you find necessary. It's not going to make a couple of third-category climbs on the next day's stage rear up like the Gavia and the Tourmalet. The curious thing, although it has no relationship with sex, is that as a kid I discovered a formula for winning – at least, sometimes. From January onwards, in school we organised a party on Fridays to raise money for the end of course outing. The following day, the Saturday, there was usually, although not always, a race. I used to worry about doing too much on those Fridays in case I couldn't perform well in the race. What really came as a surprise was that on three consecutive week-ends I won, after these parties. They were house parties and I said to myself, 'Look, it's only now, when the course is ending, that you find the secret of winning bike races.' It was a pity that the classes were coming to an end, and the parties; I had found the secret, and it promised a really brilliant year. Seriously though, the thing is to find the right balance – and that applies equally to sex."

As the Catechism warns us, the world, the devil and the flesh are the three enemies of man's soul – but what of the cyclist, and what about vegetables? The eating habits of certain cyclists constitute a mortal sin, most especially when it is proven that recalcitrant vegetarianism leads to physical ruin. So, what about meat and vegetables? Some, like the Scotsman, Robert Millar, kept themselves healthy with a mixed diet: vegetarian yes, but without spurning a good sirloin steak now and then. More complicated, and sad was the case of the Swiss rider, Urs Zimmermann. "He followed a vegetarian diet absolutely to the letter, and managed to shed eight kilos. He was a tall, solidly built rider, and he could afford to lose a bit of weight. The result was third overall in the 1986 Tour, together with a truly outstanding season which included victory in the Critérium International, and Dauphiné Libéré, second in Paris–Nice and fourth in the Tour of Switzerland. As he had gone so well, he made the following rule of thumb for himself: 'If I climb so well having lost eight kilos, then I will be flying if I lose another two or three.' The following year, 1987, was a disastrous year for him; he didn't ride at all well, and because of the severe diet he imposed upon himself he began to have problems with his stomach, and with his general state of health. So, in the matter of diet, too, you have to act with a measure of wariness."

More recently the matter of body weight was one of the battles which Miguel Indurain had to fight; however, there was an occasion when he had a scare as a result of taking his diet to extremes. "Miguel was a tall, strong rider and José Miguel Echávarri was always concerned about finding ways to improve his physique. After making a number of trips to Italy, he was told that he was a very heavy rider and that to improve his performance in the mountains he would need to reduce his weight, something which, as we saw, he managed to do, and it enabled him to climb very much better. But also, in his case, we came up against the extremes. Planning for the Giro in 1994 it was clear that Indurain was obsessed with the Mortirolo, an enormous puerto in the *etapa reina* of that edition which came near the end of the race. I don't know if his weight always had to be around 78 or 79 kilos for him to be at his best, but he became obsessed with the idea that if he got it below 78 he'd be better able to climb the Mortirolo (which is the steepest puerto I have climbed in my life: it is twelve terrible kilometres long). Miguel was brilliant going over that mountain. Pantani led over the top;

Miguel caught him on the descent; and behind them Berzin, in the pink jersey, was dropped.

"The two of them then collaborated and put more time into the Russian, but when Miguel began to climb Valico di Santa Cristina, a not particularly demanding puerto, towards the finish at Aprica, he realised that his reserves were exhausted. It was not that he couldn't follow the rhythm Pantani was setting, he could barely keep upright on the bike. He was suffering a serious *pájara*, and the reason, in my view, could well stem not only from the difficulty of the stage, but also from his lack of reserves of body fat to deal with the cold on the Stelvio (the first climb of that day). As a result he found himself with nothing left to enable him to stay alongside Pantani. If he had, he could well have won his third Giro. To perform at your best you do have to watch your weight, but never to the extent of neglecting your intake of food according to the conditions prevailing on the day."

Chapter 4

1985

*'Circumstances make clever men become what
they want to be, and able to beat weak men.'*
Mariano José de Larra

"What a day! You can't see anything in this mist. Yes…there's a
bend to the right coming up now. Then a short straight, and next
it's a sweeping curve to the left, and that goes into a long straight.
When it's like this, with practically zero visibility, or when it's
raining, you don't have time to admire the countryside. You take
the obvious precaution of slowing down, because of the road
surface and the mist, and your imagination inevitably runs wild.
That's what happened to me. Nowadays, I live with one foot on
the top of the aqueduct and the other in the capital of Spain, and
often, when I drive between Segovia and Madrid, over the Puerto
de Navacerrada in the middle of a downpour, I can't help but
remember the Vuelta of 1985."

It was the middle of May and freezing cold. What a foul day,
'a real dog day', the cyclists were thinking on that stage which
would finish in Segovia. It was raining, it was hailing, it was
misty – the best place to be was indoors. But business comes
before pleasure, and for some business meant finishing the
Vuelta, come what may. For others it meant trying to win it, and
for one, Robert Millar, it meant making sure he didn't lose it.

"In the mist and with hail falling you have to be careful on
any descent, but I know that road. I know it by heart. I know the
bend that's coming up now, and the one after that. I could almost
ride it with my eyes shut.
"Pepe Recio escaped between Cotos and the false flat leading
to the Navacerrada. I tried several times myself on the climb,
but I was watched too closely and couldn't get away. Before
the start of the descent the mist came down, accompanied by

46

hail. And a saying came into my mind, a saying very much of that period: 'If you can't escape going up the climb, you have to try going down, especially when the road is particularly dangerous.' And that day it most certainly was. Two hundred metres before beginning the drop, I attacked with everything I'd got. In that dense mist it was very dangerous to ride flat out, but that's what I did, seeking out the painted lines at the side of the road to give myself some margin for error and not ride straight off the road. I didn't turn my head to see whether or not anyone was following me; any distraction could have been fatal, causing me to fall and ruining the escape. I didn't hear anything and I had the impression that at last I was on my own. A little later I was closing in on the man who had got away – Yes, there you are, I can see you. Now I've got you. And I saw the chance of getting away, alone, but then, as if by magic, the mist disappeared.

'Come on, Recio! Come on, let's go! The two of us. Let's go together'."

The rider from Kelme puts himself on Pedro's wheel and at first he collaborates. He takes two or three turns on the front, but he's not committed to the mission. It seems the break will now have to do without him. Out of the corner of his eye he looks at who he has for company. 'I was doing alright when I was on my own,' he seems to be thinking, and he holds back. Recio is a fine rouleur, a man who climbs well in the medium mountains; he has class and endurance and he'd be a real danger in a sprint finish for the stage win.

"We are getting close to Guadarrama; there are several kilometres of flat road ahead of us. He doesn't take a turn.
'Recio, come on! Come through!'
'No.'
'Come on, man. This is a good break.'
'I said, no.'
"He wasn't going to budge, and I'm getting ready to climb El León. I'm very conscious that I'm not going to get any help from him.
'I won't help you because you'll drop me as soon as we start climbing.'

'No, man. I won't. Look, first let's make the gap bigger, then we'll see.'

'No, because I want to win the stage, and if I have to pull, then you'll drop me on the climb. No, definitely not!'

"After the effort I'd had to make to get away I decided to carry on setting the pace myself. On the hardest part of the climb I did try to drop him with a couple of changes of rhythm, but he managed to hold on to me. Going over the top I was thinking that second place on the stage would be better than nothing. So I encouraged him to take some turns. I knew that close to the finish there was a steep climb where perhaps I could surprise him and win the stage.

"I had given up all hope of winning the race itself; I was more than six minutes down – 6-13 to be precise – on the leader, Robert Millar. My initial intention was two-fold: on the one hand, fight for the stage win; on the other, make the leader's team work non-stop so as to improve the chances of my team mate, Pello Ruiz Cabestany, who was currently third overall."

Radio-Vuelta was constantly providing up to date news about how the stage was unfolding. The directors had their ears glued to their car radios and were making decisions on the run. At that point in time the news was that the two escapees had scarcely got more than a couple of minutes advantage half-way up El León.

"This is fine, only it's a shame that I'm with Recio, who is a much better sprinter than me. He's going to beat me for the stage. I don't know if it's going to be worth it in the end, because I'll finish second. On the other hand, it is on my home territory, Segovia, and that's not bad. Never mind. I'll try to get this cooperation going between the two of us and force those behind us to work."

They went over the top two and a half minutes up. From that point onwards Pedro and Recio shared the work unselfishly between them.

"The thought of winning the Vuelta never passed through my head that day; I only dreamed of winning the stage in front of the people in my home town. To my mind, what was to happen that day was simply impossible. From the summit of the Alto de El León all the way to Revenga I had the chance to reflect back on how the race had unfolded.

"The 1985 Vuelta a España had begun in Valladolid and would finish in Salamanca. We'd left the River Pisuerga behind us and arrived in Orense, and that day a young, first-year professional, took the leader's jersey; his name was Miguel Indurain.

"He was riding for Reynolds, the team I'd been with until the previous year. I was now with Seat-Orbea, a young, recently-formed team, which had signed me because they wanted to take a step upwards in the ranks of professional cycling. On the stage to the Lakes of Covadonga, the sixth stage, I took the jersey away from Indurain. That day I let myself profit principally from Robert Millar's generous work, because in my mind was the memory of losing the jersey on that very same climb twelve months earlier. I concentrated solely on following the pace set by the Scotsman; it was he who forced the selection and it was he who was responsible for dropping the danger men. I held my fire until the last third of the climb, after we'd passed the hardest ramps of La Huesera and the Mirador de la Reina; only then did I make my final attack.

"I took the stage and GC leadership, but I lost that the very next day on Alto Campoo, conceding more than three minutes. From then on the race became increasingly complicated. You cannot, or rather you should not, lose that kind of time in the Vuelta, because it is going to be very difficult, if not impossible, to recover it."

In the Seat-Orbes team, which Txomin Perurena was directing, the picture had changed radically: Pedro Delgado had lost his chances by dropping down the GC order while Pello Ruiz Cabestany, the team's alternative leader, had strengthened his position and was wearing the yellow jersey. They would have to play his card, even if they did so with a certain lack of conviction: he was still very young, possibly not consistent over a three-week race, and there were plenty of mountains still to be negotiated. Would Pello cope? Nobody really knew and that feeling persisted.

"I had to support him; he was now the leader. However, in its heart of hearts, the team was not confident that Pello would be able to maintain his grasp on the leadership of the Vuelta. A number of times Peru, the Director, told me that I ought to try to pull back some of the time I'd lost. So, on the stage to Penticosa, taking advantage of a number of attacks by Fabio Parra, I made a counter-attack, a couple of kilometres from the finish, and got away on my own. I was roundly criticised for that, for not staying at the side of the leader, my team mate."

The leader of a cycling team holds a sacred position; if needs must you will die on your bicycle for him, particularly when he is the race leader. If his strength gives out, you must ride with him, next to him, giving him encouragement, pushing him if necessary. You must protect him, support him, give him refuge in those moments when he feels he's on his own – moments that can be everlasting when a lack of oxygen turns legs into blocks of wood and the brain becomes incapable of thinking. Or when everything turns to pain, and regret and the will falters – 'What am I doing here? I'd rather be anywhere but here!' At these moments you must guard the leader's back and his spirit unless he says otherwise.

"Many people suggested that I attacked Ruiz Cabestany, among them, José María García, who was the most important radio reporter at that time. He tracked me down by telephone, hours after the finish of the stage, and had me live on the radio. It produced my first confrontation with him.

'You behaved very badly,' he blurted out. 'What you did is not what team mates do. How could you think of attacking one of your own team?'

'I didn't attack Pello; I attacked the other riders,' I replied. 'I could do it because beforehand I remained at his side, suppressing any urge to rebel in the face of a situation that was prejudicial to my GC position,'

'You attacked the leader who happens to be your team mate.'

'I didn't counter-attack until we were a couple of kilometres from the finish line and I did it to control his most dangerous enemy, Robert Millar, and I only did it after checking that Pello was OK.'

50

"García kept on like that , so eventually I said to him: 'Look, José María; you are a journalist; you know more about journalism than I do; by the same token, let me have a different opinion from you when it comes to cycling, because I am the cyclist.'

"Then he started to rant at me – how dare I say something like that? And I'm waiting down the other end of the telephone for him to let me get a word in. We are live on radio and I'm waiting for him to give me a chance to say something, because I want to defend myself against him bullying me like that. Then we were cut off. I was left hanging, with the phone in my hand. I came away feeling very upset."

When this episode took place, the Vuelta was far from finished as far as Pedro was concerned.

"I recovered a bit of time in Panticosa, and the race, at least for the time being, wasn't lost. Where it became difficult for me again was in the time trial at Pal. I lost 1-17 to the winner, Pacho Rodríguez, a Colombian who, under the guidance of Javier Mínguez, was turning out to be the revelation of this Vuelta. On stage fourteen I was caught out in the echelons, and on top of that I had a fall. And then in the time trial at Alcalá de Henares, which Pello won, I rode very badly and lost 2–15. Overall I was then 6–13 down on Robert Millar, who had become race leader. With just two days left, the Vuelta had ended as far as I was concerned. So in the Segovia stage, when I escaped with Recio, I was only looking to benefit Cabestany, or at best put on a good show in front of the people from my home-town."

The stage from Alcalá de Henares had started out at a frantic pace. Peugeot, Millar's team, didn't let anyone get away. "Everyone was controlling the race and controlling each other so as to defend whatever position they had achieved, and at so much cost, after three weeks of racing."

When the split did occur Millar found himself without any team mates. Ahead were Recio and Delgado, and behind, in the favourites' group, nobody reacted. Millar, isolated, was waiting for some movement from his more immediate rivals, and was allowing himself to be carried along. Roland Berland, Peugeot's *Director Sportif*, remained unperturbed. He seemed to be thinking that it was the men who were fourth and fifth on GC, Gorospe and Dietzen respectively, who should have been most worried by Pedro's escape; they were the ones who should have been making a move.

Pacho Rodríguez, who'd begun the day second overall, 10 seconds down, and Pello, third at 1-15, made a number of attacks on El León, but they got nowhere: the yellow jersey reacted immediately each time. 'The die is cast,' Robert Millar must have thought when, as they reached the top of the puerto, the last major obstacle of the race, he gave a show of typical British chivalry – that mixture of stiff upper lip, satisfaction and a sense of fair play. As leader and patron of the race he rode over to Pello: 'I congratulate you; you have been a worthy rival. There will be many more Vueltas for you in the future, but this one is mine.' And he stretched out his hand. 'I am grateful for having come up against an opponent such as you, because it makes my victory all the more worthy.' And he said the same to Pacho.

Pello was just amazed: 'What is this guy thinking about?' Millar's Director had been so convinced that he had the race won that when he wanted to react, he couldn't; the race had slipped from his grasp. He couldn't even find anybody to cooperate with him to reduce the gap, since in imposing such an iron-like grip on his two most immediate rivals, he had allowed others to go clear. These were the very riders who might well have lent him a hand – men like Sean Kelly or Eric Caritoux.

Some distance ahead of all this, the pair of escapees, now working together, are increasing their lead. So, an insignificant gap of two minutes goes out towards three minutes, then to four, and at Revenga, 15 kilometres from the finish, it is around five and a half minutes.

"It was then that I became aware of the situation; I realised what was happening. The Vuelta, previously so far out of reach, was turning once more in my favour.

'Recio, you're going to win the stage, for sure, but I'm going to win the Vuelta. We must give it everything here.'

'Well, come on then. We give it everything'."

José Recio's change of heart had come about after discussion with his Director, Rafael Carrasco, who didn't just encourage him, but demanded a major effort from him. 'Collaborate, Pepe, collaborate, because today we're really going to stir things up. Come on! Come on! Pitch in; today we're really going to make history.'

In the press room, set up in one of the buildings of the DYC distillery, they could barely believe what was happening. The typewriters were now silent. With every passing second the emotion was building up on this penultimate stage of the Vuelta. What had previously been an unforeseen outcome was now looking more and more like a premonition. Restrained silence, and stopwatch in hand, nobody dared blink. It's six minutes now and four or five kilometres still to go. Another 14 seconds and the Vuelta will belong to Segovia. Delgado and Recio finish their bit and bit and the man leading pulls for all he's worth. The second hand turns and never does so short a distance seem so long. But what are Peugeot doing?

"We got into the last kilometre and from then on Recio didn't take a single turn on the front. His doubts about whether I would keep my word appeared to have resurfaced. He was reserving his strength for the sprint with every certainty of taking the stage; I was empty. Some three hundred metres from the banner above the finish line he attacked. I followed him as best I could, but that was all I could do. Recio finished a second ahead of me. From then on it was pure tension. The clock ticked slowly and so many riders were about to finish. That was my impression. I asked for time checks and the latest ones indicated that I was going to take the Vuelta – just. One by one the riders crossed the line; I looked to see if I could make out Millar, but among so many it was impossible.

"Three minutes have passed, four minutes and more cyclists appear and no, still no sign of Millar. My heart is beating quicker than when I was climbing the Navacerrada. Someone tells me that the Scotsman is further behind. It's now five minutes since I crossed the line! God! I didn't know if another two minutes had gone by or half an hour, I only saw riders who had been dropped, and had the impression that the yellow jersey was among them. I didn't know when Millar finished. I learned I had won the Vuelta when they announced it over the loudspeakers.

The shouts from the DYC distillery were heard all the way to Segovia, five kilometres away.

"The following day the headline in one newspaper read: 'Spanish whisky was better than Scotch'."

Pedro Delgado was the news of the day, of the week, of the month, almost of the year, after getting the yellow jersey on the eve of the last day, on one of those stages when nothing ever happens because everyone is controlled. For Robert Millar, the defeat hit him like a shot from a gun. His frustration went so deep that the chivalry he displayed on the top of El León deserted him.

"The next day, he angrily announced to the British press that it was a Spanish coalition that had beaten him. All of us Spanish riders knew that in fact the 'Invincible Armada' had not been brought back to life. His Director lost him the race by not informing him of what was happening and how the time gaps, which Radio Vuelta regularly reported, were developing. Millar could have hooked up with any one of those groups of dropped riders which overtook him in the final 40 kilometres, instead of being so preoccupied with Pacho and Pello. In fact, Pello told me that he didn't start riding until near the end of the stage when it was already too late. As for nationalist alliances, in cycling they are more likely to be anti-alliances, with all the rivalry and squabbles that can exist between fellow countrymen favouring the foreigner. The Peugeot team must have understood that perfectly well because, a few weeks later, they sacked the Director for letting victory in the Vuelta slip through his fingers."

But the Vuelta was not over.

"On the last stage, from Segovia to Salamanca, there was no let up in the tension, despite it being the epilogue. Nerves got the better of more than one rider. The final part of the stage was run off on a circuit through the streets of Salamanca and Duclos-Lasalle, one of Millar's Peugeot team mates, tried to position himself behind me going into every corner. Then in the middle of the corner – always in the three or four most dangerous corners on the circuit – he would come through and try to block me. I'd let him do it, then jump past him on the other side. So it went on till the crowning moment. The winner. The final, definitive winner of the Vuelta Ciclista a España of 1985. My first grand tour podium, and on the top step.

"Spanish Television wanted me to talk live in Torrespaña (their main broadcasting tower in Madrid) but José María García, who was aiming to show off with the hero of the hour, who happened to be me, sent his assistants to tell me that he wanted to take me by helicopter to Segovia where they were preparing a party for me. I still remembered our brush over the Panticosa business so the situation was a bit difficult. I hate people saying that success has gone to a person's head, but at the same time I was still annoyed with García, so I told him of the earlier agreement I had made with the television people and that they didn't want to share me with him, El Butano*. But he was the most powerful man in Spanish radio and he got his own way: I flew to Segovia, and then later, in the same helicopter, I was taken to the television studio."

Luckily, 1985 didn't end for Pedro in Salamanca: he had won the Vuelta, but there was still the Tour, the race that obsessed him.

"I had an outstanding debt with the Tour: the first time I'd ridden that race I got a glimpse of myself ending up winning it, and that was something I hadn't forgotten. Then, swept along by the excitement of success, it was suggested that I should go and ride in Colombia, which was fine by me. If you want altitude training, where better than Colombia? Before heading off to France I also went to an altitude training camp with the team on Navacerrada.

"This was all in preparation for *la Grande Boucle*, and it was also thought that I would be more relaxed after the frenzy of the Vuelta. Nevertheless, I went into the Tour feeling tired; I didn't feel as if I had any spark. The first setback came in the team time trial: we were last. Even the Colombians beat us! I realised that I was only going to play a supporting role in the general classification,

---

* It seems that one of Atlético Madrid's players once saw García wearing an orange overcoat, apparently looking like one of those ubiquitous butane gas cyclinders and coined the nickname 'El Butano'.

so I thought about the Mountains prize. There I came up against Lucho Herrera, who was a better climber than me. Alright then, there were still stages to go for, but before the time trial at Villard de Lans I fell ill. What had been a slight head cold got worse, and I spent several days running a high temperature. So with my physical condition far from ideal I didn't think I had much chance of a stage win, either.

"Added to this, I rode the time trial worse than ever, so my morale was pretty low. I really was in the doldrums during this Tour, although every night when I climbed into bed I thought perhaps the next day would bring a change for the better, even though it was taking forever. But there is a saying: 'there's nothing bad that lasts for a hundred years' and so it was that towards the end things did turn more in my favour and my physical condition, after the calvary of the Alps, did improve. And the Pyrenees were waiting for me."

Every day, before leaving the hotel, the directors would get the riders together to explain the tactics to be followed, or simply to discuss the most appropriate strategy. Planning it, of course, is one thing; how it works out in reality is something very different. However...

"The 16th of July, Stage 17, was the day earmarked as the *etapa reina* – 210 kilometres spiced up by the Aspin, the Tourmalet and ending on the summit of Luz Ardiden. At the start in Toulouse we planned that José del Ramo [nicknamed 'El Gato' - The Cat] would attack on the climb up the Aspin and that Pello Ruiz Cabestany would then go on the descent. The idea was that del Ramo would be waiting for him and would pace him to the foot of the Tourmalet. Pello would need to hang on to whatever advantage he'd got and then I would take off on the final part of the Tourmalet. Pello would be waiting for me on the way down and I would follow his wheel on to the lower slopes of Luz Ardiden, where I would aim to get the stage win. As easy as two plus two makes four."

The peloton that year was dominated by a resurgent Hinault, while Fignon, his big rival, was trying to recover from his injuries.

"Hinault didn't cut you much slack, unless you were a Colombian. He was the absolute patron of the peloton. But he was a rider not without his weaknesses, especially in the high mountains, and knowing what was at stake, he reached a tacit understanding with the Colombians. He would support Herrera in his bid for the polka dot King of the Mountains jersey, plus stage wins (he got two) and would help Fabio Parra win the white jersey and a stage. In return, their Café de Colombia team would help him at critical moments on the climbs and they would not go in for any of their characteristic, crazy attacks which had the tendency of blowing the race apart.

"Half way up the Tourmalet, near La Mongie, with the battle raging and the group breaking up, I saw Hinault shouting to Herrera. He was telling him to set the pace and to set it so that he could follow it without any difficulty. This was my moment, the moment to put it all to the test, and I didn't think twice about it. I attacked; and I was away. The rest was like a film; the whole of the rest of the stage went just as we had planned it in the hotel. Although we didn't ride alone, for the first time the tactic worked out line by line. No punctures, no falls, and it all went exactly as we'd hoped. Something like that, so simple in its planning, happens once in a life time, and that time it happened. I took the stage win after a very nervous final ascent, since I began the last 14-kilometre climb to Luz Ardiden with little more than a minute in hand.

"Behind, Lucho had jumped, and with several kilometres still to ride the gap was down to half a minute. A dense fog descended on the mountain in the last ten kilometres; visibility was nil. I had the feeling that Herrera was going to come past me as if he were riding a motor bike. I looked behind – nothing there. I asked for time checks from the motor bike or the car and every time they said 'around 30 seconds', with a shrug of the shoulders. Hardly reassuring, with the best climber in that year's Tour behind you. After an anxious climb, full of doubts because of the lack of time-checks, the fatigue, my legs which felt ready to burst, and Lucho who never did appear, I got my first stage win in the Tour.

"In the end I was sixth overall, and thus finished a Tour de France which for me had begun so negatively."

The success on Luz Ardiden rekindled an ambition that had been lost because of his accumulated tiredness; Pedro enjoyed play-acting to confuse a rival. So why not a game on the last stage? And his victim – how, in this particular year, could it be anyone other than Robert Millar?

"The outcome of the Tour was settled: Hinault had the race in his pocket, and Herrera was King of the Mountains. In this competition, the Scotsman was lying second and I was third, but I was so close to him that I decided to reverse that on the final day. This is the day when the only thing the survivors are hoping for is a bit of peace and quiet, and the chance to preserve some strength for the end of race party; attacks are the last thing anybody wants. 'Look,' they say, 'after twenty-two days when you've had every opportunity to attack and show how good you are, you don't need to do that on the final day; that is a day for celebrating and chatting.'

"I'd done well that year – the Vuelta, a stage of the Tour. And yet... Something inside drove me to want to lark about. Second place in the mountain classification was within my grasp, even if there wasn't anything particularly special in that; furthermore, after all the strains I'd had..."

He weighed up the pros and cons, aware of all the commotion this would cause in the peloton, and the nuisance he'd be causing the Scotsman. Oh, what the hell. Go for it! "I finally made up my mind. There were seven classified hills, four third-category and three fourth-category.

"In truth, Robert Millar has never done me any harm; on the contrary, I have done more harm to him, especially in this year's Vuelta. The first climb is coming up. I won't move, so as not to warn him. Where I need to take points is on the next ones. His team is getting him ready for the sprint so he won't be taken by surprise, and they are telling him I'm behind. So that's that.

"Then comes the next one, a third-category, and he's obviously saying, 'If he's not going to go for the points, I'm not going to make myself look ridiculous, sprinting all by myself.' I let myself drop back in front of him; I make out as if I'm not concerned about the sprint. I can see him; he can see me, too, but he's not paying any attention to me. I let a couple of other riders start to sprint for the points and when I realise that Millar no longer has a chance because he's boxed in, I accelerate. I overtake the first two and the Scotsman, having left himself with no time to react, gets nothing.

"On the remaining hills, there's a furious fight between us both, and I outrun him each time, but again I cross swords with Duclos-Lasalle who is trying to niggle me to benefit his team mate. Millar is furious with me and kicks up a real fuss. I tell the others that I was only sprinting for the mountain points, I wasn't being crazy, that after that I would stop. That pacified the peloton, which was concerned about the day turning out to be a good deal harder than they'd anticipated.

"With that it seemed that everything was settled. After all that song and dance I ended up snatching second place in the mountain competition from Millar. I don't know if he likes me any more or less these days, but in 1985 I must have been a real pain in the arse for him. A few years later our paths would again cross in the Tour."

Chapter 5

Blasted Cold

'Health is the right measure between hot and cold.'
Aristotle

Friendship is a valuable gift in cycling because the combination of a ten-month long season and communal living (not only between members of the same team) is very conducive to illness, and that is one of the worst aspects of this extraordinarily competitive sport. It's not only the intrinsic pain, but the peculiarity of the problems that accompany it. For the most part, it is the cold and the vagaries of the weather that bring about the sickness that cyclists suffer from. Perhaps the ideal place for cycle racing would be some Caribbean island: sun, pleasant temperature and no extremes. But then the epic dimension of cycling – what truly makes it so enthralling – would be lost.

Colds and even flu have to be overcome in the saddle; so too does gastroenteritis, and numerous other 'itises'. And it's no good thinking you can temporarily retire to deal with your health problems in a sensible way. To withdraw is to concede defeat and in a big stage race that is a total disaster.

"In the 1983 Vuelta I got a stinking attack of flu. I was in such a terrible state. If your health is not there, nor is your cycling. A rider depends one hundred per-cent on his physical capability. Good morale is also essential, and some warm weather, too; but when your health is poor you just don't function properly: you have no strength, and if you have no strength there is no way on Earth you're going to be able to push hard on the pedals. So you just don't perform. In the course of three weeks you are constantly exposed to the elements, and they can be friend or foe according to whether it's the rain, cold or heat. Even on the same day the weather can vary hugely, and of course, colds are always potentially there, lurking."

Riders need to be careful with medication, and with the classical remedies like Frenadol, which contains caffeine and is prohibited, or Couldina which also cannot be taken. Even a wide range of children's cough syrups are banned. The list is long; and the propensity of riders to fall ill is wide.

"It was cold and raining heavily when we rode out of the Valley of Arán, into the Viella tunnel heading towards Sabiñanigo. I was in high spirits because I'd finished third the day before. As we emerged from the tunnel we went straight into a snowstorm. The mountains, the edges of the road, the road itself, everything was covered in immaculate white; but it carried on snowing and it became freezing cold. Hinault and Saronni, foreigners and patrons of the peloton, suggested a collective protest – 'We can't carry on in this.' The Vuelta's organisers agreed to neutralise the race for a good stretch.

"We were ferried by car for some 70 kilometres, but with my lack of experience, all this caught me quite unawares. I had no dry clothes to change into when we restarted the stage. When we crossed the finishing line in Sabiñanigo I was shivering, and even after a good hot shower I couldn't get warm. As you might expect, I was ill."

It's really hard to fall ill away from home, where being cared for by your family does you as much good as ever the medicine does, and getting over the worst in your own bed, well looked after and knowing that you'll want for nothing is the quickest way to recovery. But in cycling…

"I was in a bad way that night; my temperature was over 39 degrees, and in the morning there was no noticeable improvement. I went down to breakfast and, as I often did, exchanged opinions with other members of the team about home-made remedies for overcoming the flu. There are various concoctions for curing colds, while evading the thorny matter of doping. It's a question of looking for effective solutions because, more often than not, conventional medicine turns out to be inadequate.

"I don't know how it happened; I don't know if it was my idea or if it came from José Miguel Echávarri. It could well have been mine because I've always tried to keep myself well-informed about anything related to my job. The fact is that we stumbled upon a remedy for curing colds."

There was also some urgency about putting it into practice because, for a variety of reasons, the Reynolds team had been somewhat reduced in numbers.

"Some had abandoned, and the rest of us were needed particularly to protect Julián Gorospe, as we were counting on him for the General Classification. So, José Miguel didn't want to lose me, just like that. We had to find a cure for my flu, and get me recovered for the sake of the team."

The previous day's storm had largely subsided, although you could still feel the cold which seeped into the rooms through the cracks in the wooden window frames of that dilapidated hotel in Sabiñanigo. Not far off, the snow, clinging to the mountainside, threatened another icy day. In the dim light, behind locked doors, Echávarri and Delgado set about counteracting the effects of the flu. The net curtains danced and the large red and black checked curtains rustled with the passage of years since they last saw the wash tub. For better or worse, the director and the rider took up their respective positions. Pedro, his torso naked, lying face down on the bed, watched every detail of José Miguel's attempts to light a cigarette. José Miguel did not smoke and so every drag became an exaggerated coughing fit.

'Let's see, Pedro. It's a question of stimulating some particular points on your back with heat. Is that right?'

'Yes. Two centimetres to the right and then two centimetres to the left of the spine at the level of the seventh vertebra.'

'Wasn't it the sixth?'

'Maybe so. OK, then, let's do it again on both sides.'

With this remedy his fever would subside, and possibly the head cold, too. Above all, it was vital that Pedro made the starting-line that morning. So, José Miguel got down to work. He smoked like a chimney, puffed out more smoke than a steam engine and brought the glowing cigarette close to the areas Delgado indicated.

'José Miguel, you're burning me!'

'I am sorry. I'm trying to be careful and to bring the end just close enough not to burn you. I haven't touched your skin with the cigarette.'

'Well, go on. Is that it?'

'I think so.'

Echávarri had put smoke in his eyes and, despite the crack in the window frame, the room stank of tobacco.

'Come on, then. If we carry on here I'm going to end up even worse.'

And did it work?

"In the course of the stage, the Panticosa time trial, I was extremely cold, terribly cold; but before the start I'd felt very hot, with a burning sensation down my back, and we hadn't managed to effect a cure. The flu – because I think that's what it was – was incubating and I don't know if we slowed it down a bit or not, but the fact is that I was another three days on warm milk and brandy before going to bed, infusions, inhaling and more normal methods than a cigarette on your back, before I began to feel a bit better. In other words, I resorted to the usual methods that cyclists use to fight against colds and sinusitis, the common illness of our profession, even though they don't very often have much effect.

"Cycling is one of those sports where you're most exposed to the cold. I know that from experience, because I have taken part in other sports and I have spoken with other sportsmen. My first really icy experience came in 1978, during a stage of the Aragón-Béarn, just after I made the move up from Juvenile to Amateur, with the Moliner-Vereco team. Alongside Machín, or De La Fuente, or Cabrero I was just a kid. They were the favourites and my job was simply to cope with the attacks and to get through the stages. The *etapa reina*, which had us going over the Soulor and then the Aubisque, started out grey with a forecast of rain. When we got into the mountains it did start to rain, and my strength began to fail. Little by little the cold got the better of me even when I was climbing, and the descent from the top of the Aubisque to the stage finish in Laruns was really dramatic, and quite unforgettable. Those 16 kilometres went on for ever and I was shivering so much I couldn't control the bike. It was in

June, the end of June in fact, and I could scarcely believe that you could get so cold at that time of the year."

Abrupt changes of temperature provoke real races among the cars following the peloton. The sun suddenly shines and the riders cover a dozen kilometres at a brisk pace, still wearing their rain-capes; they break out into a sweat. From that point onwards they are constantly calling for their Director's car so they can hand over their arm warmers, leg warmers, thermal jackets and all the luxury items of clothing which, years ago, nobody had even dreamed of. Suddenly a cloud in the high sierra discharges every drop of water it's holding – and the race is back on. Some don't have time to recover what they've just handed back and they simply settle for getting cold and wet.

"When I was a Juvenile I was used to one-day races, where it was just a matter of a vest, a jersey, shorts, a bicycle, the road and a blanket (and the blanket a matter of choice). And you don't worry about anything else. In the Aragón-Béarn I realised what it is to be cold and how important it is to wear clothing to deal with the cold and the rain. Often, because of the effort of climbing a col you didn't feel like carrying the additional weight. It's all an extra encumbrance. Then it begins to rain. Then it pours and pours and you don't even have the team car to provide you with something to put on; you've been dropped and as usual the Director is up ahead with the leaders, so you've no choice other than to get cold – and even colder on the descent."

That's in June and similar adventures are more usual in February or March, even in the 'Race to the Sun' (better known as Paris–Nice) which sometimes doesn't ever see the sun.

"It was in that very race in 1982, in my first year as a professional, where I again came up against the cruelty of freezing weather. This normally happens to you in your first years as a rider when storms can take you by surprise, because you're not used to them. I remember that out of the nine days that the race lasted only once did I see the stage winner raise his arms because on every other day I'd been dropped.

"I was very uncertain of myself in that edition; I was just getting to know the job. I remember, in the process, the third stage which ended in Saint-Etienne, where I went over the only completely snow-covered mountain pass in the whole of my racing career. There was talk of cancelling the stage because of snow on the final climb, but there was no sign of it as we were climbing and so there seemed no real grounds for the protest. That is until we got to the last kilometre before the summit, where suddenly the road seemed more like a snow field. So too, the three or four kilometres downhill, which turned the descent into something between comedy and tragedy as far as staying on the bike was concerned.

"At first you could ride on it, if you were careful enough, because the virgin snow offered some grip. We carried on descending, some sliding off the road in scenes more ridiculous than dangerous, until the snow began to lose its consistency and the tyres began to sink into it and do peculiar things. Luckily there were no serious falls, but what with the effort on the climb and the stress on the descent that day the cold was more bearable. As I said, that stage was within a hair's breadth of being neutralised, but as it was Paris–Nice... That day, since I was going better, I finally finished together with the leaders, but because of the snow, I still didn't see the winner – in this case Sean Kelly – raise his arms.

"The nightmare of being in my first Paris–Nice, with the echelons, the cold, the rain, the snow, meant my morale was at rock bottom, and that's where it stayed. I, a climber, couldn't follow the speed of the main group on the climbs. After being dropped, once again I felt humiliated, and in the middle of the descent I was caught by a number of riders, fortunately including a couple of my Reynolds team mates (Carlos Hernández and Jesús Hernández Ubeda). The three of us tried to mock that dreadful day by singing. It must have made a comic scene: frozen stiff and singing in the rain. Anyone who saw us would have thought we should have been in straitjackets. And what a state we were in. I was so physically and psychologically exhausted that I didn't have an ounce of energy left, especially not for turning the pedals."

And just when it seems that there'll never be a worse day on a bicycle, another ghastly day comes along. Another criminal stage looms over the horizon to test the readiness of the human body to endure not just torrential downpours, but a torture which bit by bit undermines your physical condition and so ends up tearing your psychological strength to shreds. It is when you're descending mountain cols that the cold becomes most extreme, and unbearable. At a speed of 60 to 70 kph your body registers between five and ten degrees lower than the surrounding temperature. It is what's called the thermal sensation. Without question the Gavia stage in the Giro of 1988 beat all the records for torture in the last thirty years of cycling.

"Yes, the *etapa reina* of the cold, to give it a cycling name, was that famous Gavia stage. One rider, Johan van der Velde, was first over the summit of the colossus with a small lead over the favourites. He crossed the finishing line at the bottom, 25 kilometres later, 43 minutes behind the winner, another Dutchman, Breukink."

Climbing to an altitude of 2,621 metres on a narrow road, its surface broken up in a number of places, and a dirt track in others, and having to cope with persistent rain, is both hard and complicated, because the muddy patches that settle on the tarmac demand an extra effort from the cyclist. The wheels slip and frequently your drive on the pedals is empty, and that kind of effort is exhausting, and it gets you nowhere. 'Thank God we'll soon be on the downhill,' riders say to motivate themselves.

To prevent traffic jams among the cars following the race, spectators were prohibited from driving their cars up; the organisers required them to cross the Gavia two hours before the race. The road, built by the Germans during World War II, only allowed room for one car to pass. Even without cyclists, the gradients of up to 14 per-cent on this gigantic col, were imposing. And with rain and snow even more so.

"They warned us of the storm, a typical Dolomites storm, and told us that if the bad weather continued the day's racing would be cancelled. Roberto Visentini was leading a pressure group to have the stage annulled while, even before the bad forecasts, Torriani (the Giro's Director), was kind enough to cut the first part of the stage... but we rode the remainder, all the same."

As a parenthesis to the epic on the Gavia, the following day's stage, which included the Stelvio, was neutralised. The organisers did not dare go through another event like that. Riders, journalists and all the followers went up the serpentine road of that legendary climb in their cars, after having been warned of the possibility of avalanches. The forces of law and public order demanded maximum precaution. On that grey day not a single car horn sounded. It was as silent as the grave. We didn't even dare to speak out loud in the cars. The riders continued to think about the woes of the previous day.

"That day we had started in the rain and, aware of the suffering that was in store for us, we put jackets on top of our jerseys. In addition, the teams assigned one car to go to the top of the Gavia with more winter clothing, food and hot drinks, since they could foresee that the stage was going to be horrendous. When we started out on the Gavia – a climb of nearly seventeen kilometres – Van der Velde went away by himself. We all looked the other way. A little later the asphalt disappeared and the road turned into a quagmire. The gradient, the rain and the mud began to make the selection. I don't know how many kilometres of mud we had to climb; I think it was around about five. Our tubular tyres were sticking in the sludge, while we looked for patches where it was harder so we could ride over it, but it was all much the same. Now and again we came across some grooved wooden planks placed across the track. At first we didn't know what they were doing there until we realised they were to channel the water that was coming off the mountainside. At each point we had to make a little jump with the bike so as not to come off.

"I was not doing too well in the General Classification; I was 14th at 4'-43", and the conditions did not exactly invite any heroic deeds. But, little by little I started overtaking other riders; I was receiving time-checks from the team and I knew I was getting closer to the favourites. All of a sudden the mud gave way to asphalt which encouraged me sufficiently to link up with the leading group. Then the rain turned to snow. On the first part of the climb I had been wearing neoprene gloves (a new thermal material at that time), but they started to become a nuisance when I couldn't hold the handlebar tightly enough to pedal strongly on those slopes. I put them back in the pocket of my jersey. I also rolled my arm warmers down to the wrist, but as we approached the summit I started to feel something extraordinary on such a demanding ascent: I began to feel cold."

The hard-pressed riders climbed, alone or in a group, and from time to time some spectator, looking like a ghostly shadow wrapped in a blanket, cheered them on. For all the good it did.

"I had become so cold and so tired that the arm warmers, which previously had hindered me, now seemed useless against the cold. I put them on and tried to put the gloves back on before I reached the top. It proved impossible, and I thought it might be better to leave it for the false flat of the summit. The cold was becoming more intense. As soon as I went under the banner, indicating the special category summit, the Reynolds helpers were there with a bidon of hot tea, and a dry thermal jersey. I took everything on the move; I didn't want to lose time because I was getting close to the leaders. With some difficulty, I managed to put on the jersey, but couldn't get the zip done up. I was shivering. I slowed down a bit and I still couldn't manage it. I had to stop, and Enrique, the mechanic, zipped it up for me. 'And now, for the gloves,' I thought, because there was another twenty kilometres of descending, plus a bit more to the finish. Yes, yes…the gloves.

"I wanted to do the descent as safely as possible. The safety of the cyclist, especially when descending in the cold, depends mainly on his capacity to react quickly; it's more important than his reflexes. The hands need to be protected at all times so that they can respond in an emergency, to brake hard or to control the bicycle. But the thing was that I couldn't manage to fit my fingers in the correct holes of my gloves. I got so annoyed as I became aware that the group was moving away, and I could do nothing to prevent it. It was impossible. Minutes went by and my chances of getting a good position in the General Classification were fading away.

"Echávarri and Enrique got out of the car immediately to see what was happening to me. They tried to help me, but they couldn't get the gloves on me. My fingers were still too weak,

I was too upset and too cold, so I decided to give up. Let it be God's will!"

Totally frozen, Pedro started the descent with his mind set just on reaching the finishing line; that would be a remarkable enough feat in those circumstances. It never occurred to him that he stood any chance of victory; at that precise moment his only concern was survival.

"On the way down I witnessed scenes that I could never have imagined: there were riders who had left their bike at the roadside and were running on foot in the opposite direction, simply to get some warmth into their bodies; others were stamping on the road, or beating themselves all over with their hands to fight off the terrible cold. As for me, I was almost fainting, and I didn't know whether what I was seeing while I shivered violently was real, or a product of my imagination. I came out of one curve and I found a French rider coming in the opposite direction: he was going up while we were going down. I tried to bring myself round because I thought I was starting to have hallucinations, I was so cold. Did I take the right crossing? It was Dantesque!

"The scene didn't seem real, but anything goes when you are fighting such cold. Some just poured the can of hot tea all over themselves. Others sought to lessen the effects of the cold by peeing on themselves. In an extreme situation – and this certainly was – it's a case of anything that helps..."

Some riders were going through such a bad time that they decided to descend off the Gavia in the team cars, and they couldn't care less if they were disqualified. The organisers were fully aware of this, but turned a blind eye; they knew the peloton would be reduced by a half if they decided to intervene.

"It was a terrible stage. We were shivering so much we were barely capable of controlling the bike; we were going down, weaving from side to side. Everyone had their brakes on all the time because our hands had lost all feeling and you try not to go too fast or you'd be heading for a certain fall. I remember how difficult it was to overtake the eldest of the Madiot brothers. I was afraid we'd end up colliding: what with his shivering, and my shivering I didn't think there was room enough to overtake him safely, even though the road was wide enough for several riders. We were putting our lives at risk, without even being aware of it. All we wanted was to finish and get the stage over with as soon as possible."

Delgado crossed the finishing line, it was I, Julián Redondo, and two other journalists who helped the masseur put some warm clothing on him and give him a hot drink, but he barely managed to hold the bidon. What a state he was in!

"When I finished, the only thing I wanted was to go straight to the hotel and have a hot, hot shower even though that may not have been the wisest thing to have done when I was showing signs of frostbite. But that's what I did. I needed to feel my body warming up, to dream about sweating, sweltering even. I was so cold! I swear I spent at least half an hour in the shower, yet I still couldn't get rid of the cold that was so deep inside my body. I certainly would have liked to have stayed a bit longer, but at that moment my room mate, Omar Hernández, burst in. He didn't even take his clothes off; he got straight in the shower with me, and I had to let him get under the gush of warm water in spite of myself.

"There were some who didn't even have the opportunity to think about getting undressed. Javier Lukin, for example, a team mate of ours who was so shy he used to feel embarrassed changing his clothes in front of his own room mate. He reached the finishing line in a wretched state, pretty much like everybody else. They took him away quickly, wrapped him in blankets or overcoats provided by local people, because it really had been an epic stage. He was then taken to what you might call a kind of field hospital where the Giro's podium girls were taking refuge. They undressed him and put some dry clothes on him. When we asked him, full of envy as we were for such a wonderful experience, what he'd felt when those beautiful girls took his clothes off, he denied it completely. He insisted we were pulling his leg. He hadn't even been aware that it was happening."

Can money compensate for that kind of suffering? And the question is not about the Javier Lukin episode – being rescued from the cold by a chorus of angels.

"Irrespective of the good contracts I've had, it has always annoyed me when people asked how much did they 'give' me for racing a bicycle. They didn't 'give' me a penny; rather I earned it. No matter how much money they 'give' you, on a stage as ghastly as that one on the Gavia, you would exchange every last penny of it for a bit of warmth, or a seat in the car, without so much as a second thought. Riders race for the love of it. A fifteen-year-old boy doesn't think about the money; his dream is to take part in the race, to raise his arms in a victory salute. Money comes later, and even then it's not the most important thing. What keeps you in cycling, what helps you put up with all the suffering is not the money; it's the pleasure of winning and the excitement of competing."

The fact that money is a powerful incentive is self-evident. We all know that: money makes troubled times easier. This must have been what one of Pedro's sponsors in his junior years thought.

"Pedro Gimeno, a supporter of mine in Segovia from when I was fifteen until I turned eighteen, always paid five thousand pesetas into my current account as a reward, every time I won a race. I looked forward to that money. He didn't give it to me; rather, he paid it into my account, thanks to which I avoided the temptation of spending it immediately. At that time, it was victories I was after, and I didn't attach so much importance to the money. Nevertheless, this friend of mine, rewarding me and at the same time trying to secure a future in cycling for me, was implying that my dream was worthwhile."

The Spanish Inland Revenue also benefitted from Pedro Delgado's economic rewards: "Yes. We all pay tax. For us cyclists, though, that is a bit of a thorny issue. All the money you can earn in your career is during a span of, at most, some ten years. It doesn't go on longer than that. We pay half of the money we earn in taxes; or to put it another way, we end up handing over five year's worth of our victories and our suffering to the Inland Revenue. With the passing of time, you are left with the feeling that they have taken away our money and our sacrifices, all at the same time."

Chapter 6

Double Fractures

'Most of the evils that men suffer come from men themselves.'
                                                            Plinius

"How about that then! First and second on the stage. That was what was going through my mind as I escaped down the Joux Plane, behind my team mate Ángel Arroyo, who was out on his own, up ahead. It was the Tour of 1984, and the stage ended in Morzine. However, in that edition, it was not so clear to me that I stood a realistic chance of winning, which I had done the year before. In 1983 Laurent Fignon won the Tour which got away from me, and in which Arroyo came second. This year's Tour also had his name written on it, only this time he displayed such superiority over all of his rivals that, unlike the previous year, he was just untouchable."

Fignon was riding for the best team in the race – Renault. Directed masterfully and strictly by Cyrille Guimard, they were not going to leave the merest crumbs for anyone else. Fignon could win on any terrain, if he put his mind to it, and his team mates ran away with whatever else was left. They racked up a total of ten stages. Just about anyone would have won the Tour if they'd been riding for Renault in their glory year of 1984.

"The rest of us could only fight to improve our overall position, and maybe win a stage, so we were not going to let this one get away. It had gone well for us, with Arroyo now clear, alone, and with a sufficient gap. As soon as we went under the banner at the top of the Joux Plane, we started descending at full speed towards the finish in Morzine. I remembered my exploit the previous year in the Pyrenees, coming down from the Peyresourde, when I was dubbed *Le Fou du Pyrénées*. [The madman of the Pyrenees]. I felt strong. I wasn't going to win; my mission was to keep the other riders sufficiently under control so they wouldn't jeopardise my team mate's victory."

LeMond, Fignon's team mate, was also fighting for a good position in the general classification. He was third, while Hinault, second overall, was only some 30 seconds back.

"LeMond was riding at full pelt and I was glued to his wheel. Flat out! The only one who could keep pace with us was Fignon; neither Hinault, nor Millar, nor any of the others in that group could stay with us at this speed. Too fast, perhaps? The fact is that halfway down the descent, on one of those bends, LeMond ran off the road and came down. That didn't stop Fignon, who loved to humiliate Hinault, from continuing that crazy descent. One curve, two, and then in the third curve he lost control of his bike and went straight on. I looked behind and realised I was alone. That's when I told myself: 'Hey, first and second on the stage! Just like last year on the Puy de Dome!' And I kept descending as fast as I could. I was just a few kilometres from the finish-line, as the gradient began to level out, and I could picture the next day's headlines. I continued at full speed so that LeMond and the rest couldn't get back to me."

It was going to be another glory day for Spanish cycling.

"I was full of confidence and I'd descended fast. I'd taken the curves with ease, all at full speed. I could feel myself cutting through the air, and the impact of insects on my face. As I approach the end, I start to take a bend to the left. I think it's opening out now; I open myself out too. But no, it tightens again. I am taking it badly, I stop pedalling, I lean a bit more, and I brake as much as I can to avoid going off the road. As I try to correct my line, braking heavily now, the front tubular explodes, and I crash against the concrete parapet.

"Painfully, I managed to stand up and I could see I had a cut on my right arm. It scared me at first, but as there was only a bit of blood, I decided not to pay too much attention to it. 'It's not serious,' I told myself. One rider went past me, then another and another; one of them almost crashed against me: it really was a dangerous curve. With some difficulty I got back into the race."

Cyclist really do seem to be made of rubber. They fly over the handlebars and make pirouettes in the air before landing.

For spectators the sight is terrifying – 'he's killed himself!' But the man who's just taken this great tumble picks himself up, feels his bones for any breakages (although many continue with a broken bone anyway), brushes himself down, picks up the bicycle, fixes it if it's possible, and then off he goes dancing on the pedals.

"I noticed the pain was stronger than usual. Cyclists get accustomed to falling off from the time when they are kids, and are quickly able to identify the seriousness of an injury. Coming off so often makes you learn the hard way; you learn to follow in the slipstream of another cyclist; you learn to think strategically. The life of a cyclist has many ups and downs: punctures, rain, oil, gasoline, gravel. A thousand elements on the road that can cause an accident.

"At first glance, the injury looked less serious than I had originally imagined. However, my right shoulder was hurting a good deal, and when I got on my bike again I realised something was out of place. I always get on my bike on the left side, lifting first my right leg, tightening my toe-strap, and then doing the same with the left foot. This time, as I was about to lift my right foot I felt an acute pain in my collar bone: 'Pedro, this is serious,' I told myself. I had never felt that sort of stabbing pain before, but I still managed to finish the stage. The finish line was really close, only four kilometres away. What a pity; we could have done something really special. I found it hard to complete those kilometres because the pain intensified as my arm got colder, but in the end, I crossed the finish line.

'What happened to you? You were second,' one of the team assistants asked me.

'What do you think happened? I took a whack against a parapet.'

'Look at that cut in your arm. And here, on your head.'

'My collar bone is what really hurts. I think it's broken.'

'Let's get you to the race doctor.'

At that time, most of teams were not accompanied by their own doctor, and the only recourse was the obligatory race doctor. I was taken off to see him, and left there.

'You only need a few stitches in your arm. There isn't anything unusual, as far I can see. You haven't got anything serious.' This was after he had examined me.

'Well, I think there is, Doctor,' and I pointed to the place which was most painful – my right shoulder.

'No, there's nothing; you're just making a fuss. It's natural. You gave it a good bashing and the more it cools the more it will hurt. But it's nothing serious, don't worry.'

'Doctor, I think there is,' I insisted.

'All right. Let's see then.' And he took another look at my arm and shoulder. And then, as obstinate as before: 'No, there's nothing. There's no fracture.'

'Doctor, there is. I've got a broken collarbone and it's hurting like hell.'

"I went on and on so much that he ended up taking me to the hospital in Morzine. There, I was X-rayed, and they confirmed my moaning was not in vain. My right collar bone was broken and on the point of slipping out; they immobilised it straight away so that I could recover as soon as possible. This was to be the only serious injury in my entire racing career.

'Well then, you were right,' confirmed the Tour doctor. 'But it is so clean and there was no distortion, I didn't notice it.'

'So, all this pain was not for nothing!'

'Yes, yes. Well son. I'm sorry and I hope you get well soon. It's nothing serious'."

Meanwhile, in the hotel where Reynolds were staying, there was increasing anxiety because nobody knew where Pedro Delgado was. It was now more than three hours since the end of the stage and he had disappeared. They began calling the police, then the clinics, and just as they were dialling the number for the hospital in he walked through the hotel door, completely unruffled and with his arm in a sling. Ángel Arroyo was coming down for dinner and met him.

'You've had a real whack, haven't you?'

'Yes, you can see, it's the collar bone.'

'OK then, so now you head home; my dinner is waiting, and I don't want it to get cold.'

All this looked so ordinary, so clinical, so commonplace, as if nothing had really happened. This is how you must take things in cycling, with the same attitude that doctors and nurses adopt to cope with so much drama. Cyclists become cold-hearted, impervious. So, Pedro went back home the next day. It was July 18; he had lost his fourth place in the general classification of the Tour and the leadership of the King of the Mountains, which he was disputing with Robert Millar – of course it had to be him! It was within reach, but…

"A month later I resumed training in Segovia."

When a cyclist breaks his bone, it is a double fracture: the bone itself and the emotion. It's so frustrating to lose the chance of helping your team win, or of winning yourself, whether it be the overall or a stage win. Broken bones heal with time; frustrated expectations are ruined investments. However, cyclists cope with even these reversals with a special kind of fortitude.

Delgado experienced very few injuries in his career. He did not suffer, for instance, from tendinitis, which was widespread in the peloton. He did fall ill at various times, but nothing really important. However, his first serious injury sent him straight to hospital, and from there, back home.

"In our profession, falls are quite commonplace. We don't think about it, but there they are; they happen even in our training sessions. I remember one of them in 1992, on the road from Fuente el Saz to Torrelaguna, in the province of Madrid. I had a bad, dramatic, even comical crash. I was training for the time trial. José Luis Pascua Piqueras, my personal trainer, was following me in his car; I was riding on the 'Cabra', which is what we called the time trial bicycle. It was all about adapting to it while still making maximum effort. We were doing interval training on long straight sections of road, riding in the most aerodynamic position. I would be pedalling with my head bent forward, my chin glued to the handlebar and my eyes fixed on the white line that separated the hard shoulder from the road, trying to imagine a time trial. And doing it flat out. 'You have to ride at 160 or 165 beats per minute,' Pascua told me.

"Without losing sight of the white line, I pedalled in that position with all my strength. I felt confident, too, because José

Luis was just behind. I was riding full on, using all my strength. Those days of interval training were very intense. Suddenly, I crashed against something with the right-hand side of the handlebar. I wasn't even aware of what I'd hit. The next thing I knew I was flying through the air, and crashing back to earth, rolling over and laying there motionless. My collar-bone hurt, my legs hurt, my whole body hurt. 'Have I broken something?' I was devastated; I was pale and stretched out on the road. I felt awful, really awful.

'The collar-bone, the collar-bone!' Pascua was shouting.

'What bloody collar-bone?' I replied.

'But, what were you doing? Didn't you see the van?' he shouted at me again.

'What bloody van! Why didn't you warn me? Of course, I didn't see it.'

My body hurt so much that I couldn't even feel angry. The pain in my legs was excruciating.

'Pedro, it's a four kilometre-long straight, how could you not see it parked there?'

'I tell you; you should have warned me. What a whack! Oh, my legs!'

'But it's a four kilometre-long straight. How could I imagine you would not be able to see the van? You had plenty of time.'

'Sure; but I didn't raise my head because I thought you were behind me.'

'What happened to you? Are you all right?' said the owners of the van, a crew from Telefonica. They were fixing a fault at the top of a telegraph pole.

'I don't know but…'

'And how come you didn't see the van? It's parked correctly. What an idiot!'

And it was parked properly, with hardly a wheel touching the tarmac, and yet I crashed into it. In a grimace of pain, I replied, for the umpteenth time, that I didn't see it.

'Well, I didn't see it.'

I was getting annoyed at their incessant questions about me not seeing the van … on such a straight stretch of road, and … so long. The only thing I knew was that I couldn't pedal because of the impact, so we loaded the 'Cabra' in Pascua's car and we went straight to the doctor to forget the whole thing as soon as possible."

Luckily, he had no broken bones. The fractured collar-bone on the Joux Plane and this inconsequential incident on the Torrelaguna road were the only two accidents he suffered that were worthy of mention. "I didn't even have tendinitis, one of the most common injuries among cyclists at that time. Not once. Maybe I caught just the occasional cold. It can be said that I enjoyed good health. I have been lucky not to suffer injuries that would have prevented me from training for a time. The collar-bone injury kept me away from the bicycle for three months; after this recent incident it was only two or three days. I have really been lucky."

Another common disease among cyclists is gastroenteritis. Just a sip of cold water on a hot day can wreak havoc. On the hottest days of the season diarrhoea has no mercy for even the greatest of champions. Greg LeMond, for example, was involved in one of those incidents in the Tour of France in 1986, on the way to Futurescope. It truly was what you might call a 'messy' story.

"It was one of the stages in the first week – a flat, fairly easy stage. However, a cross-wind got up, and the typical echelons were formed. Then, LeMond, one of the favourites and Bernard Hinault's team mate in La Vie Claire, began to have problems.

"Cyclists like him are always closely marked by the peloton, so, it's sensible to keep near them. Whenever there is a break or any other dangerous situation, especially on flat and windy stages, it's good to stay alongside them, because if they are caught on the wrong side of the split there are more of us who can collaborate, and with a group of domestiques it is easier to get quickly back to the peloton. What's more, they are men who ride very well on the flat and, whether they escape or not, it's good to stay around them. But LeMond was dropping back. 'That's strange,' I thought. 'He must have punctured. That's a bad time for it.'

"After a short while I saw three of his team mates waiting for him. A few kilometres further on and they were already dropping back. I realised that nobody was on his wheel and I saw I had a chance to ride comfortably protected without the pressures of the echelons. As I approached his wheel, I saw the back of his cycling shorts were stained. I also noticed quite an unpleasant smell. I looked at his legs and I saw some trails on the inside of his legs going right down to his feet. In spite of the speed, the bad smell intensified until I realised what it was all about. Aaaarggh!"

'What a stink!,' says one of my team mates who was riding just behind me. 'My God, nobody can stay next to LeMond!'
'Why's that?'
'Uuughhh! Can't you see? Just look at him. He was trying to shit but he ended up doing it all over the place.'
'You're joking! He should have stopped for a moment, shouldn't he?'
'Yes, but who's going to stop with all these echelons! And at this speed! Well, first he tried to shit in his cap, but he got it all over himself, and because of the wind it splashed over one of his team mates. That's disgusting, isn't it! Have you seen their faces? No one can stay next to him.'

"After a few kilometres I couldn't sit on LeMond's wheel any longer; I preferred to have to deal with the side-wind rather than follow him and end up vomiting. So I went off to fight in the echelons on my own. In the meantime, I saw how other riders were doing the same as me: they'd get behind LeMond, only to veer off to find a more agreeable place, even if it meant running the risk of getting shoved out of that echelon. Despite the dramatic situation and despite the risk of the peloton splitting, someone was always in the mood for jokes.
'Hey man, move up. Make a break. Oh, shit!' some of them said to him.
'Either escape or drop back, but don't come around here!' others were shouting at him.'

"A great void was formed around him, only filled with the two or three team mates who stayed with him. When the situation became increasingly calmer, I had a chance to get a good look at him, and I noticed just how filthy poor LeMond really was: his shorts, his legs, the bicycle, all oozing with shit. Life can be strange; in an echelon, everybody is packed so tightly together, almost on top of each other to protect themselves from the wind, but that day it was so striking that no one was hanging on to LeMond's wheel."

In the Tour of 1990, amidst all the drama, Delgado became the star of yet another comic sketch. The same old gastroenteritis was the reason for it.

"I started to feel something wrong in my stomach on the way to Millau, where Stage 14 ended. Stomach cramps came and went. After a while they came back again, getting stronger by the minute, and I couldn't help thinking about LeMond. Of course, I wasn't inclined to want to go through such a similar nasty, messy experience. So I had to bite the bullet, and try to cope with it. I told myself incessantly, 'I'll stop, I won't stop' – this refrain going back and forth all the time. Miraculously, I endured it, but I was really scared because it was an uphill finish, ending on the top of Causse Noir: it wasn't that hard, but I couldn't afford to lose any time. It was on that day that I had planned to attack in order to win back a few seconds or more on a healthy LeMond, and pull back some time on Chiappucci, who, at that moment, was leading the race: this, after all, was my terrain. The situation was really uncomfortable, I was having a dreadful time but not because of my effort. My stomach was being pulled to pieces, I felt I was going to have to stop, and so the chance of launching an attack faded away completely. I was painfully aware I couldn't get off the bicycle because we were arriving at the climb where the stage ended. So, finally, I decided I had to endure it, come what may.

"Two kilometres from the finishing line I made a move, whether to snatch back a few seconds, or to get over the line as soon as possible and find some relief, I am not sure. Marino Lejarreta, won the stage, shortly followed by Indurain, whilst I arrived seventh, 34 seconds back. Immediately after going under the final banner, I kept on riding to get as far away as possible. I did a fantastic, post-finishing line sprint!"

The journalists who were waiting for his appearance were taken by surprise; they wanted to ask him why he hadn't attacked earlier, they wanted to hear his account. Only one of them, Chico

Pérez and a TV cameraman insisted on going after him.

'Pedro, listen…!'

'Not now, please! Later!'

'But man, do me a favour. Stop for a second!'

'Not now, I can't!'

'Listen, it's for Television-Madrid.'

'I'm going to the team car. Follow me!'

Once there, after some 400 metres, Chico Perez and the camera man were breathless after chasing him.

But as soon as he arrived he rushed out towards a bit of waste ground far from the crowd.

Chico didn't give up, he kept following him; he didn't understand anything until, after a while, he saw Pedro stop, get off the bicycle, crouch down, pull down his shorts and…then he understood why he hadn't stopped.

A few days later, on 15 July, 1990, the year when Indurain won his second Tour stage, Perico lost any chance of winning the French race.

"I felt weak, constantly dehydrated, I had suffered colitis ever since Millau, and it seemed I had no way of getting better. Two days later came the *etapa reina* in the Pyrenees. That morning, on the way to Luz Ardiden, I told Miguel that he should do his own race and forget about me, that it would be difficult enough for me just to finish. Fortunately, he did listen to me and ended up winning the stage. My state of health was kept secret in the team to avoid giving clues to rivals who, like so many supporters, were expecting me to attack in the mountain. But that day was merely about survival, and getting to the finish as honourably as possible on what was an extraordinarily hard, 215-kilometre stage, over the Aspin, the Tourmalet and up to Luz Ardiden – and also to keep myself in with a chance to finish on the podium."

But Pedro's health was so precarious that, after he'd finished the stage, Pascua Piqueras commented, 'I have always admired Pedro, but today I admire and respect him more than ever.'

"I ended up shattered at the top of Luz Ardiden. Had I not fallen ill, and with Indurain in the streak of form he was going through at that moment, I am sure we would have made a lot of trouble for LeMond and his team mates. How lucky he was! What a third Tour he won! I always thought he showed symptoms of vulnerability in both the last two Tours he'd won. Chiappucci, who was in a pretty favourable position in the race, launched a series of compulsive attacks, without making use of his advantage. Given that he was the race leader, that would have been the logical thing to do, but his fierce competitiveness, coupled with his rashness, perhaps deprived him of the final victory in a race which I had certainly lost by then.

"In the end I finished fourth in Paris, but I was feeling worse every day. I was on the point of quitting, but I didn't want to lose the podium. It was not for myself, but also for the team mates who had worked so hard for me. I felt I was in a deep hole, unable to recover physically because the gastroenteritis persisted, and in the final time trial I lost my third place to Erik Breukink."

Chapter 7

The Value of Yellow

'The ideal is in thyself, the impediment too is in thyself.'
Carlyle

We used to play football at school, but no game was ever as important as one where we wore a proper 'strip'. It didn't matter if the two sides were uneven – ten against nine, say, because the teacher had kept some Tom, Dick and Harry in at playtime for writing something stupid on the blackboard. The important thing was the strip – shorts, shirt and socks. That is the distinctive badge of the team; it motivates you and it excites you to the point where the first time you wear it you can't sleep for thinking about it. If that happens with youngsters, just think what getting your first yellow jersey in the Tour could mean – whether it was the one that Pedro Delgado missed out on in 1983, the one he never stood a chance of getting in 1984, or the one that deceived him in 1990.

Yellow is the emblematic colour of champions. It's hard to get your hands on it. If it were easy, it wouldn't be worth the effort. The yellow of the *maillot jaune* came from the pages of a newspaper, later to become a universal symbol. In the same way, the pages of another newspaper gave birth to the Giro's *maglia rosa*. But no newspaper reported what once happened to Jesús Rodríguez at the end of one particular Vuelta a Murcia. He didn't win it. Rodríguez had been born for other work: he was a magnificent *domestique*, a reasonable climber and one night he saw the light, as his good friend Pedro Delgado recalls.

"I was in the front seat, next to Jesús, the driver. I was the co-driver, and what a help I was! I fell asleep the moment we left Murcia. We had just had dinner – only a snack, nothing more than a sandwich – but that and the accumulated tiredness from the race, along with the gentle drumming of the car did the rest: I nodded off. I'm not sure if that was before or after the two who were snoring on the back seat."

A football player finds it difficult to sleep after a match, whereas a cyclist doesn't usually have any difficulty because he has a 'match' every day. What he cannot easily put behind him, however, is the emotional reaction to something that happened in the race: the escape group which dropped him, or which he didn't manage to infiltrate; the mountain col which left him nailed to the asphalt at the very bottom; the sprint which he lost by a few millimetres because of a moment's hesitation; or the victory he did achieve. In one of so many sleepless interludes Pedro fidgeted in the seat.

"First, I opened my right eye; then, I opened the left eye. I saw the headlights of a car coming straight towards us…I looked round and saw Jesús had also fallen asleep at the wheel. I gave him an elbow and shouted, 'Wake up, quick, you're going to get us killed! Stop!'

"I threw myself on him to wake him up; the lights were coming towards us, getting closer and closer.

'We're going to die. Do something. Brake! Brake! Turn right, quick!!'

While he braked, we both grabbed the handbrake and yanked it upwards as hard as we could. It was a matter of life or death.

'Help. Oh my God, it's coming!'

"At the same time, we heard one of the back doors opening as one of the two sitting behind, the one on the right, jumped out of the car in the middle of all this hysteria.

'Bloody assholes!' he yelled. 'What the hell, the car's stopped! It isn't even moving! Bloody hell!'

"We were scared to death! What had happened was that after the last stage of the Vuelta a Murcia, which was an amateur race in those days, we wanted to get back home as soon as possible. The race had finished at around eight in the evening and, after the prize-giving, a shower, that quick bite to eat before the journey, we left. It was now gone ten at night and we had 400 kilometres ahead of us before we'd arrive home – a four-hour journey, without a motorway in those days. It would have been wiser to have travelled later but...

"As soon as we started the journey we told Jesús to let us know when he needed a rest, if he felt tired or sleepy, because we all had our driving license. However, it seemed that, once he reached that point, he saw we were all sleeping like logs and, instead of waking us up – 'I didn't want to annoy you,' he explained – he pulled over to have a little nap himself. And then, of course, I open one eye and see a car coming towards us, and when I saw the driver sleeping my heart leapt, and – well, you know what happened.

"When we decided to start off again, with our hearts still pounding fast, and wide awake after the scare, we had a good time recalling the situation. First, it took us an age to get the car going because we had to release the handbrake which we'd yanked up so fiercely. We thought we were going to be stranded when we couldn't free it. And Jesús, a rider like the rest of us, wasn't able to compete for a month because of a pain in his right knee from pressing so hard on the brake pedal.

"To anyone without a good knowledge of the cycling world, what happened in the car might sound absurd, but it wasn't. Obviously, those kinds of situations don't happen every day of the week, otherwise they would stop being anecdotes; but nor are they that unusual either. At the end of a tour all you want to do is head off home straight away. After going through the anti-doping test, if you're called, having a shower and getting some energy back with a bit of food inside you, you leave as fast as possible. The journey is usually long and at night, and that's after five or six days of racing, with your energy spent. You're as anxious to get home as you are exhausted. This is why that tragic-comic situation in the car is just another aspect of cycling, albeit a somewhat risky one."

Among the most precious aspects, of course, is winning the yellow jersey; it's as rewarding as your first victory. You can only appreciate its value when you win it, although Pedro insists the colour yellow never meant anything special to him.

"I reckon the very first time I heard about this jersey was in the 1982 Vuelta a España. It was my first year as a professional and in the Reynolds team we were working tirelessly to help Ángel Arroyo, who was leading at the time, keep hold of the jersey. I was fortunate enough to feel in 1983 that yellow had an affection for me, that it was tailor-made for me. I sensed that in my first Tour, which I only narrowly failed to win; I was so close to winning it that, for a while, I imagined the jersey was mine. I was reckoning on it in the following year's Tour, too, but that year Fignon was way out of reach for anybody to take the jersey off him.

"In that year's Vuelta, however, I did at least get to wear it – for five days. Then I knew what it meant. I had that feeling of relief, the sense of accomplishment it gives, the respect it commands in the peloton. It's something you don't really understand when it is others who are wearing it. And so it was, every year, at the beginning of every season, I used to dream of wearing that yellow jersey perpetually, in the Vuelta or in the Tour. I got into my head the idea of winning it in some epic, glorious manner. I couldn't imagine what a surprise the Vuelta a España of 1985 would bring me on its penultimate day, and in my home town, Segovia."

That young boy with a sharp Adam's apple, who had been discovered by Moncho Moliner in the Provincial Championship of Segovia, ruled in the Vuelta and achieved things he had long dreamed of. But he still had some scores to settle with the Tour.

"I was still determined to wear the yellow jersey that I'd come so close to in 1983. But this remained a remote possibility because, crucially, in the time trials I was losing five or six minutes to my rivals. After taking part in the '83, '84, '85 and '86 Tours, everyone who had been a cyclist or had ridden the Tour told me I had to ride it with more strength and to have more confidence in myself. They suggested I should sneak into a break to balance my losses in the time trial. But, however much I tried, I never managed to get in the right group of escapees. It was always some others, more fortunate than me, who succeeded. It seemed I would need to look for a different strategy, if I wanted to win.

"I always felt it was in the high peaks where I stood a chance. But I was not gaining as much time as I needed in the mountain stages to compensate for what I was losing, sometimes by the bucket-load, in the time trials, be it the individual or the team trials. Little by little I saw my chances fading, and the Tour began to look very different from the way I had seen it back in 1983.

"To be honest, I wasn't very keen on the idea of winning the Tour if I could only do so by courtesy of infiltrating an escape group. I really loved being the leader of the race, even more if it were the Tour, but I didn't want to win it that way, because I felt it would be undervalued. But of course, that doesn't mean I didn't put all my effort into it. And I never gave up, even when, for one reason or another, things went wrong.

"So, the jersey seemed to elude me, and it wasn't until 1987, when I got it on Alpe d'Huez, that I felt reassured once more about my chances of winning the race. And I got to wear it without being gifted it in an escape, or by any other advantage. I got it simply by suffering every day, keeping my concentration, and doing a good job in the time trial. In other words, maintaining a certain regularity and only going for the 'yellow' in that territory where I was always at my best, in the mountain. That was clear to me after the victory in Villard de Lans. It was a victory in an impressive stage.

"In the final days of that '87 Tour, the main favourite was the young Frenchman, Jean-François Bernard (riding for Toshiba), after the crushing blow he had delivered in the mountain time trial on Mont Ventoux*. Ahead of me was his fellow countryman, Charly Mottet, from the Système U team, who with Fignon – a true expert in the art of the ambush – in their ranks, had just about been able to control the race up to that point . On the other hand, there was also Stephen Roche, and the Colombians Lucho Herrera and Fabio Parra.

"The 19th stage began with a certain measure of calmness because in the second half of the stage we were confronted with five serious obstacles: two first-, two second-, and a third-category. The prospect of all this, together with the pain in our legs from the previous day's mountain time trial, meant that nobody was eager for battle, at least not until Jeff (Jean-François) punctured on the descent of the first pass, but it was fixed quickly, and he was back with us again at the feeding station. There was the usual brief moment of relaxation while we grabbed our bags, then Fignon and his team began to accelerate; it was the start of a second-category climb, and once the first teams had got their

* Only Herrera (at 1–39) and Delgado (at 1–51) had finished within two minutes of Bernard.

bags the pace became furious. Some brave souls just threw their bags aside but very few were inclined to take that risk, because in those day you were not allowed to take solid food from the car. When I got my bag I had to react quickly: I could see Système U and Roche's Carrera riding flat out on the front and the peloton already stretched to breaking-point. I took a bidon and a bit of food out of the bag and threw the bag, with the second bidon and the rest of the food away. This was one of those 'everyman for himself' moments.

"The upward slope helped me gradually to get closer to the leading group – a group of some 15. Apart from the absent yellow jersey, we were the leaders on GC. Fignon was frantically asking for everybody to take their turn on the front because we were climbing at an extraordinary 35 kph. Behind, I imagine Jeff was attempting to stabilise his situation, but his casualness through the feeding zone had cost him, and would eventually result in him losing 4-16 that day.

"The stage was turning out to be very hard, thanks to the speed we were riding at. On the last climb to Côte de Chalimont, I could see the signs of fatigue on everyone's face, so I decided I would give it a try. Only Roche kept with me and when we arrived at the finish line I thought he had let me win the stage, because he would be taking over the jersey. He eventually admitted he was suffering badly and just didn't have the strength to challenge me in the sprint. From that day, I was absolutely convinced I would win the Tour. I was full of energy and my morale was sky-high. I knew the Irishman had been able to stay with me when I made my move, but he was vulnerable. I had this single idea in my mind: 'tomorrow I will get rid of him.'

"And so it was to prove. On the climb up to Alpe d'Huez I attacked very strongly and managed to drop him, and I remember saying to myself as I crossed the finishing line, 'the yellow jersey is mine.' The dream I had in 1983 was coming true. And I hadn't been given any 'gifts'. Riding my own race and making the most of my strengths at the right moments had been more than enough. From that moment on, I promised myself I would not let the Tour go. I even think it was at that moment when I lost my obsession with the unattainable yellow."

In his apprenticeship, during his years as an amateur, Delgado's goals had been clear and precise, and he'd managed to secure them with calculated displays of strength.

"Until 1982, when I took part in my first Vuelta a España, my goal was stage victories, especially in mountain stages, where my physical qualities shone most clearly. There's one I especially remember. Every time we raced in Asturias or Santander, I felt an extra motivation because those particular mountainous regions brought out the best in me. On this occasion, the start was in Ibio in Cantabria. Ahead of us were 125 kilometres, according to the route-book, and a number of passes, some of them well known like the Carmona, the Obalza, and the Hoz; it's an area made popular by Alberto Contador, thanks to his attack in the 2012 Vuelta, where he made the definitive move that would win him the race. As I say, this was a really hard route for an amateur race. We set off at around four in the afternoon, mid-August, and it was very hot. Just as I was about to take my bicycle, Tomás Nistal, the Team director, blurted out: 'How can you ride your bike in this state? Have you seen it?' I had not even noticed. Then he pointed at the left fork. 'Well, have a look at that. That thing you see there is a little crack. You shouldn't ride today unless you want to crash.' But I really did want to ride and I thought the crack was not that serious."

Nistal reminded him that this was a hilly race, that roads were not in good condition, and that he had to be careful and pay more attention to what were the tools of his trade.

"The truth is I'm a bit hopeless with my bike. I was never renowned for caring about it, and nor was I finicky with the mechanics, some of whom could spend the whole day fiddling about with it. I did not pay too much attention to the crack in the fork, reckoning that it would last a few more days, at least. Nistal shrugged his shoulders and, as we didn't have a mechanic, I went to the start line as if it were not a problem. We had to scale the Puerto de Carmona, first one side, then the other, and in between these two there were a couple more passes to be dealt with.

"I escaped on the first ascent of the Carmona and Javier Ízcue, a Navarran riding for Reynolds, jumped after me. I was in the Moliner-Vereco team. For quite some time he followed me, maintaining a gap of some 300 metres. I did not know what to do: should I wait for him or should I push on, since we were not yet at the halfway point? Finally, I decided to go for it and push on, because I was feeling strong. But whether I was climbing the hill, or coming down it, there he was, always the same distance away. All this was making me feel somewhat uneasy, but I told myself it was nothing and to make an all-out effort, and on the second ascent of the Carmona, I went for broke – I had to in order to drop him. Then I heard some strange noises and felt some odd vibrations when I took the corners and rode over the potholes, but I didn't pay much attention to it; I put it down to the poor road surface.

"This last effort finally disposed of all my rivals because I could not see a trace of Ízcue, nor of anyone else. I reached the finishing-line at dusk – the 125 kilometres turned out to have been more than 150 – and at that moment I could raise my arms as calm as you like, while all the pursuers arrived after dark, with the headlights of the following cars illuminating the road. After passing through the crowd I went to put the bike on the roof rack and, as I loosened the quick-release on the front wheel, I heard the noise of one of the forks crashing against the asphalt. I will never forget the director's frightened look. 'It's only by a miracle you haven't killed yourself. All day you have been foolishly playing with fire.'

"This anecdote in which I flirted between the recklessness of youth and the risks I ran on those dangerous descents made me feel even prouder of what was an unforgettable victory. My God, it turned out to be an extremely hard stage, and I won it in the most unusual circumstance – with a broken fork."

More than once Lady Luck has smiled upon him.

"In other tours I took part in around that time, I used to fight every time for a good place or for the occasional victory. My dream was to be the first, but without worrying about the yellow jersey. We heard talk about the 'yellow', but that was as far as it went; we didn't pay any more attention to it. The important thing was to be first over the line, like when I won the Vuelta a Tarragona in 1980 with the Gaylo team, or when I won the Vuelta a Murcia with Reynolds the year after. That wasn't without its peculiarities.

"It was 1981, and I was doing my military service, and also enjoying leave to ride in the Reynolds team. The race was auspicious as I was the leader. We were coming into the definitive stage and, on paper, it shouldn't have been too difficult for me to win it. But we found ourselves facing an unexpected handicap: of the eight in the team who had started the race, there were only three of us left: Enrique Aja, who was in very good form at the time; Jaimerena, the weakest, and me, the leader. So, in the morning, before the start-line, I tried to get some help, just in case. Not a chance; everyone was only too aware of the weakness of my situation. So, there I was with just a couple of team mates to try and control the last stage. It was one continuous assault, breaks proliferated and with 30 kilometres to the finish it was only me and Aja left. My lead overall was a meagre half a minute. That should be enough in an amateur race, if there is an entire team rallying round the leader. But with just one team mate it was going to be very difficult, since everyone else could see they had a chance of winning.

"Halfway through the stage, amidst utter chaos, Ángel Ocaña, who had been with me in the Moliner team, took pity on me.

'Hey, do you want me to lend you a hand?' said Ángel in that Granada accent of his.

'Both hands, if that's possible. You see, with only Aja …I don't think he will cope much longer. If you help me I'll be eternally grateful. Things are getting difficult, Aja is riding out of his skin, and I need to save my energy for the final bit, the climb to Cresta del Gallo.'

"It was on that climb where my lead would be in the most serious danger. With the excellent collaboration of Ocaña and Aja I managed to keep control of the race all the time. I didn't let anyone escape on the way up.

"On the way down – I don't know why – I was stricken with doubts and a fear, or a premonition, that I could fall and, as happens so often when you have that feeling in your bones, you do end up on the ground. And then you can say good bye to the general classification. So, I try to be careful. I'm in a little group;

we take a bend to the right. Watch out!, Gravel!: two hit the deck, I get hooked up with one of them and crash!, I'm down as well, just like my premonition. I get up immediately and I'm off again. All this is just six or seven kilometres from the finishing line.

"We finish the descent of the Cresta del Gallo and, just as I go through a level crossing I hear a very strange 'click'. Is it the frame? Is it broken? Then another 'click' – softer this time. I look, and I can see it's the quick-release lever – it's revolving, with the front wheel loose! I run the risk of a hell of a crash the moment I hit the first bit of rough road. As bold as brass I lock the lever while still on the move; it's something I have never repeated, and would never do again in my whole life. The position is fearfully dangerous and I cut my finger slightly on the spokes, but my obsession with victory overcame all caution. With victory, the bitter-sweet taste of the risk gives it an added spice. That was the first tour I won that year, and I won it while I was still doing military service, with hardly any training. I was well satisfied."

A year later he made his debut as a professional, also with Reynolds. And he took part in the Vuelta a España for the first time.

"I felt the change from the amateur to the professional category. It was April and I still had the weight of military service in my legs. The race started in Santiago de Compostela with a nine-kilometre prologue where I came ninth. I have never excelled in individual time trials, but such a beginning to the Vuelta exceeded my wildest expectations. However, the leaders of the team had to be Ángel Arroyo, or José Luis Laguía or Julián Gorospe, the latter being a specialist rider against the clock. Youth was his only obstacle. But the Vuelta got tough for him in the Reinosa stage because of the echelons. My morale was high because of that first day, and I passed the test well enough. It was like this until the day I had to face one of the most difficult stages I've gone through in my life. It was only 150 kilometres, which was good because races longer than 200 kilometres (very typical at that time), scared me. The fewer the kilometres, the less likely you are to suffer a *pájara*, which was an obsession of mine in my early years."

And furthermore, the Puerto de Mont Repos was on the way – so much the better. An easy route and a mountain. This could be his day.

"Yes, yes! As soon as we left Zaragoza, a strong wind began to blow from the side, the famous wind coming off the Moncayo, well known in that area. Very soon it was every man for himself, riders elbowing each other to find shelter against the wind; echelons were formed and after a few kilometres I found myself in the second group. Then Ángel Arroyo had the misfortune to get a piece of paper stuck in his spokes; he couldn't continue until he had stopped and removed it. Echávarri, our director, did his best to regroup the team and we set about an intense chase to get back to the front group, where all the favourites were. They were always in sight, ahead of us on the long straight road, but we couldn't manage to reduce the distance. Our turns on the front were perfectly synchronised, but our strength was failing. As we left Huesca, already in the foothills of Mont Repos, we managed to put Arroyo into the front echelon, or rather, some of my team mates managed to do it; I was dead. I couldn't believe I had only ridden 80 kilometres. Simply thinking that I still had to climb the puerto made me want to give up and go home. I did my best to recover and I managed to reach Sabiñanigo but with a huge *pájara* and ten minutes behind the stage winner. All I could think about was that bloody wind, and that cycling was just not for me.

"I ended the Vuelta in 30th position, almost 47 minutes down on our team-leader, Arroyo, for whom, more than once, I ended up exhausted at the finishing line, after pulling on the front for many kilometres. Out of curiosity, the director released me from that pacing duty in the last flat stages so that I could regain some strength for the penultimate stage that would take us through the Guadarrama mountains towards Segovia. I knew the area very well, so I would be able to help Arroyo. Such a typical piece of team-strategy – and it crumbled the moment we started the first puerto of the day, the Navafría, when I was one of the first to be dropped. Thank God I had been rested for that day before, because I'm not sure I would have been able to finish otherwise. I was totally worn out. Arroyo may have been familiar with what it meant to wear the yellow jersey; I learnt how hard you had to work to keep hold of it."

Chapter 8

Decisions

'There is nothing so difficult as making a decision.'
Napoleon

"All the events in my racing life, the moments I suffered a *pájara*, all the attacks I made and those I thought about making, my yellow jerseys – they are so recent and fresh in my mind that I don't even realise that I am now retired. And, like other decisions I took throughout my life as a cyclist, the decision to retire was mine alone; and those decisions are no different from those that any one might have considered at some point in his life.

"However, when facing and reliving all those memories, you cannot but feel inclined to doubt the benefits of voluntary retirement. All the good moments force you to find better ones in places where you are already familiar. So many stories, so many experiences – it's the comradeship, the atmosphere, the good life that you can only find in cycling, which makes the decision so hard to take. I guess it also happens in other sports. But in my sport, the one that was once my sport, the one to which I had devoted the best years of my youth, with all its moments of happiness and sorrow, and passion and dreams, deciding to quit was so hard for me.

"To stop working – giving up – in short, opting for retirement, comes as the result of a number of warnings. Life provides them for you, without you having to ask. When the puerto becomes harder every year; when the wind blows stronger with every season; when the rain feels colder, more hostile, even wetter with every spring; when every time you are away, for however short a time, you find yourself missing your family and your friends; and thinking about everything that is waiting for you on the other side of the barrier, beyond the finishing line, and the crowd and the hotel.

"And when in every interview they ask you the same old questions: 'When are you hanging up your bicycle?' or 'How long are you going to carry on racing?' or when a fanatical supporter shouts at you from the kerb 'Perico, time to give up!' or 'Perico, you are done for!' you understand that the last finishing line is near. There is no 20- or 25-year-old cyclist who gets bombarded with those kinds of questions every five minutes, not even every season. There's something there that points towards the end. I didn't take that decision on any one particular day. I came to it little by little."

He thought about those questions he was asked and managed to find the answers: 'Although you are already an old cyclist when you are thirty, I would still like to last until I reach 32.'

"Then, when I turned 32 I felt like a little child, just as I do now. But you switch your mindset when the newly arrived team mate, a new professional in his twenties, tells you: 'I feel so excited about cycling by your side, I have been following you all my life, I started to cycle because I wanted to be like you, I have a poster of you in my room, above my bed. I would like to bring it to you one day so you can sign it.' Words like that would make anybody end up facing reality, and I told myself: 'Oh dear, Pedro, you are so old, too old for cycling anymore.' It seems like yesterday when that young kid on his bike was asking for my autograph. Yes, what I hear is embarrassing, I feel awkward, I understand I have become an oldie."

This is hardly a new story; it's a cycle that repeats itself again and again.

"When I was nearly 22 I became a professional, and as I observed veterans in the team like Eulalio García, Rafael Ladrón de Guevara, Jesús Suárez Cuevas, all of them around their 30s, I got the feeling they were really old, just as I became old to my admiring neo-professional. I bore witness to the retirement of all those cyclists, one by one, and I told myself that one day I would grow old too. As I am now, and contemplating a world looking backwards. But in my case, I have been lucky: nobody forced me to retire; it was entirely my decision and what is more, Miguel Indurain would eventually become my replacement, which gave me an opportunity to enjoy my last years of cycling a lot more."

Pedro was not affected by the generational change; quite the opposite, he continued to maintain a prestigious place in the international peloton, but his role had changed.

"In 1993 I realised that I was not fit for the Tour anymore; I struggled to keep up with the peloton. In 1991, the year of transition, I was still optimistic because I felt strong in the mountain stages. But in 1993, it was a quite different story: every day became harder, more uphill. Particularly, I remember with amazement the 158-kilometre Stage 6 between Evreux and Amiens. The riding was flat out from the start, non-stop attack and counter-attack. The kilometres went by so quickly. The lined-out peloton split, and then came back together again. Halfway through the stage I found myself at the back, a very difficult position because you run the risk of being dropped. I tried with all my strength to move up, but for every ten places I gained, aiming to go on and get past another ten, I incomprehensibly lost them again. I remember with real anguish the last hour of the race because I had the feeling that, at any moment, I was going to lose contact. My punishment came on the long straights, when I had a chance of making out the leading group: I could see the attacks constantly going off the front. Finally, I arrived with the main group, after a nightmarish day on the bike, at an average speed of 50 km/hr, behind the stage winner, Johan Bruyneel.

"There were better days, but after that stage, and other mountain stages where I couldn't cope with the pace of the strongest riders, I told myself, 'The Tour is stronger than me, and if I am not stronger than the Tour, it must mean that I shouldn't be riding it.' And I made the firm commitment that I would never return to the Tour again.

"But I didn't want to grovel either, so I decided that I would ride one more Tour as a professional cyclist – the 1994 Tour – so as to remove the bitterness of the previous year and to try and leave the supporters and myself with a good taste in the mouth before saying a final goodbye.

"Postponing my retirement made it less hard to take the decision. It would be an abrupt change in my life and I knew that it would have to come at some point, but I resolved to have a decent retirement. As a passionate cyclist, it would be simply too much for me to put up with pointless and excessive suffering in races, where the only outcome would be disappointment and melancholy.

"I don't consider myself anyone's idol, but if that were the case, what would that young neo-professional who was so excited about riding with me, think if he saw me capitulating like that? Dignity above all else. And 1994 did work out nicely. The decision was already taken; it was inevitable, and I had to accept it; I was aware of the metamorphosis and of the importance of the decision. If that were not the case, I would still be pedalling instead of writing this book."

Delgado's cycling career has been marked by three transcendental decisions: the last one, the painful one, has just been told; the other two were of quite a different nature.

"The first of these decisions was taken in 1975, when Moncho Moliner came to Segovia to sign me up. I could play basketball, which I was quite fond of, although at that time I didn't know I wouldn't grow taller than 5ft-7ins, and I was also good at cross country running, which had a strong tradition in Segovia. But I finally took to cycling, which brought with it a few drawbacks to an ardent sports fan like me: it meant I wouldn't be able to run, for instance, or swim or play football. But none of this really bothered me because I wanted to be a cyclist. At first I didn't listen much to anyone's advice. I just did what I wanted to do. But of course I tried to be fit on racing days to perform better. I changed little by little. As I won more races I realised that I was becoming an important cyclist within my category, and that to maintain that level every year would become increasingly demanding."

He excelled. Pedro Delgado was an exceptional junior and a very promising amateur. His victories didn't go unnoticed because some of them, like the one in Ibio, were remarkable achievements. In 1979 he got an important call from someone who had been involved in cycling for a long time, Santiago Revuelta, manager at Teka.

'Good afternoon, can I speak with Pedro Delgado please?'
'I'm his mother. Who's calling?'
'My name is Santiago Revuelta, from the Teka team.'
'Hold on, I'll call him now.'

"I already knew about Santiago Revuelta because he had both an amateur team and a professional one. The talk was so long that my ears still hurt even now. He insisted I had to move on to the professional ranks, that he wanted to make me an offer, that I had to count on him, that I had to become a professional rider now because I was so talented…I told him I was a bit scared, that I still had to do my military service, that maybe in a couple of years I would. And he told me I shouldn't be silly; he insisted that I would be able to do the military service as a professional because I would get lots of military leave. To be honest, I was very grateful for his call. I got the same stuff from Rafael Carrasco, Kelme's director, and from Javier Mínguez too, who had been in the same professional team as Moncho – the Moliner Vereco outfit. But I wasn't persuaded; first, I would do the military service and get that out of the way, and then I would become a professional."

He proceeded accordingly, and he went on to serve in the army. However, his second decision was not to postpone his entry into the professional ranks.

"I went from being a junior to an amateur during 1978, because I had outgrown that category. I needed to challenge myself with new and stronger rivals. The end would be becoming a professional, without forgetting my studies. The thing is that in 1982, after serving my country, I was still undecided. I wanted to be a cyclist, but it was not clear to me how I could earn a living from it, and I decided to start my training as a paramedic. To my family all this seemed odd, especially my wanting to become a professional cyclist. My father didn't find that particularly funny: 'This is a young boy's madness; he'll grow out of it,' he thought. 'Yes, you win races,' he said, 'but it's one thing to play a sport because you like it, and it's a different thing to make a living out of it.'

"At home they understood my urge to get better and that turning professional was only one more step, but they also considered that I was a student, and that obtaining a degree would be the best way of securing my future, certainly better than turning the pedals. And then they wondered how I could make cycling compatible with my studies. I pondered the same dilemma. The year 1982 was not particularly good. I won two professional races – Sabiñanigo and a critérium in Ávila. I felt especially proud of these victories because I wasn't fully fit for them, mainly because it had been difficult to achieve my best level in such an anti-sports environment as the Army. Moreover, I didn't have enough time to devote to training. In the mornings I either had to train or attend school, I couldn't do both things at the same time because in the afternoon I had an internship at the hospital.

"All this worried me somewhat, because I couldn't do all these activities to the best of my ability. On the other hand, there was my medical training; I passed two courses, but I couldn't undertake all the work required at the hospital because I was racing. So my training was completely mishandled. I found myself falling between two stools because I was neither studying nor cycling as I should."

He reassessed the situation. He didn't listen either to those who continually told him he was 'champion material', and that he could earn a good living from cycling, nor to those who suggested cycling was 'a waste of time'. Those clichés, you are 'champion material', or 'a rough diamond', sounded so unfamiliar to him.

"I was in the Moliner team at the same time as Cabrero, Machín and de la Fuente. These three cyclists, in my humble opinion, were much better than me. They won a lot of races and it was normal for them to finish in the top five. They really were 'champion material' as I used to be told I was, but none of them made it. On the other hand, what raised my hopes was that I had rubbed shoulders with other cyclists in the amateur ranks, like Alberto Fernández, Marino Lejarreta, Faustino Rupérez, Ángel Arroyo and Juan Fernández, who were now making it as professionals.

"I had to make a decision: In 1983 I decided I would quit my studies as from October, and I would put all my effort and all my time into cycling. If that year wasn't fruitful, or I didn't feel comfortable, or I felt it was too much for me, it would not be a problem: I would pick up my books again and finish my studies."

And that's what he did. He struggled in the '83 Vuelta – Hinault's most costly win ever, and then he discovered the Tour. It was goodbye to books and to studying. The 1,000 little pesetas he earned at weekends as a junior, or the monthly 15,000 or 20,000 he earned in his last year as an amateur received a splendid boost when he became a professional.

"I have always been lucky at key moments. In those years, it was not too difficult to move from amateur to professional, but it was also true that wages were meagre; some riders even paid to become part of a professional team. They wanted to pay me one million pesetas a year, an incredible amount for a boy from Segovia. A millionaire! I could earn a million pesetas at the age of 21*. When I saw that in capital letters my mouth watered. I was told by two sports directors at that time, that Julián Gorospe and I were the two best-paid new professionals in Spanish cycling, although you never know if that was really true."

It was in 1983, after the Tour and during the Vuelta a Burgos that Chico Pérez came to see him at the hotel, and Pedro almost fainted.

'My offer is 30 million pesetas for a three-year contract.'

'Chico, you are crazy!'

'Not really. Look at it this way; it's 15 million for each leg.'

'You must be kidding, Chico.'

'Would you like sixty?'

'Oh my…'

'That was the amount I offered,' Chico later said, 'but he didn't accept it. It would have made me rich because he was the cyclist of the future. He was a great cyclist, as he eventually became, but mainly, he was a celebrity. The proof? Go into a market in the

---

* The rate of exchange was 200 pesetas to the pound at the time. As a junior he had earned £5 over the weekend; as an amateur, £75 to £100 per month. A million pesetas was an anual salary of £5,000.

rush hour, when it is crowded with women, and shout "Perico!" Everyone knows who you are referring to – the winner of the Tour, the one once tested positive, the one who arrived late...'

Finally Pedro decided to devote all his time to cycling.

"I was torn between the two. I really wanted to continue studying, and it saddened me to have to put all that to one side – I even considered enrolling in the Universidad a Distancia* – but the reality was that I had a promising future as a cyclist, and the Tour of '83 had given such a boost to my confidence. I was getting good results, even better abroad than in Spain. I was not deterred by that fear of crossing the Pyrenees, which was so pervasive in Spain. It was all the same to me whether I was racing in France, Italy or Switzerland. I was not scared to sign up for races abroad, I adapted easily."

His successes and his quality were becoming well known, both at home and abroad; from the very first moment he set foot in the Tour, his competitiveness delighted everyone, and his reputation grew rapidly. His good performances in France in July launched him into what, at that time, and still today in many cases, was the cyclists' El Dorado – the post-Tour critériums. Only the best were chosen, and the last week of July and early August became one continuous period of racing, travelling to and fro from France to Holland, from Holland to Belgium and vice versa. It was a punishing round, especially after 21 gruelling days in the Tour, but it paid handsomely.

"In one of those critériums, in Holland, I was approached by a gentleman who talked about the creation of a new team and they wanted to make me an offer. He said they needed a star with 'champion material' – that was me. It was 1985; I had won the Vuelta a España and my confidence was growing, day by day."

Delgado, whom everyone called 'Perico', felt flattered. It was an interesting and tempting offer. The only 'but' was that it was a foreign team, and a new one.

---

* The Spanish equivalent of the Open University

"I pondered whether I should go abroad or stay in Spain. I have always been an adventurous person with a strong will to succeed. I always liked to do things better, and even if I did not get obsessed when things didn't go too well, they were a cause of concern to me; for instance, my performance in the time trial, or my problems with echelons. I used to think that foreign cyclists must have a special formula to ride faster against the clock, or to turn an echelon into something more or less normal. I was attracted to the adventures of all this. It is like when I took my first decision, to move to Valladolid. In this case, to be honest, the primary motivation was economic, but I did consider other important factors as well. After barely a week, I signed, somewhat impetuously, a preliminary agreement. Once I had done it, I wondered what the hell I was doing in Holland. I didn't understand a word of Dutch, I knew hardly anything about the country and its customs. Everything was new. 'Well then,' I thought, 'I will learn English, which is widely spoken here.' After all, it would only be for a year. I wasn't over keen on the idea of extending my adventure."

In the end, he did not delay his decision any longer and signed a one-year contract. So, in 1986, to Holland, but after crossing that Rubicon, the doubts continued to buzz round his head, even though he could immediately see the benefits. He went from pessimism to euphoria in a trice.

"I felt encouraged by the thought of all those Spanish workers, emigrants without a secure job, who had to move to Germany, France and so many other countries. Their circumstances were so different. But then, as if I didn't have enough doubts, I happened to run into one of the best cyclists in the world at that time, Francesco Moser, the hour-record man, and he only added to them. We were both flying from Quimper to Paris after riding a critérium. He knew that the following season I would be part of a Dutch team.

'Pedro, you are crazy!'
'Why?'
'How can you even think of going to a Dutch team?'
'Why not?'

'Well, it's good to ride in a foreign team; I would even recommend it.'

'Then, what is the problem?'

'You're going to learn a lot there; but at this early stage of your career, I'm not sure. I think you should have waited a couple more years before signing for a Dutch team.'

"Although he didn't say it to me, I believe Moser was thinking that I would have done better by signing for an Italian team, like Marino Lejarreta (who signed for Alfa-Lum) because the culture shock would have been less abrupt. But the offer I had received had come from PDM... and they were Dutch, and once the contract came into effect, I was cheered up even more when they told me I would be racing a lot in Spain – in other words, just as I was already doing. I was to be a member of a foreign team, but it was based in Spain. It wouldn't be all that different. And in future years I came to realise even more clearly that the decision had been correct and a very positive one. Apart from the distance imposed by the language barrier I felt very well looked-after."

And he had occasion to become convinced that cyclists, whatever their nationality, are plagued by pretty much the same demons. He discovered that, on the very first day of strong winds.

"It was a race in Holland, and as usual, the first thing I did was to open the curtains to see what the day was like. I found myself face to face with the tops of the trees bent over by the strength of the wind. Mother of God! What's going to become of me among all these flat-country greyhounds?

"I went down for breakfast with my morale at rock bottom, half expecting to see a celebration around the table among my team mates, rouleurs the lot of them, facing what was to come. But no. There was total silence, and long faces. 'Something has happened,' I thought to myself. 'What is it?' I asked them. They all looked at me in amazement, and asked if I hadn't seen what kind of day it was. 'Of course' I replied, 'but does that put you in a bad mood?' They all began to rant about the blasted wind. 'Bloody hell,' they said. 'Have you ever seen a more filthy day than this? Just our luck!'

"Then there were Dutch exclamations identical to those any Spanish rider would make. When there is a cross-wind in Spain we are on the alert, listening intently, and nervous of what's coming. We used to grumble: 'Now the Dutch or the Belgians are going to make our lives a misery in these conditions, and we are going to be left here at the back of the peloton with no chance of winning.'

"But after that race, I knew that it was the same everywhere. Nobody likes a cross wind, and the echelon formation – however pretty it is to watch on television – means a pitched battle among the riders. It's every man for himself: the level of aggression to be in front is so high that they push and shove with their elbows and their handlebars; they bare their teeth like wild animals; they swear like men possessed; and they'll do anything to defend their position. The danger of crashes or of splits in the peloton is ever-present, with all the consequences that has if one of the favourites is involved. And there is no way round it: you just knuckle down and get on with it, and tell yourself to put up with it and that's it! It's all the same – whether for a Spanish team or a foreign team: the pleasures and the pains are similar, wherever you are. The best thing undoubtedly is to settle down in the race, because you can't change the weather conditions however much you wish you could. From that day onwards the fear when confronted with those kinds of days just became a part of the job, in spite of all that multi-lingual yelling and shrieking which translated into the same thing, everywhere."

Chapter 9

1988

'The greatest victory is beating yourself.'
Calderón de la Barca

'Perico, this is Alfredo from Channel 3 in Segovia. How are you?

This was one morning in April 1988.

'Hello Alfredo, you've just caught me. I'm on my way out.'

'Look, it's my boss, José María García; he'd like to have a quick word with you. He'll call you straight away if that's OK by you.'

'Fine, but straight away because I've got to go.'

'OK, OK, we'll call you immediately.'

After a couple of minutes the phone rang again.

'Hello, Pedro. How are you?'

'Oh, I'm very well.'

'How come you're not riding the Vuelta?'

'Because we want to win the Tour and we are going to put everything into achieving that. For the Vuelta we have riders like Gorospe, Miguel Indurain or Ángel Arroyo. So the team can fight on two fronts – the Vuelta and the Giro – and above all, I can have the perfect preparation for the Tour.'

'Oh. I see, well that seems very good. I was also calling you because I've heard you are going to be doing radio commentaries for Cadena SER.'

'Well, yes. I have considered it and I decided to do it.'

'Oh, come on, how can you do that?'

'They called me, and the idea seemed very attractive. I told them it was fine, splendid.'

'When did you reply to them?'

'I've already committed myself. I'm the one who decided.'

'But, just a minute, Pedro. If you are the number one in Spanish cycling, you know with whom you need to be. You need to be with radio's number one. I don't believe you're going to get that if you choose Cadena SER. You could see last year how Álvaro

Pino and I formed a good pair. I tell you, cycling's number one has to be with radio's number one.'

'Well OK. You're right, but the fact is I really get on very well with the people from Cadena SER.'

'But have you signed anything?'

'No, not yet, but I have given them my word.'

'Words can fly off with the wind. Until it's signed and sealed, you can always change your mind.'

'I can believe that, but the point is I've given them my word...'

'Alright, alright. You know what you are doing; but think about it – carefully. Goodbye.'

'Goodbye.'

* * *

In 1987, when he was still with the Dutch PDM team, Pedro had mulled over the idea of swapping the Vuelta for the Giro, as a better way of preparing for the Tour, but such was the reaction he'd received that he decided to leave things as they were. 'I'll do it some other time,' he concluded. However, the seed had been sown in his mind.

"1988 was a really hard year for the team, although not so much for me, owing to the important decision we announced during the Tour of the Basque Country. We made it public that I would not be taking part in the Vuelta a España. We came in for a lot of criticism: some people didn't believe it; the Vuelta organisers threatened to remove Reynolds from the list of teams taking part, if I wasn't going to ride. But I had changed since the previous year: I knew that I had a realistic prospect of winning the Tour, without having to rely on somebody letting me take minutes out of them, or through some lucky breakaway. I had observed how, in 1987, the Giro had served as an excellent preparation for Roche. What's more, Hinault, Fignon, and LeMond had all followed a similar route in getting ready for the Tour, and it had served them well. It was something I needed to try."

The decision was taken, definitively, and Reynolds found themselves riding the Vuelta only after an unprecedented controversy. Many people felt very disappointed with Pedro and it earned him more than one enemy.

"José María García, who was said to have had a big interest in Unipublic (the organisers of the Vuelta), was very upset with the decision I'd made. And that wasn't the sum total of it: after hearing that I wouldn't be riding the Vuelta, he then discovered that the Cadena SER radio channel had made me an offer to commentate on it. From when it had first been mooted, I'd fancied the idea of following the Vuelta as a commentator. So, after weighing it up, I gave it the OK.

"García was the top radio sports commentator in Spain, and it was he who was principally responsible for putting round the idea that I was unpatriotic for not going to the Vuelta and that such a decision was a public disgrace. I believe, however, that what really hurt him to the depths of his ego was that his broadcasting rival, Cadena SER, was announcing over the airwaves at all hours of day and night: 'Pedro Delgado is doing the Vuelta…with Cadena SER'."

Little by little, things returned to normal, the controversy gave way to the race itself, and life carried on, although not without the argument leaving its mark.

"The days passed normally for me; I was getting ready for the Giro. The Vuelta started, and with it, my collaboration with Cadena SER. And from that point onwards José María García began to criticise me in that over-the-top style of his. And it was not just me he directed his ire towards, but also my team mates and our sponsor. So, instead of 'Reynolds' he used to talk about 'the team from Navarra'."

With the Vuelta over, the Giro began shortly afterwards.

"I went off to the Giro with the intention of putting in a good performance, while not losing sight of the fact that the aim was preparation for the Tour. The criticisms rained down, more for not having ridden the Vuelta than for going to the Giro: 'a grave mistake and he's going to pay for it,' they said. In addition, the Giro didn't turn out to be at all a positive experience; I didn't ride particularly well. At the very beginning, on the Capitello Matesse stage, I lost practically three minutes. I was certainly disappointed, but I didn't attach too much importance to it; after all, I was there primarily to prepare for the Tour.

"After Capitello Matesse came that mythical day on the Gavia, and not much else. I liked the race, yes; but because of our unfamiliarity with it, my director and I made some serious mistakes, which in the long run became apparent. I wasn't as mentally prepared for the race as I should have been. Even if I had wanted to contest it with greater conviction, at the critical moments I always had a ready excuse for not giving it everything: 'Pedro, you need to take it easy; it's in the Tour where you have to put it all on the line.' In short, with that kind of mental attitude, I wasn't aggressive enough and, bit by bit, the race slipped away from me, until in the end I was left with no chance whatsoever."

The question remains whether taking part in the Giro as a way of preparing for the Tour turned out to be a decisive factor in what happened later. Pedro believed then that it was, and remains convinced, even to this day, that it was a good decision.

"The experience was very good. José Luis Laguía, to take one example, went through a very interesting metamorphosis. He had ridden the Vuelta, and immediately afterwards he started the Giro; he was 'dead', not so much physically as simply demoralised. He hadn't known until almost the last minute that he would be going to Italy. So he arrived, reluctant, unmotivated, exhausted, and with just one idea in his head: 'I should be at home. I don't want to ride the Giro. Nor the Tour either, for that matter, but after three hard weeks and all the tension of the Vuelta, this really is too much. I just feel so tired.' These phrases were repeated over and over again. José Luis was normally a happy-go-lucky person, but now he seemed permanently miserable. Instead of a cyclist we had a corpse in our midst, and instead of keeping quiet about it, he did nothing but complain – about everything.

"As the days went by, in a tough, three-week race, following on from another, similarly demanding tour, you would expect someone in the physical and emotional state that Laguía was in, to get even worse. But no, exactly the opposite happened. At the end of the first week, he had recovered his spark, and was his usual witty, amusing self. 'Incredible, but this is cycling,' he remarked. 'I am back again.' The change came about because on the flat stages of the Giro, the first 150 kilometres were usually ridden at a tranquil pace, in one large group and without an attack worthy of the name. It was only in the last 50 kilometres that the race would explode. This gave José Luis time to recuperate physically, and most especially, psychologically. The Giro grinds you down, like all three-week races, but it doesn't pressurise you as much as the Vuelta, and it leaves you in good shape for the Tour. Nowadays, the Giro is different. They have changed the profile of the stages, the routes, and even the way of racing."

Once he was over the frustration of not shining as he would have liked in the Italian race, Pedro confirmed that the Giro had put him on the launch pad for the Tour; he felt he was in impressive physical form.

"The team, on the other hand, was weighed down by the stress, since we weren't getting the results: the Vuelta had been a disaster; I hadn't won the Giro – in fact my performance had been weak – and the criticism was mounting. Thus we began the Tour, full of nerves, and our principal detractor, the all-powerful José María García on Radio Atena 3, had 'the team from Navarra' well and truly in his sights. The sponsors were very ill at ease with this constant sniping from the media. For my part, I let it pass over me; I concentrated on the race and, as if by coincidence, found one small recompense for so much criticism at the finish of the team time trial. We went very well, coming in just 1–02 down on Panasonic. After we'd crossed the line, I went off to the team car to change into some dry clothes, and who should turn up but one of García's collaborators, Pepe Gutiérrez.

'You've done a tremendous time trial. I'm absolutely delighted.'

'Thanks.'

'Could I ask you some questions?

'It's up to you…'

"With that reply I was trying to remind him of what we'd been going through in recent months, but that didn't seem to have dawned on him, and live on air as we were, he put the question to me.

'Here we have Perico Delgado. How did the time trial go?'

Pepe followed my movements while I was drying off the sweat, keeping the microphone close to me, waiting for my answer. As I didn't reply he repeated his question, reporting that I was changing. Once I'd finished he put the question to me again.

'You are all pleased with today's time trial, I imagine?'

Again, silence. The seconds ticked by; the silence was deafening. On the radio, fifteen or twenty seconds without a sound is a lifetime. Pepe cleared his throat, then finally, off he went."

July advanced and, little by little, Pedro was getting into the Tour. Mentally he was on top of it, and he knew that physically he was, too.

"After we'd got through the first few, typically nervous days I was feeling very positive. On the way to Morzine, the first mountain stage, I found myself climbing easily. The following day we faced the *etapa reina*, which culminated on Alpe d'Huez. I felt full of strength and my morale was sky-high. The start was crazy: very fast, one split after another, and we went through the first 100 kilometres in a little over two hours. Then we arrived at the foot of the Col de la Madeleine. The banner, announcing its 28 kilometres to the top provoked a chorus of hysterical shouts, calling for a slow-down, since at the speed we'd been riding everybody's legs were aching. All that had a calming effect on the peloton; the stage became more sedate.

"Although initially we were not climbing particularly quickly, because the race had been so fast up to that point, the peloton immediately fractured into a number of smaller groups. Some three or four kilometres from the top, Arroyo urged me to attack. I replied that it would be better to wait. A short time later he said it again: 'They are dead; now is the time to settle it.' I preferred to wait. I told him that the team (Miguel Indurain, Omar Hernández, Jesús Rodríguez Magro and he) should join together and take advantage of Indurain's ability to descend at high speed. 'Warn them all,' I said, 'to ride on the front as soon as we are over the summit.' At the bottom was the feeding station and immediately after that you are on to the first slopes of the Col de Glandon; I was hoping not to give a moment's respite to anyone still with us.

"Everything went to plan: we arrived at the feeding station in a group of some 10 or 15 riders, with the race completely broken up. I told Indurain to continue forcing the pace through the feeding zone so as to prevent anybody from picking up any food, which would be essential on a day like this. Halfway up the climb Omar Hernández stepped up the pace, and two kilometres from the top I attacked.

"With some 50 kilometres still to ride to Alpe d'Huez, only Steven Rooks was able to follow me. We shared the effort, bit-and-bit, all the way down and then on the level valley road. Behind us, the Colombians were pulling strongly, which was very unusual for them. But this time they didn't let us ride free, and so prevented us from building a big gap. Close to the finish-line they caught up with us. But the principal objective – to bury some of the favourites, like Mottet and Bernard – had been accomplished."

Rooks won the stage and Delgado recovered the yellow jersey which Roche, convalescing in this edition of the Tour, had snatched from him in Dijon the year before. The French, with Bernard and Mottet practically eliminated, and Fignon retiring after a tapeworm was found in his intestines, found themselves with nobody left to contest the race.

"The day after Alpe d'Huez was the mountain time trial at Villard de Lans, which I won, as I had done the year before, and put more time into my pursuers. I felt in control of the race; the Pyrenees were still to come, but it would be enough for me simply to follow their wheels, and go on to the offensive only towards the end of the stage to add a few more seconds to the advantage I had over my most immediate rivals: Parra, Theunisse and Rooks. There was no need, as there had been the previous year, to attack from far out, because none of them could match me in the time trial or in the mountains. The Tour was practically won."

Fabio Parra, Lucho Herrera, Theunisse, Rooks and Breukink were identified as Pedro's only opponents, and in the Pyrenean stage that followed they attacked as often as they could – and Reynolds dealt with all of them.

"The team coped very well: Indurain climbed the Peyresourde perfectly (that day he revealed to me his potential in the high mountains) and all the way to the Tourmalet I was never left isolated. From then on there was just a handful of us left. Climbing towards the final summit, Luz Ardiden, I sat off the back, from where I could keep on eye on how the rest were doing; the French TV commentator interpreted this as 'Peguico' being in difficulties: I was dropping back, but he didn't understand what I was really doing. Nor did my own Director: even he thought it was a sign that I was weakening. After a number of attacks by Fabio Parra, to which Rooks responded immediately, I realised that we were all pretty much exhausted and, just like the day before, again with three kilometres to go, I decided to switch to attack with the intention of destroying them psychologically. They were going to be fed up to the back teeth with me. And everything would have gone as smooth as silk, were it not for the famous positive in Bordeaux. Yes, the positive…"

It was 19th of July.

"Ever since I put on the yellow jersey I'd been sharing a room with the French rider, Dominique Arnaud. After the finish of the second part of that long, split-stage day, while I was taking a shower, I seemed to hear on the French television some mention of a possible positive doping result. I dried myself off and came out of the bathroom.

'They've said that somebody in the Tour has tested positive, somebody important.'

'My God! Who could it be?' I asked. 'That's bad news.'

'They said they'll say more in an hour's time.'

"Dominique showered himself and we continued talking about it. 'Perhaps it's somebody who's recently won a stage. Who would that be?' we speculated.

"Within the peloton a certain amount of bad feeling had grown up towards the race organisation. On a number of occasions we had criticised Xavier Louy, the race director. We in the Reynolds team were annoyed because during the stage to Luz Ardiden some of the Dutch Superconfex riders, like Nijdam, had climbed the cols by hanging on to the cars, and nobody had said anything about it. Arroyo, who was sick and had to abandon, was absolutely furious at their cheek – the whole lot of them hanging on to the team cars. And the race judges didn't say a word. There was not so much as a peep out of them. A couple of times Arroyo confronted the riders, and the director. They ignored him, and the race judges were complicit in this because they didn't apply the rules. This practice became widespread on any mountain stage, and we Spaniards, in particular, criticised it. 'On this stage it was a disgrace,' we told them. 'Cars overtaking us, towing their riders.' This was becoming such an extraordinary Tour that the business of the positive hardly came as any great surprise."

Two hours had passed since the finish of the Bordeaux stage. The Reynolds team were in the Mercure Hotel, and in one of their rooms Pedro was receiving a recovery massage. The television was on.

'The rider who has tested positive is Pedro Delgado,' the newsreader began...

'What? Did you hear that?'

'How can it be me? That must be a mistake!'

Delgado went off looking for José Miguel Echávarri. There was nobody in his room. Soon after that Francis Lafargue, the team's public relations man saw him.

'Listen, Pedro. Yes, it does seem to be true. They hinted at that to us this morning, and we didn't want to say anything to you about it because we didn't want you getting into a state.' Then José Miguel turned up.

"I was in a surreal world. This was not possible. What is all this about? I felt I was being robbed; I was outraged. And people here, there and everywhere. The usual hullabaloo."

Julián Redondo was in the huge garage at Bordeaux de Lac that was serving as the Press Room: 'At about eight in the evening, Claude Sounders, the Tour's Chief Press Officer, came over to us. Juan Manuel Gozalo and I were saying that the race was over, that Paris was only a stone's throw away, and that we'd be celebrating the victory of another Spanish Tour winner, after Bahamontes in 1959, and Ocaña in 1973: Pedro Delgado.'

'Julián, do you know about the positive?'

'A positive? From whom?'

'From Perico.'

'Come on Claude, you're kidding us. Ok, I know perfectly

well that you would have preferred Fignon to win, but the tapeworm…'

'I swear to you it's true. Perico has tested positive.'

We froze. We couldn't understand it. 'They must be having us on,' we said. We understood it better when we noticed, a few metres away, all our colleagues from *L'Équipe* in a huddle and talking in low voices. Guy Roger came over to remove the doubt. There was no need to ask. 'It's true. It's Perico.'

* * *

The day was never-ending, permanently on watch inside the Reynold's hotel. Echávarri gave a press conference and insisted on his rider's innocence. That night Xavier Louy went to see him and suggested – indeed, requested 'for the good of the Tour and for cycling's sake' – that Delgado should withdraw from the race. José Miguel contacted Luis Puig, President of the International Cycling Union, who emphatically told him not to withdraw his rider. The matter was going to be taken further. The following day Javier Gómez Navarro, Secretary of State for Sports, and Cecilia Rodríguez, Director of the Sports Council, together with Luis Puig arrived at the Tour to put a stop to this outrage.

"Wherever I turned someone was asking me if I was going to abandon. I answered: 'I am carrying on.' Yes, I was going to finish the Tour, and I was going to win it because physically I was very strong and I felt I would win it legally. 'The race is mine and nobody is going to make me quit. And if they give me a 10-minute penalty I'll still win.' With that, I went off to bed.

"It took me a long while to get to sleep because I was in a highly emotional state. For only the second time in my life I took a sleeping pill (the first was during the 1986 Tour, when I was told that my mother had died). With all that going on I woke up, between dreams, startled. What had come into my mind was the water that is offered us by fans encouraging us from the side of the road. Would they have set a trap for me? Are there people capable of doing that sort of thing? It was all crazy; the possibility that I drank water from some spectator was slight, and furthermore, that it was contaminated seemed impossible to me, but I didn't stop wondering about it as I tried to find some explanation for the positive drug test. This couldn't be real. I felt sure that when I woke up I would discover that this had all been a nightmare. Dawn broke, and the positive test was the reality."

In the Paris laboratory where the urine samples were analysed, an eagle-eyed assistant discovered probenecid in Pedro's sample. Probenecid was not a product banned by the UCI, although it was by the Olympic Committee, who considered it a masking agent. In September, as a result of Delgado's positive test, the UCI would also include it on their list of doping substances. However, the person on duty prematurely released the result as if this were some run of the mill matter, which it most certainly was not. Procedures were rapidly set in motion to clear up the scandal.

"All this coming and going was beginning to weigh me down, but I continued to resist any suggestion that I should withdraw from the race. 'Why am I going to abandon? After all it has cost me to get this far?' Nobody in the team wanted to disturb me. They knew that the problem was serious and that it was necessary for me to be left alone. One of my biggest worries was how the public would react in the morning when I went to sign on before the start."

The next day the race would be neutralised from Bordeaux as far as Rouelle, and the journey from the hotel to the signing-on control, a matter of some kilometres, seemed to Pedro to be no distance at all. The news which filled the front pages of the French papers was not pleasant to read and the fear was that the public would be shouting insults and whistling their disapproval. Echávarri preferred to park their car at the entrance to the town, rather than in the race zone.

"The reception we feared so much, turned out to be quite extraordinary: they were chanting my name; the people were supporting me; they were encouraging me to carry on. It was that which gave me the security and courage to stay in the race. The stage was short, but what with my positive and the yellow jersey on my back it was very hard. It went through the Massif

116

Central, over territory very similar to Galicia, and the attacks came non-stop. Both the team and I coped with them well, and we got through the day. In Spain there was a growing current of sympathy towards me and in the peloton I sensed there was a gratifying measure of solidarity. At least, an emotional solidarity – the race was quite another matter. Almost everybody came over to encourage me. I felt it giving me strength and a measure of support; I came round to the idea that Paris was waiting for me. Half way through Stage 21, the Puy de Dôme stage, I was informed that everything was resolved and the matter cleared up. There was no positive.

"For now I had to forget the matter and face the race with optimism, as if nothing had happened. The time trial was over a 48-kilometre route, and I made every effort to win it; I really needed that to redeem myself and to demonstrate that I was a worthy winner. However, some five kilometres from the finish, and with the best time up to that point, I began to weaken. I think it was due to all the accumulated tension caused by the whole business. I finished fourth, a few seconds behind the winner, another Spaniard, Juan Martínez Oliver."

And then came the day he'd so looked forward to, Sunday 24th July, the final stage.

"I saw the culmination of a dream which I'd caught a glimpse of in my first Tour: to be the winner; to stand on the top step of the podium. And there I was. Even so, I still had one small fright. Two hundred metres before crossing the finishing-line for the last time my team mate, Herminio Díaz Zabala came looking for me to congratulate me. We joined hands so as to cross the line with our arms raised. Suddenly I hit a pothole (the Champs-Élysées is paved with cobblestones and is very uneven) and we almost ended up crossing the line in mid air. It seemed this Tour was always destined to be just one thing after another."

Pedro Delgado, with his spotless, brand new yellow jersey, escorted by Rooks and Parra, took over Paris, like thousands of his compatriots, and got ready to enjoy the formal ceremony with all the intensity that the occasion demanded.

"Listening to the Spanish national anthem, the silence which that moment produces, with everybody's looks converging on me – it makes you feel as if you are floating several feet in the air. During the minute while the music was playing, the Tour passed in front of me in rapid flashes. I am on cloud nine; all the sacrifices – the battles, the freezing cold, the heat, the criticism and the praise – they have all been worthwhile. I have got what I have sought so much, a complete victory. Once the ecstasy of that minute had passed, I was like a puppet; they carried me here, there and everywhere. And all I wanted was to have a rest, and get away from all that hubbub into my hotel room, by myself, and free from everything that had happened during those last, long three weeks."

The day didn't end there; it carried on for hours with the obligatory Tour party. In those days, the Lido de Paris used to invite the winner and his team to a dinner and a cabaret. With his Reynolds team mates, Pedro arrived at that most famous of Parisian venues, not forgetting to take his radiant yellow jersey with him. After the dinner and with the performance in full swing, the showgirls called him up to the stage. He went up and posed with them, carrying the *maillot jaune*. After the required series of photographs and a few words to the guests attending the show, he rejoined his companions at the table. At that moment it dawned on him that the precious jersey was missing. Francis, our PR man who had accompanied him to the stage, must have it. 'No, I haven't got it. I'm sure you had it,' he replied. Oh, no. The jersey he had so longed for had disappeared. Suspicion fell on the Lido's head waiter. He swore over and over again that he knew nothing about how it came to be lost, but the emblematic jersey did not reappear. One way or another it really seemed that Delgado couldn't win.

"The years have passed and although I tried to turn the page on the business of the false positive drug test, I have come to realise that I will never be free from the shadow of doubt that remained after my victory. It didn't do much good that *L'Équipe* and the ASO organisation recognised the mistake, but that acceptance didn't occupy a fraction of the space, nor receive the front-page media attention, as when they were trying to throw me out of the race – one small, practically invisible note in the press, weeks later acknowledging their error. Furthermore, heads rolled inside ASO; they sacked the Director of that Tour, Xavier Louy. That didn't in any way compensate me for all I'd had to go through, but it was better than nothing.

"Even today, there will be journalists or newspapers that try to remember my Tour as a 'stained yellow jersey'. The system got it wrong by me, but that same system which likes to puff its chest out with pride is equally keen to hide its mistakes and to blame others, so as to appear the more worthy because of their lack of professionalism. The UCI demands professionalism from riders and teams 'for the good of cycling', but as time goes on I have come to realise that they lack the very professionalism which they demand in others. There is a long list of errors committed against cyclists by this organisation; some don't have the capacity to defend themselves against an institution; others do. And yet, even though they might have received some recompense, 'the doubt is more cruel than the worst of truths,' as Molière said, and against that doubt, you are defenceless.

"Now, seen from the distance of the time that has passed, what they did to me was unforgivable, all the more so in a race like the Tour, with its huge organisation. If I had been an American with their lawsuits, I could have sued them for a tidy old sum, but at moments like that you don't think about money, but rather about dispelling any doubts and giving legitimacy to your victory. The pressure I went through was enormous, and I seriously considered abandoning; that thought came and went for hours after the disastrous announcement. The definitive push came before the great public reception at the start of the stage in Ruelle sur Touvre; that was the turning point. From that moment onwards I completely gave up any idea of abandoning.

"On the matter of the substance which appeared, I could have taken it quite freely every day and in whatever quantity if I'd wished, since it was not prohibited in professional cycling, nor in other professional team sports. To some of those who think badly of my victory or who question whether my victory was legal or not, I would say this: 'Yes, probenecid is used to mask testosterone, but I would have needed to have taken it every day;

to take it just for one day, and not on other days, would have had no effect whatsoever. It would necessarily, therefore, have appeared many times in my urine sample, since as leader of the race I was tested every day from Alpe d'Huez (stage 12) to Paris (Stage 22), but that did not happen."

1. The Moliner Junior team, 1976 (Pedro Delgado, age 16, centre)

2. With Moncho Moliner at a race in La Rioja, 1977

3. First Tour de France, 1983: Pedro descending the Peyresourde into Luchon and to finish second on the stage behind Robert Millar. The French named him '*Le Fou des Pyrénées*' – the Madman of the Pyrenees. A week later, after the Alpe d'Huez stage, he would be lying second overall. "The Alpe d'Huez climb, where I felt in stupendous form, gave a huge boost to my confidence. That's when I first thought that the Tour was a race that I could win."

4. Tour de France, 1984. "We found ourselves up against Fignon in his pomp, and he was unbeatable." Fignon won five stages, and finished the overall winner by a margin of more than 10 minutes. Here, on Stage 18, the leading group tackles the Col du Galibier. From l to r, Robert Millar, Pascal Simon, Pedro Delgado, Patrocinio Jiménez, Phil Anderson, Edgar Corredor, Laurent Fignon, Eric Caritoux, Jean-Marie Grezet and Sean Kelly.

5. Vuelta 1985: Stage 18, on the road towards Segovia, with José Recio. The Kelme rider took the stage. Delgado overturned a 6–13 deficit to take his first Grand Tour win.

6. Vuelta 1987: with Lucho Herrera (1st overall) and Raimund Dietzen (2nd)

7. And riding against Herrera again later that year in the Tour de France, where the Colombian took the Mountains jersey.

8. Tour de France 1987: third on the Mont Ventoux Time Trial.

9. Tour de France 1987: Stephen Roche holding Delgado's wheel on the Col de Joux Plane. Over the summit, on the descent into Morzine, he will take back 18 seconds on the yellow jersey.

10. Giro d'Italia 1988: the unforgetable Gavia stage…

11. … and at the finish.

12. Tour de France 1988, climbing
to Luz Ardiden

13. After the Tour, presenting a yellow jersey to King Juan Carlos

14. Barcelona, October 1988, Pedro Delgado sitting with the only other Spanish Tour winners at that time: Luis Ocana (1973) and Federico Bahamontes (1959). The occasion was the celebration of the 25th Montjuic Hillclimb.

15. Three stage wins and a second Vuelta victory in 1989, although pressed hard throughout by the Colombian, Fabio Parra. Here, riding into Brañilín, in pouring rain.

16. Tour de France 1989: late on the starting ramp. "This was the year when I felt I was at my strongest ever. The start of the prologue in Luxembourg, possibly the biggest mistake in my entire career, cost me my second Tour without a doubt."

17. Tour 1989; 500 metres from the finish at Superbagnères, Delgado with Robert Millar (who will win the stage) and Charly Mottet just behind. "And what a great trio we formed, as we combined perfectly, sharing the work and riding bit-and-bit to the finish. Behind us the PDM men were pulling, but all they managed to do was to save the bacon of the two leading protagonists: LeMond and Fignon."

18. Vuelta 1990, and Miguel Indurain leading from the surprise winner, Marco Giovannetti, who gate-crashed the Banesto party. "From this year on, and without any traumas, the batton was passed from Pedro to Miguel."

19. "The Vuelta in 1993, and the uphill time trial on Navacerrada convinced me that I was not going very well that year, It was a case of 'wanting to but not being able to'. I finished 6th overall."

20. "I took the decision in the course of the 1993 Tour to quit cycling; my legs were no longer what they had been in the mountains and I didn't want to end up grovelling. I did occasionally attack, but these were acts of treason – attacking in the valleys so as to scrape into an escape group and to be up ahead, waiting for the arrival of the 'capos'. That way I could be alongside Miguel and able to lend him a hand. My final 9th place overall was a joy to me."

21. Pedro, during the Bola del Mundo stage of the 2012 Vuelta a España. In 1995 he began a new career, and since then has been commentating for Spanish television and radio at all the major international road cycling events.

Chapter 10

Marked by the Stars

'In all rituals simplicity is the best extravagance'.
Confucious

'A person who says she is an astrologist called; she wanted to speak to you,' said Luisa, one of the young ladies at the Pasadoiro hotel.

"I was at the team get-together in Navacerrada, preparing for the Tour, just like every year. This was in 1988, and barely two months later I would be bringing it home. I had just finished my regular training and was getting ready to go and eat. It hadn't been a hard day because the following day I would be doing some interval training, and so I'd ended a little early. I was trying to be as focused as possible, but all too often I didn't have the peace and quiet I wanted; there was always some journalist, photographer, or fan hanging around, wanting to interview me or have a chat with me. At other times the phone didn't stop ringing. This was one of those times, but what caught my attention was that this person was an astrologist. I'd never taken much notice to what they say, or to what they write in their columns; however I do admit to having read them. Mind you, I then immediately forget about what they've said. Whatever did she want? I had lunch and then went up to my room to rest for a while.

'Pedro, you're wanted on the telephone.'

'Who is it?'

'No idea.'

'Alright.' I stopped watching the three o'clock television news. 'Give me the phone.'

'Hello…'

'Hello, let me introduce myself. I am Vicente Cassana.'

'Pleased to meet you. What can I do for you?'

'We are astrologers. We are also great cycling fans, and we

would very much like you to tell us the date of your birth, the hour and the place.'

'What for?'

'Well, you see, we are convinced that you're going to win the Tour de France this year, and, simply as cycling fans and as practitioners of astrology, we would very much like to know exactly how your stars are placed, but we do want you to know that things are looking very good for you...'

'Alright then, if that's all there is to it...I was born on the fifteenth of April, 1960 at...' And that's how the conversation went. A couple of days later they called me again.

'Pedro, you know that you're definitely going to win the Tour; you're not going to have any problems.'

'Well, that's wonderful, isn't it.'

'Yes it is and, as you know, we've said that you're not going to have any problems. However, I am sorry to say that we do see something strange here.'

'I am going to win, but there is something strange. Is that what you're saying?'

'Yes. It's an unusual thing in the heavenly bodies: a crossing between two stars which is going to make something happen, something that's very bad for you.'

'How?' I didn't attach much importance to any of this, but I did pay attention; the conversation was amusing me. 'Carry on.'

'It could even force you to abandon, but if you are sensible, and we are sure that you are a very sensible person, you will cope with it perfectly well. You will come out of it successfully because eventually everything will be clarified...'

'Clarified? What will be clarified? Can't you be more explicit?'

'Don't worry, because you're going to win the Tour.'

* * *

"I was nowhere near getting close to imagining what would eventually happen. In this light, it just seemed odd, at first. I was not surprised that they saw me as a favourite for the Tour. After all, the year before I had been on the point of winning it. But it did make me laugh, that idea that the movement of the stars would force me to abandon if I were not very careful. I had to get ready for some huge surprise; I had to be strong; but I would overcome it, and carrying on riding. Wow!"

Vicente Cassana's omen from the stars remained stuck somewhere at the back of Pedro's mind. How could he possibly be marked by the stars? His confidence about the future came from his training, from the strength he was building up, and from the experience he had accumulated in previous Tours. However, who knew what cards he'd been dealt which would shape his destiny in the July of 1988?

"At first, when the news came out, I didn't imagine what was about to happen. But as soon as the thing unfolded, and I became increasing entangled in it and needed to take a grip on it, the words of the astrologist came into my head: 'You are going to win the Tour, but you will have to be strong and fight against quitting the race.' How could I have thought, a month earlier, about anything like that? At that moment in time I was in agreement with the astrologist – how right he was. But of course, what he was talking about was a drug-test positive, and that would have meant an immediate return home, if it really was a positive. I also thought that Vicente Cassana's words might actually come to my defence and, even if unconsciously, encourage me to fight back.

"From my point of view, the explanation was beyond doubt. So what then? When everything was clarified I thought still more about him. How right he had been. I was almost expelled from the Tour. He also told me about another curious detail on my star chart. He said my biggest triumphs would be accompanied by big controversies. I immediately thought back to the Vuelta of 1985, although that had been more a chance occurrence. Never mind the Tour of 1988, what about the Vuelta of 1989? After that, it really did seem to be ordained by the stars – and was always going to be so – that I would have powerful friends and powerful enemies. While none of this turned me into a keen follower of astrology, after everything that had happened, it did tickle my curiosity. So, now and again, I would read something about the esoteric, the occult, biorhythms and that sort of thing. I was never a fervent devotee of any of this, but it is certainly true that at a particular stage of my life I did delve into them."

In ancient Rome there were priests who examined the entrails of victims so as to make premonitions. Cyclists don't go that far, but there are some who, in the attempt to improve their performance, will try holding on to a burning nail, or occasionally resort to methods which, although innocuous enough, perhaps, are unorthodox in the extreme.

"We grab hold of things to give ourselves some necessary security or confidence in what we can do, especially in critical moments. Back in 1984 the Reynolds team was competing in the Setmana Catalana. We were in Andorra, and José Miguel Echávarri got hold of a calendar of biorhythms. With that, and with the birth-dates of the riders, he nosed into their emotional, their intellectual and particularly their physical state. He was constantly going around with it, and whenever we saw him, the first thing we'd ask him was, 'How are my biorhythms today, then?' He'd reply, 'Well, now, they seem alright, but perhaps not as buoyant as they might be. Possibly in this stage you'll have to suffer a bit more; your biorhythms are not going to be much help.' As soon as I had a bit of spare time I bought a book about biorhythms. I've still got it at home. I read it to find out about these new things. I have always been very curious and because I like reading a lot, that day I switched from the usual novel to this treatise on biorhythms. I don't know if it did me much good, but it was entertaining, and that was good enough."

José Luis Pascua, Pedro's trainer ever since 1983, explained that with any training exercises he would always apply himself with rigour and discipline. 'He set about it like an athlete, whereas cyclists, not so much now as they used to be, were far more anarchic when it came to training. Take Arroyo, for example. I called him "Barullo" [Bedlam]; he was always getting himself into some noisy state of confusion. If Pedro felt that he could make some improvement in his training, the first thing he'd do would be to ask me. We'd discuss it, and if he was right, which he usually was, we'd go ahead with it.' The effectiveness of that method didn't stop Pedro from trying other possibilities.

"At the end of 1987, the year when I almost won the Tour, I discovered sophrology. Mariano Espinosa taught me and seemed very proud to have me as one of his students. My uncle Miguel introduce me to him, through his children, and once he knew that we were related, Mariano said to him 'Tell Delgado to get in touch with me. Sophrology will help him improve his performance'."

Pedro had already let it be known that he was curious about it, so he got in contact with the sophrologist.

'My cousins have told me that you could improve my performance.'

'You haven't been deceived. I work with horse-riders, chess players, gymnasts, golfers … and, they all find it helpful I can assure you, you are going to perform better and more strongly.'

'You are sure of that?'

'Whatever happens, I am not going to do you any harm. If you like, we can meet up some day and I will show you – without any obligation – what sophrology is all about.'

'That's fine. To give it a try…'

'What is your problem?' he asked me.

'What I would like is to be able to perform better in time trials.'

"We set about that, and the most positive thing I got out of it was learning how to breathe with my stomach. That is a technique which scuba divers use, and also singers. And yes, it did work for me; it improved my time trialling. The other aspect of it was to visualise the time trial in your mind, before riding it, to psyche yourself up with good memories, to think back over the best rides against the clock you've ever done. That is more or less what all riders do. The fact is we have something of the child in us, so at decisive moments, or just when we are slightly depressed, we try to motivate ourselves, to rediscover our optimism, strengthen ourselves by recollecting the best moments of our careers. Mariano Espinosa was pleased to have worked with me. He told me I was a very balanced person, so sophrology was not essential for me. On the other hand, it could help me during the most difficult times to overcome any kind of lean spells."

Superstition also has its place in cycling. When medicine doesn't work, or conventional techniques don't bring about results, the cyclist, the masseur, the mechanic, and even the director, look towards alternative 'sciences'. Pedro insists he has never had need to turn to methods or procedures that are, to a greater or lesser extent, unconventional. However, he has seen such things. One day he went into the room of his friend Ángel Arroyo and found him making a bonfire in the wastepaper basket.

'Perico knows something is going on but he hasn't a clue what,' Arroyo said, between laughs. Then his mood changed. 'Yes, I had to burn a wooden rosary for some days, because they had been giving me the evil eye. But truthfully, I prefer not to talk about this because for me it is something really serious. I have more faith in the woman who helped me than in the doctors.'

Ángel had gone down with brucellosis in 1985; he went from one specialist to another, and all that did was make him go from bad to worse. Nobody was able to come up with a remedy for his problems. He just couldn't get back on his feet again. Finally, he resorted to a quack healer from around where he lived and, little by little, he got better. There are popular beliefs, sometimes mere superstitions, which (perhaps by chance) have a real impact.

Francisco Javier Fernández Rojo, nicknamed el Rubio [the fair-haired], a masseur who was always in Javier Mínguez's team, had a picture of an owl. Someone had given it to him as a present, and apparently it used to tell him what the future held. It tipped him off that Miguel Indurain would win seven Grand Tours, and because of that, even before his first victory in the 1991 Tour, it advised Mínguez to sign up the Navarran rider. 'Pay him whatever he asks.' He had a rough idea of his market value. The owl also warned him that Rominger was going to beat Montoya in the Vuelta in 1992, and that the Swiss would even win another two Vueltas. It didn't whisper much else to him because when little Montoya lost the Vuelta to Rominger, Mínguez got hold of that picture of the owl and smashed it on the floor in front of Rubio's disbelieving gaze. 'From now on, whatever will be will be,' Javier Mínguez declared, in a furious temper.

Over and above what many would label 'quack theory', or who knows what, there are the smaller superstitions, foolish sayings, coincidences, bits of nonsense, crazy expressions, rituals, trivial and non-religious customs, or whatever you want to call them.

"These are the little habits you pick up from your childhood," says Pedro. "When I was 16 years old, we were short of race clothing – it was one or two pairs of gloves for racing, nothing more. And if I happened to win a race, those particular gloves that I was wearing on that day I would put on again in the next race. And if I won again, as soon as I got to the front in a race with mountains, the first thing I'd think about was the gloves – 'are these the winning ones?' I had that habit in my early years. Then, as a professional, you are fortunate enough to find yourself with an abundance of race clothing, and you end up not differentiating between one pair and another. They are all the same."

These fixations don't belong exclusively to the Juveniles; quite the contrary, in fact. Fully grown men, true champions, also have their little superstitions which they are incapable of ridding themselves of, whatever harm it might do to their image.

"Greg LeMond wore the same cycling shoes for three or four years. They looked dreadful; quite disgusting. The peloton, in unison, told him that they were a disgrace – you could almost see his feet through them – and that he had to change them. And LeMond refused, point blank. 'They bring me luck,' he insisted, and there was no way he would change them. I do believe it was in those shoes that he won the Tour in 1989."

Not everything is medication; not everything is sorcery; not everything is obsession; there are other remedies, as old as mankind, which are endorsed beyond any doubt by scientific rigour. Every now and again they become fashionable, most especially because their effects are proven to be positive. As, for example, acupuncture, in which Pedro has complete faith.

"Because of our difficulties with doping, acupuncture helps us to cure and to prevent those blasted coughs, and one injury or illness after another. This type of healing was not very much embedded in cycling in my time. Miguel Ángel Rubio, ONCE's physiotherapist, known to many as the Blindman, did a great deal, especially with the needles, to help sportsmen to get better, and recover from small injuries as well as from more complicated ones. Mind you, you have to go to an expert, someone who knows about acupuncture, because there are plenty of charlatans around."

Another of Spanish cycling's good masseurs, and a grand person, is Manu Arrieta. He not only works wonders with his hands, he also makes use of other remedies which come from his home. Who knows how many he has treated with his mother's potions – and he revers her.

"Manu's mother is now an old lady. She knows all about plants, flowers and roots that come from the mountains, and with them she prepares creams and holistic medicines. 'Mama's ointment' is famous in the peloton. For the cyclist who is forever troubled by boils and abscesses it comes as a blessed relief; it is really good. Half-way through the Tour of '89, when we were in the Massif Central heading towards the Alps, I was in agony because of a callus I'd developed on my foot. What with the chafing of my shoe, the vibration from the road, the water they threw over you, and the sun beating down all day, what had begun as a little raw patch had grown and become a real pain. On the day of the mountain time trial I finished thoroughly fed up: things hadn't gone at all as I'd wanted; I hadn't pulled back any time on LeMond, nor on Fignon; and the callus was getting worse by the day. I decided then to cut a hole in the shoe, and smother 'Mama's ointment' over the affected part of my foot. The result was that after three days the callus had vanished, all by itself, and that was thanks to that concoction. The cream for removing corns, which I'd bought some days earlier from the pharmacy, had done nothing for me."

When Sean Kelly withdrew from the Vuelta in 1987*, it was a saddle boil that forced his retirement. If Ramón Mendiburu, then the director of Kas, had put more trust in a pair of journalists – Benito Urraburu and me – it is likely that that particular Vuelta,

---

* Sean Kelly, with a 42-second lead over Lucho Herrera, was forced to abandon the race 14 kilometres into stage 19 because of that boil. The Colombian went on to win in Madrid two days later.

instead of travelling to Colombia, would have gone in the direction of Ireland.

We had dined in the parador at Albacete, where we were sleeping that night, and were chatting with Manu Arrieta over coffee. He was telling us that with his mother's ointment he had got rid of a boil which had come up on Laguía's forearm. At this point Mendiburu appeared, with his usual poker face. We asked him how things were with the team, and about Kelly, who now seemed the certain winner. He said that they were fine, and he didn't want to tell us any more. We could see that he didn't like the direction the conversation was heading. Alright, that was up to him. But if only he'd stayed he would have discovered 'Mama's ointment', because Manu was quite happy to share it with riders from other teams And possibly Kelly's boil would now be just an anecdote and would never have become a reason for abandoning the race. However, be that as it may, it is that which we now always hear about.

Chapter 11

The Moncloa Ashtray

*'Happy is the man who has never known the taste of fame —
to have it is purgatory, to lose it is Hell!'*
Bulwer Lytton

After his victory in the 1985 Vuelta, and even more so after
winning the Tour in 1988, the fame of Pedro Delgado spread
across all levels of society; as well as being recognised as a great
sportsman, in a flash he became one of the most popular and
highly sought-after celebrities, and a sensation among journalists,
especially those with a particular interest in his private life.

Whereas the sporting press naturally celebrated his cycling
achievements, the yellow press discovered in Delgado a new
gold mine, a prime target for headlines, yet another source of
scandal, just as his astral chart forecast ... and 1988 would be the
year when it would all start to happen.

Pedro's presence on the top step of the podium at the end
of July, surrounded by the magnificence of the Champs-Élysées,
with his name on everybody's lips, was an excuse for hundreds
of Spaniards to visit the Eiffel tower, have dinner in Le Procope,
stroll through the Latin Square, stop at the Lido, and cross the
River Seine by steamboat, and, of course, the obligatory visit to
the Bois de Boulogne or the Pigalle (even if that had perhaps
lost some of its charm). These Spanish tourists would then boast
of having seen Notre Dame, the Louvre, the George Pompidou
Centre, the Sacre Coeur and its staircase, and would carry home a
cart-load of postcards purchased along the Melancholy Walkway.

Among the visitors and very close to Pedro's father, Julio,was
Miss X.

"As had become normal in Segovia in the previous few years,
trips were organised to see the last stage of the Tour, with the
excuse of seeing their countryman who, this year, had finally

won. So, the event became doubly valuable: they witnessed my victory and they also visited Paris. Many travelled by bus; the more affluent did so by plane. My father travelled in one of those planes, as he wanted to be present to see his son's victory. He arrived a couple of days beforehand and came to see me at the hotel. He was accompanied by my auntie Boni, who lived in Paris, and also by a girl I knew from Segovia. 'Congratulations my boy, you're going to win the Tour.'

We fell into each other's arms and I thanked him.

'Congratulations Pedro.'

My friend from Segovia gave me two kisses and, as I was expecting, she alluded to the fright she'd had when she heard about the doping.

'Then all hell broke loose in Segovia! Luckily, everything was cleared up.'

'Yes, thanks be to God.'

The Segovian lady continued holding on to my father's arm, and when the people from the tabloids turned up, there were more and more pictures taken.

'She must be his girl-friend, surely? She comes from Segovia, and with Perico's father. She is Perico's girlfriend, no doubt about it'.'

Miss X didn't shy away from the lenses and, pleased with the confusion, perhaps, she let go of the father's arm and jumped on Pedro, the son.

"And more and more pictures. Between one click and another click, I realised the photographers had the idea that they were recording me for posterity with my girlfriend. I tried to tell them they were wrong. I repeated that she was not my girlfriend, but to no avail: flash after flash; photo after photo.

'Well, we know she's not your girlfriend,' they said with a conspiratorial wink.

'No, she isn't. So please don't take more pictures; she isn't my girlfriend,' I insisted, time and time again.

"No response; they ignored me completely. But I didn't want to get into a discussion with them because that would seem like admitting they were right. There were still two more stages left, two more days of competition, and I had to focus on the race. But I thought to myself: 'What a mess! And my girlfriend was at home, in Madrid. Ludi, who is now my wife, preferred to keep out of the grandeur of the moment because she was aware of what was in store in the last days before arriving in Paris: hustle and bustle, a collective madness. But Miss X was still there with the photo-reporters. More and more photos, more confusing publicity, what could be done about it? But I couldn't imagine what was brewing. After all, I was just trying to relish the happiness that came from winning the Tour."

'Pedro?'

'Yes, hi! How are you, sweetheart? What a joy!' It was Ludi, calling from Spain.

'Everything OK?'

'You can imagine.'

'By the way, who is the girl standing next to you in the photos in the magazines?'

'Here we go,' I thought to myself.

'I suppose you are referring to a girl from Segovia.'

'Which girl?'

'A girl I know, she came along with the crowd from Segovia. Why do you ask?'

'Because she's all over the magazines and they say she's your girlfriend.'

"As if all the mess with the doping hadn't been enough, now I had this. I tried to go over the whole thing: Miss X, the photographers, my father...I could imagine Ludi seeing the pictures in the magazines, my future in-laws ...

'Well, who do you think she is? She's a girl from Segovia; she's just a girl I happen to know!...' The situation was pretty delicate, difficult even, until everything was finally cleared up."

Pedro's first contact with the world of celebrity did not happen overnight; although not an expert in this kind of thing, he wasn't a fool, either.

"I got to know the celebrity magazines when I won the Vuelta in 1985. All the popularity on the finishing line of the races then spilled over into everyday life. I went from being an ordinary citizen, a relatively well-known cyclist, to being 'Pedro Delgado, the man who won the Vuelta'. And then in the Tour, it was Perico here, Perico there, Perico everywhere. I became a celebrity. What had happened in 1985 couldn't compare to the explosion that took place in 1988.'

Well known in Europe, and famous in Spain, he could barely take a step without being stopped to sign an autograph. And once the doping issue was sorted out, journalists from various fields couldn't get enough of him. However, the clarification continued to make the news even after being verified by Doctor Manfred Doenike, head of medical control at the Union Cycliste Internationale (UCI). After all, it was a question of mitigating the effects of an injustice.

"My positive was headlines in the most prestigious European newspapers, but the clarification only appeared on the inside pages."

Even innocence leaves a trace of bitterness.

"Without any doubt, the business of Miss X was the first time I came up against the world of the gossip magazines. But I was going to have more clashes with the *paparazzi* later. One day, Ludi and I went out for dinner with some friends; we were in the restaurant completely normally – I say that, but from time to time I would be approached by somebody and asked to sign an autograph for his little child or for a friend. Everything was completely normal. Or rather, almost everything.

'Look Pedro,' said Ludi as we left the restaurant. 'I think I have seen someone taking pictures of us.'

'It can't be of us, just ignore them. You are always thinking about the same old things!'

"And just when we were about to get in the car, click! The photographer was there; Ludi was right. The situation was quite annoying; it was a question of our privacy. I tried to cope with it; I wanted to understand the *paparazzi*, but it was impossible. They strike from behind the car, or you turn a corner and they immediately start taking pictures, no more than a metre away from you. They infringe your privacy in the street and then you begin to feel uncomfortable because, even though you have nothing to hide, they don't approach you in the normal way.

"In the end, I had a very poor impression of these people who were always pestering me. But it became much more upsetting after what happened when we were leaving another restaurant in Madrid, in the Plaza de Oriente. It was the same old story, the wretched photographer again, still on the hustle as soon as we stepped out into the street. Ludi and I went off in different directions. Then we were both chased: one photographer trailed her and another was after me. Suddenly a female journalist stood up in front me.

'Hi, are you Perico? I'd like to ask you some questions.'

"I usually don't complain; but this was different because we were being chased. And they took pictures of us without our permission!

'Well, I'm not going to answer your questions,' I replied. 'Before taking your pictures, you might at least have asked us.'

'Well, you don't really care...'

'Well I do, I absolutely do. I have nothing to say to you.'

"On top of this, the tape recorder was running. Then she started ranting.

'You know what? You're a show-off. Who do you think you are? You let success go to your head.'

"She was shouting at me, in the middle of the street. I felt totally embarrassed. And she wouldn't stop insulting me with her tape recorder on. I soon understood that she was hoping to create a scene; she was being provocative and was clearly expecting a violent response from me while the photographer had his finger on the shutter. Perhaps because I was not entirely unfamiliar with this kind of situation, even though I don't recall any of them being quite so unpleasant, I tried to ride out the storm, not to be provoked while I headed for the car trying to forget about the damn lady, who kept haranguing me. I felt really hurt. What did all that have to do with my professional career? But that was only half the story. I was approached by the photographer when I was about to get in my car. What does he want now?

'Perico.'

'What's is it?' I was on the defensive. Although he may have wanted to apologise.

'Can you sign some autographs for me please?' I turned to stone.

'I'm from Segovia and I wonder if you could sign some autographs for my kids.'

How dare he ask me for an autograph after the scene he made! I didn't know what to say. But the look I gave him was quite unmistakable.

'Come on, you must understand we have a family to feed…'

That hurt me even more. I got in the car and we dashed off. Have you ever!"

That is the price of fame and popularity, which does not always, nor even normally, get so unpleasant. The other side of the coin are the fans who appear to know more about the private life of their idols, who in turn never cease to be amazed by them.

"On the first Sunday in November at the end of the 1987 season, I was invited to a critérium in Japan, together with other European professionals who'd been prominent during the course of that year: Italians, Belgians, French, Dutch, the Irishman Stephen Roche and me. After the race, the organisers decided to buy our bicycles from us and then auction them. We were also asked if we could possibly donate anything to the auction – a jersey, shorts, the cap or the headband that was so fashionable then. I had never been to an auction sale, and I had quite a good time there. The bidders had to pay in cash, which I found surprising. I thought they would pay with a cheque because a racing bicycle, at that time, cost around a thousand pounds or more. Well then, first the bicycles were auctioned and then the rest of items. And then it was the turn of my PDM headband."

Changing the yens to pesetas, the starting bid for Perico's headband was around five thousand pesetas (£25).

"Of course, I don't speak Japanese, but it's not difficult to understand what's going on in an auction sale. A few people bid for an item and after two or three offers, someone manages to get hold of it. The auction was going smoothly until my PDM headband was shown. There were four, even five bids. The excitement increased and, after the expected course of events, only two bidders were left: two ladies.

'Fifteen thousand,' said one of the two.

'Sixteen thousand,' said the other.

'Seventeen thousand,' replied the first lady.

'Twenty-five thousand,' replied the second lady again.

The room became as silent as the grave; the auctioneer was about to end it; you couldn't hear a fly buzzing. Suddenly, one of the two ladies burst into tears; between her little sobs, she couldn't be comforted. She didn't have any more money and couldn't buy my headband. People were initially flabbergasted, then they smiled. And me – I can't deny it – I did feel proud."

But not all the tears you shed in this life are echoes of sadness. The little Japanese lady was upset because she had no more cash available that day. Who could have predicted that she would find herself up against such a fierce competitor for a souvenir of Pedro.

"The person who came off best from all that was Ludi, because every time I was approached for an autograph she was given a present … for her trouble. 'I wish it were always like this,' she said, referring to all the times I was asked for my autograph."

These were unexpected situations. Pedro was not surprised anymore when a member or a team assistant asked him to visit one of his friends who was his greatest fan.

"We competed in the Clásica de San Sebastián and our masseur, Manu Arrieta, asked me if I could see one of my supporters, who was also one of Arroyo's, as he would be very excited to see me in person.

'You'll see how happy he'll be,' said a delighted Manu.

'We went there to say 'hello'. He lived in a small village near San Sebastián, and he also had a garage and workshop for body repairs and repainting; we turned up without any prior warning. When we entered we found a middle-aged man, around 50 years old, who was staring at us without blinking – first at Manu, then at me. He didn't say anything, not a word. Manu, somewhat surprised by this, said 'Hi, how are you?' But he didn't make a peep. And just when we thought he was going to say something, he burst into floods of tears, non-stop. What wailing! What sorrow! What could we do?

'Manu, how could you do this to me?' the poor man stammered. 'How could you do this to me?' He was sobbing his heart out, and we thought that rather than making him happy, we had scared him to death.

'But Manu, you should have told me. I almost passed out! Why didn't you tell me before? This is really embarrassing! Oh my God, how happy I am!'

"Once he had recovered, I signed a couple of posters for him, but he didn't know how to thank me enough.

'Pedro, please bring me your car; I can paint it, fix any scratch, anything you need, I'll give it a new lease of life. Bring it to me please!' he begged me.

"There are times when the ones who suffer the consequences of my popularity are my own supporters, as happened in the Vuelta of 1993. I was not performing strongly and things were not working out as I'd wanted; nothing was going well for me. We were in Asturias, and had begun the day at Cangas de Onís on the stage that would finish on the Naranco. The day before, ending at the Lagos de Covadonga, I'd been behind the leading group and, all the way up the climb, I'd been trying to get back to them. It was raining a bit, that fine rain, more like mist, which the Asturians call the 'Orbayu', with the sun occasionally poking through. After only 50 kilometres, I felt the need to pee. You can always stop if you really need to when you are riding calmly. However, if the stage is hectic, then you must deal with it on the bicycle.

"The trouble with peeing on the move is that not only can you end up getting wet all over, but so too might some distracted bystanders. What can we do about it? That's just the way it is, and it doesn't upset us. In fact, we riders are quite used to it. Sometimes, we ride off the front of the peloton, then stop so all the other riders can see us, and then if they were planning an attack, they can delay it for a bit. After that, it only takes a few seconds and then, straight away, you are in among the cars, then back into the race. And that's it.

"At that moment, as the race permitted it, I tried to find a spot in the ditch free from prying eyes. We were crossing the area near Llanes around the coast, on our way to Gijón. In Asturias you can find quite a few little hamlets along the road; I tried to find a secluded place in between one hamlet and another, where I could take a pee without being seen. I was on the left side of the road and cars were passing me by, and just when almost all of them had gone past and in the middle of a long, warm pee, a lady crossed the road. Apparently, she had not seen me as she was looking at the cars. Suddenly, I heard a voice: 'Oh my God! I was so looking forward to meeting you, Perico, and this is how I get to see you for the first time.'

"I wanted the earth to swallow me up! I wasn't scared as much as completely taken aback by what the good lady had said. She was so looking forward to meeting me! I was so embarrassed. I apologised, and she said please don't! But after a while I laughed about it, although I'd only been half finished."

Quevedo, the famous poet from Spain's Golden Age, was said to be recognisable even from behind, but Pedro, apparently, was recognised from every direction. That is why it is not surprising he got invited to the famous restaurant, 'La Bodeguilla', by the President of Spain, Felipe Gonzalez. It's interesting, though, that the invitation to the restaurant coincided with the first general strike in Spanish democracy. The banquet was on 13 December, 1988; the strike took place the day before.

"The dinner was in honor of Franz Vranitkis, Chancellor of Austria, who was on a state visit. At that time, the President's office invited celebrities like me, or the film actress Carmen Maura, together with distinguished local or foreign politicians, to these events to make them more informal. We were arranged to sit at round tables; the chief of protocol was sitting next to me, and he asked me about the Tour, and about cycling issues. The dinner was quite informal, not at all pompous, but nevertheless, to me, the event still felt rather serious. Once coffee was served came the speeches. The first was Felipe González. I noticed they had left a written transcript for me, entitled: 'Speech by Felipe González'. Ah! Very well!. Next, the Austrian Chancellor, and another transcript. Great, because he'd read it in his own language.

'If you don't understand it,' the chief of protocol told me, 'you can take it with you and read it, like that of Felipe's.'

'Yes, that's better,' I replied.

'You can also take the menu as a souvenir.'

'That's very kind, thank you.'

"We still had not finished our coffee, when another waiter, dressed in a frock coat, showed up passing around cigars.

'No, thank you, I don't smoke.'

'Come on, take one or two,' the chief of protocol intervened. 'They are very good; they are Havana cigars. You can give them to someone, to a friend, to your dad…'

'My dad doesn't smoke either.'

'It doesn't matter! Take them, these Havana cigars are really good.'

'Well then, thank you; I recall one of my uncles is a smoker.'

'You see? He'll be grateful. These cigars are really good.'

"While I was putting the cigars away, trying not to break them, and while paying attention to the speeches so as not to forget them, I remembered the souvenirs you usually get in restaurants. A jar here, an ashtray there, a toothpick case; you know, the kind of presents you have to accept so as not to appear ungrateful. While I was thinking about all this, he repeated, 'Don't forget the speeches, nor the cigars. Don't forget them, you are in front of the President.'

"Then, while I was making these mental notes, someone gave me an ashtray. 'Look, an ashtray too,' I thought. 'I mustn't forget that.' I must admit I am always a bit absent-minded, but I'm not ungrateful, and I didn't want to appear so at such an event.

"At the end of the speeches, the event got a bit more relaxed and conversations started up.

"I was somewhat the centre of attention as I had just won the Tour! So, when the time came to leave, I was photographed with everyone, with Solchaga, the Minister of Finance, who told me he was from Navarra, and what about cyclists from Navarra. In other words, just what you would expect. And little by little we approached the door. I had the speeches, the cigars and the ashtray, yes, the ashtray, with me. Then, the President's wife, Carmen Romero, came out. 'Perico! I was so looking forward to meeting you! You have a real following here in Spain. Come on, let's take a picture that I can show to my kids.'

"And in the picture, the President's wife, the President, myself, the cigars, the speeches and the ashtray.

'You are all right are you, Pedro; you haven't forgotten anything?'

"Everything was running very smoothly when, on my way out I was approached by a butler who kindly walked me out. We exchanged a few words.

'You know what? I really like cycling. Er! Excuse me Señor Delgado, you have been so lucky! How many Ministers wish they could have taken one of these ashtrays with them! They asked me so many times! You are so lucky...'

'What? No, really?'

"I didn't know what to say. I felt embarrassed. 'I thought it was just a present, like the cigars, and I didn't want to forget anything. Please, can you take the ashtray back? I really didn't want it as I don't smoke. Everybody's been giving me ashtrays lately. Anyway, I am sorry.'

'Please, you can keep it. Don't worry; these ashtrays are really beautiful.'

'For once in my life I didn't forget the souvenir...'

These are the strange paradoxes of fame. When one thinks one is known everywhere, and then, not everything in the garden is rosy. This was not the case with Pedro, who tried to behave properly and pass unnoticed. But something happened to him that was worth mentioning.

"One day before the Clásica de San Sebastián I arrived with Ludi at the hotel Pellízar, where the team was lodged. It was a bit late and my team mates were already having their dinner. So, I thought it would be a good idea to eat out, and I asked in reception if they could recommend a 'nice place nearby'.

'Arzak is just round the corner, do you know of it?'

"I remembered I had dined there once before, with the mayor of San Sebastián and with Pello Ruiz Cabestany and his parents. It was definitely one of the best restaurants, a temple of cuisine.

'Yes, I think that's a very good idea. Besides, it's not even eight o'clock, so I'm sure they'll be able to find a table for us even without reservation. Can you please tell us where it is...'

'You can walk, it's just around the corner.'

It was August, and such a lovely day, the temperature pretty warm, just ideal. Ludi and I were dressed quite casually: Bermuda shorts, T-shirts, flip-flops – very summery, in fact. 'It's a top class restaurant, but I have been there before, and they were really kind,' I said to Ludi, without paying much attention to what we were wearing. They had just opened when we arrived, and were still arranging the tables. We met Juan Mari Arzak at the door accompanied by two waiters. We went in confidently and joyfully with a resounding initial greeting: 'Halooo!' It was as if we were at home.

'Halooo!' replied Arzak without changing the tone.

'How are yooou?' I continued in this sing-song tone.

'Very well, and yooou?' He seemed to be echoing my voice. 'How can I help yooou?'

'We would like to have dinneeer please.' If we continued like that, I imagined we would end up singing zarzuela.*

"I had just won the Tour and I was instantly recognised, and I thought this would happen everywhere. This was not mere conceit; it was just the way things actually were. Sometimes people would say to me: 'Don't be so serious; we know who you are.' This was why Arzak's cheerful response made me think he remembered me, not only for winning the Tour, but also for the last time I had dinner there with Pello.

'So you would like to have dinneeer?'

'Yes, we would love tooo.'

'I'm sorry but we are fuuull,' he said with the same smile.

'You won't have a spaaace for us by any chance?'

'Nooo.'

'Well then we must gooo.'

'Byeee.'

'See you sooon.'

"And so we left. I thought he would give us a table, that he was joking because the restaurant was empty at that time. But he didn't, and we found ourselves in the street looking for another restaurant; first we went to the hotel to get the car. We didn't

---

* Zarzuela – Spanish musical comedy, with scenes fluctuating between song and recitation. The form dates from the seventeenth century.

think any more about it, but when we got back at around eleven, I was told by the hotel receptionist that Arzak wanted to speak to me.

"Apparently, he wanted to apologise for not recognising me; he couldn't believe what had happened and was terribly upset. It seemed he'd been calling every half an hour to see if we had arrived back at the hotel. I looked at the time; it was very late. He must be very busy, I thought, and so decided to forget about it. But he called again; by now it was too late and reception didn't put him through to my room. So he asked what time we would be leaving the hotel for the Clásica.

"At nine o'clock the next morning the telephone in the room rang. 'Pedro, Pedro Delgado?'

'That's me, who's speaking?'

'It's me, Juan Mari Arzak. I would like to apologise for not recognising you yesterday. You are kindly invited for dinner whenever you wish. I felt really embarrassed when I realised it was you. How could I not let you in for dinner? I could have given you a table. Please, accept my apologies.'

"Arzak's is a quality restaurant, and it has an outstanding reputation, so maybe I should have worn a tie. One would expect guests to dress smartly, with a jacket and long trousers at the very least. There I was, sun-tanned after the Tour and wearing Bermuda shorts; I must have looked like a tourist."

For a winner of the yellow jersey, this was the most comfortable thing to be wearing, yet the least appropriate for Arzak's restaurant. Sometimes fame plays tricks on us.

Chapter 12

From Yesterday to Today

'What is wealth? Nothing if it's not spent;
nothing if it's squandered.'

Bretón

The quote heading this chapter might not be the most suitable for what follows next, but it can stay there, because the thought behind it, the talent of the man who expressed it and the truth that his words capture are so good.

"When I see myself with a Mercedes, I get a better appreciation of how different my life has been since I decided to become a cyclist, and a rider of some note. In those years before my retirement from competitive cycing, when I was travelling to races, sometimes in my comfortable car, sometimes by plane, I would look back and invariably feel nostalgic towards my first car, a Seat 600. In fact, it wasn't even mine; it belonged to my sister, Marisa, who used to lend it to me.

"At the beginning, getting hold of the 600 was one of my goals because I was tired of travelling by bus, or by train, and tired of arguing with the ticket collectors because of the bicycle. I was so looking forward to coming of age, turning 18 and getting a driving licence. How much I wanted it! With a car I would be able to make my own way to races, entirely independently. Then, lo and behold, I failed my driving test first time. But I passed it second time round. When? On December the 28, the Day of the Holy Innocents, which in Spain is the equivalent of April Fools' day. It was a coincidence, so I had to make sure the pass was legal, and not a joke."

Pedro's first rides in Marisa's 600 were a real experience, an explosion of joy, giving him a freedom which he loved as if it were the most precious gift in the whole universe, even if now and again that sense of inebriation brought its own problems.

"Marisa lent me her car so I could get to races at weekends. On one of those trips to Valladolid, I was driving along a flat road, and it felt like driving a Porsche or a Rolls Royce. It felt out of this world. It didn't go all that fast, but it took me everywhere, and I could do the round trip on the same day, even in the same morning. That meant I had the free time and the freedom of movement I was so much looking for. But one day, when I was on my way to a race in Ávila, my 600 suddenly became really sluggish. It was a horrible day, with sleet in the air and a head wind blowing, and uphill the speedometer wouldn't go over 30 km per hour. I was in despair. It took me an hour and a half to make the 65 kilometres between Segovia and Ávila. 'I would have been quicker by bike,' I said to myself.

"I assumed something was wrong with the car. Marisa only used it to travel through Segovia so she didn't need to drive fast. So I took the car to a friend's garage; he put in new spark plugs and a few more things, and the 600 became a bullet again. How it went! I had a try and on the first straight I reached 120 km per hour. Look at that! I'd never seen that before with this car. For me it was lightning fast. I was very proud of my car; well, of my sister's car".

Pedro used to meet with other cycling companions to travel together to wherever they were racing. One particular weekend the event was in Santander.

"We met in Venta Juanilla, at the foot of the Somosierra pass, going towards Burgos. Camarillo, Rodríguez Magro and Barcala were waiting for me. I was racing towards them in my formidable 600 and the idea was that I would take over one of the team's SEAT 124s at the meeting point. This was a wider, faster and more comfortable car. As usual, I was running late, but I was confident I could do the 60 kilometres easily enough at top speed. I was delighted that the car was going so smoothly, but then it started to rain and I didn't like that at all. The road, which had sunk in the middle and was very patched up, became treacherous. Going round the first couple of bends, the tyres seemed to be responding perfectly well on the wet surface, but on the next bend the car skidded off the road and crash! There we were – the car, the bicycle and me –lying upside down: the 600 bent and on its roof. Fortunately, I came out unscathed, and some neighbours from Casla, where the accident happened, helped me put it back on its wheels again. However, the back of the car, near the engine, had been severely damaged, and I was left stranded at the roadside. I could imagine my team mates waiting for me at the meeting point and cursing me because I hadn't shown up. It's a pity we didn't have mobile phones in those days, I could have told them to wait for me".

Nowadays cars are much better, of course. There's no comparison.. And roads are wider and better surfaced. Road transport, despite the sad weekend statistics, has improved enormously, just like everything else. Sometimes people get nostalgic for the good old times, which can still be as good as the present times, particularly when the subject is hotels. In this respect, cyclists must feel privileged in Spain as they come to realise other countries are not all they are cracked up to be.

"In Spain, the hotels where we spend so many days are pretty good, and you can eat quite well. They are not bad in France either – these modern hotel chains, even if sometimes they are not very roomy. But the food – that's what's wrong in France. Yes, I know it's paradoxical, in a country that is famous for its gastronomy, for its sauces, for the elegant arrangement of its dishes. Yet I would say we cyclists don't eat well there. In Italy, it's the other way round: the hotels are poor, some of them downright awful, but the food is so much better. Cyclists need lots of carbohydrates, and there's plenty of that in their many varieties of pasta, and they taste so good. Cyclists get used to sleeping in a different bed every night; they have no choice. If they didn't, they wouldn't be able to pedal next morning. And they are not a fussy lot; cycling makes them capable of putting up with hardship without complaining. As time has gone on, the cyclists' working conditions have dramatically improved, and they have noticed that improvement. However, from time to time things do slip.

"In the Giro of '88, I got quite a negative impression of Italian hotels in general. Even so, they were far better than the ones where we lodged in 1991, which were really dreadful. A couple of times we complained to the Giro organisers. We told them more than once that it was very difficult to get all the rest we needed in the awful hotels – if you could even call them hotels – that they put us up in.

"There was one that stood out among the rest and not exactly for good reasons – 'The Moderne', even if its name did sound suggestive and intriguing. Commenting on the list of hotels was our favourite topic of conversation, and surely this hotel had to be good, we thought. With a name like 'Moderne', it has to be. 'What's more, we're in luck! With the time trial we'll get to spend two days there.' The team was overjoyed.

'By the way, where is it?' We were in the team car.

'Next to the train station. It won't be difficult to find.'

'Let's ask someone in this square.'

'Excuse me, where's the Hotel Moderne please?'

Before replying, the man looked at us in astonishment, his eyes as wide as saucers.

'You see? It must be a superb hotel; that is why he looks amazed. He can't imagine cyclists staying in a five-star hotel,' somebody in the team said.

'Well, to me it looks like he was taking pity on us. He's wondering why on earth are these poor souls staying there?'

'Come on! Don't put a jinx on it.'

'Just follow this street, you are going right. It's just over there,' replied the man, who seemed to me to be looking somewhat embarrassed.

"From the outside it looked a disaster; inside, when we crossed the hall it was even worse, and the rooms were as bad as you could possibly imagine. It was horrible! My God! Where have they put us? And we have to spend two days here! It was depressing. Many of the rooms did not have a shower, and we had to go down the corridor to find the shared bathrooms: only two per floor. A few of the riders got an en-suite bathroom, but the team assistants had to find their lavatory at the end of the corridor and there was no telling what kind of surprise you might encounter there. Someone found a prostitute with her client getting themselves cleaned up.

"They've stuck us in a whorehouse. Nice place for a rest! And our resting time coincided with the girls' rush hour! It was

146

dreadful. I was lucky that my room was not close to any of their 'offices'.

"Carlos Vidales, the team's mechanic couldn't sleep a wink. The room adjacent to his was in full swing, 24 hours non-stop. The situation was not only unpleasant, but somewhat tricky in the corridors, and Carlos, as you would expect, was very concerned about it.

"Obviously, there were more complaints to the Organisers. We were there to race, and we had to take care of ourselves. It's not that we were fussy; we were always willing to adjust to any situation, but this was different. It really was the last straw. So, on the next day we agreed to move into their hotel. And what a difference! It was a four-star, maybe five-star hotel, at least that's what we thought. The rooms were really modern, ample, with beds as big as football pitches, wide-screen TVs, background music, mini bar, a soft carpet, a marble bath surrounded by mirrors, soft towels, even a bath robe. What a change! Since the Giro of 1988, I had the feeling that all Italian hotels were crap, until we discovered the hotel where the organisers stayed. And that's what they had every day, while we, the cyclists, could go to hell."

The Tour organisers are more careful about this kind of thing, although they have also made their mistakes, even if not as grotesque as in the Giro. Nevertheless…

"From the 1983 Tour until at least the 1986, seldom did a week pass without us having to stay in a school or a youth hostel. They'd put several teams in huge communal dormitories, where the teams were separated by what looked like a sort of partition wall made by the masseurs. They used blankets from the beds, so we could enjoy some degree of privacy. Everything was shared: fifty toilets, fifty showers, and lots of other cots. The typical restaurant in these places would be enormous, and the quality of the food questionable, to say the least. Since all the teams suffered equally, none had any advantage over the others, and nobody made a fuss, even if it was obvious that this kind of place was anything but ideal for professional sportsmen in the middle of a competition. Luckily, these sorts of places have been used less and less in the Tour. This is why you really shouldn't criticise a cyclist when you see him in a good car, travelling here and there by plane, or in a luxurious hotel. You may see it some of the time, but it certainly isn't always the case. Every coin has its reverse side, which we cyclists know only too well".

Sometimes hotels will turn away a professional team, even when they have made a prior reservation, the moment they discover that they are a group of cyclists.

"They used to say they were really sorry, but they didn't want them in the hotel. Maybe there had been a bad experience in the past, I don't know. Sometimes they complained about the smell of the massage oils that hung around in the room and took a couple of days or more to clear. They came very close to calling us dogs. Fortunately, this doesn't happen anymore; it used to happen years ago, in the 70s and beginning of the 80s. Now most hotels welcome us – we are seen as a godsend – because often the owners themselves are cycling fans. There has been a massive transformation in favour of cyclists, in spite of those Italian hotels. All in all, there has been a great improvement in the recognition of cycling."

Just as hotels and food are different in Spain, in Italy or in France, so too are their supporters.

"Italian supporters – here I'm referring to those standing at the roadside – always say the same thing, whether we are riding flat out or at a snail's pace: 'Piano, piano.' [Slowly, slow down. We want to see you, and we can't do that if you go past so quickly.] France is different: whether we are riding fast or slow, they always cheer us on and encourage us. They love to see cyclists. French supporters are overjoyed at the sight of cyclists. This is especially the case in the Tour, but in other, less prestigious races, the shout of encouragement can change into an insult when we stop the traffic. And in Spain, especially as regards the Vuelta, the supporters are different again. All is fine when we're riding fast, but ride slowly, and it's terrible. They even start to throw things at us. Only a few supporters react like this; but I assure you, they get on to us if we ride slowly. In certain parts of the country, we used to be savaged even if we did ride fast, because we were interrupting their work, so some said. Or we bump into the usual hooligans that you find in any sport, and they insult us with all manner of names – 'scrounger' 'cheat' are perhaps the kindest words they spit at us. This is what we have to go through. But, all in all, we prefer to see supporters at the kerb."

But sometimes it's the supporters themselves who suffer the cyclists' bad temper. Pedro has been involved in some animated altercations with supporters.

"It's when we're climbing that we run the biggest risks, because supporters encourage us so passionately that they can sometimes knock us over when they get too close. More than once I've had to slap them aside. There is a conflict of interest. The fans are waiting for hours to see you and even to be able to get there they have to put up with all kinds of difficulties because on the big puertos the traffic is stopped for a good while beforehand; others get there on foot. What they really want is to see you and the advertising caravan, the so-called 'multicoloured snake', cheer you on, give you water, feel the effort you are making, your breathing, your fatigue, and if it's hot, to be able to spray you with water to cool you off, which can be counterproductive.

"We are exhausting ourselves on the climb, so the first time they spray you with water, it's fine, but every hundred meters? That's too much. You start climbing the pass when a supporter offers you water with a sign, and you say yes or no with a nod or shake of the head. After a while you get another one and you reply again. But there comes a point when you simply can't pay attention to these signs, because all your effort is going into the racing. Then your silence is interpreted as an acceptance and they start watering you as if you were a plant in a garden. You get soaked, but they continue drenching you, until you lose your temper and you sweep them aside. When you are making such a brutal effort, feeling soaked to the skin is not comfortable, at least for me it wasn't, and also your jersey gets heavier when it's wet. I truly apologise, for myself and on behalf of any of my colleagues to all those supporters on whom we have unleashed our bad temper.

"As you arrive at the hotel, the talk among the riders who crossed the finish line some minutes later than you is totally different, and we have to put up with the recriminations of our fellow labourers, because those of us at the front have 'left the well dry'. In other words, the supporters, eager to see the riders, have emptied all their reserves of water on the leaders, so there wasn't a drop left for those bringing up the rear, and they are the ones who struggle on the climb, who were most in need it. The team director will always keep the men in the front group well hydrated; those who come behind, will have to fend for themselves."

Supporters are also biased, like in football. In Italy, for instance, until the arrival of Miguel Indurain, who won over everybody with his humility and his prodigious class, foreigners like Hinault and Fignon had their ups and downs with the local heroes – Moser, Saronni, Visentini or Bugno.

Especially in the time trial stages the French did have a hard time. And when the road got steeper, the team cars drove with their doors open to push through the crowd. In Italy too, there are those who support Chiappucci and those who strongly support Bugno. It was the same in Spain, not long ago.

"Spanish supporters are very hot-blooded. In the '92 Vuelta, because of the great rivalry that developed between Jesús Montoya and me, he got a hostile reception from the crowd as we came into Segovia. I tried to calm the waters because I knew the score. Whether we like it not, we cyclists are also companions and we try to win and compete, each in our own way. And sometimes, instead of helping, these supporters make things worse for us. Gianni Bugno was knocked off his bike by a fellow countryman as he was climbing the Galibier in the '92 Tour. This friend of his saw Gianni getting away with Fignon, and wanted to give him a push so that Miguel wouldn't catch him. Instead of pushing him forward, he pushed him sideways, and ended up knocking him off. I had a perfect view of the manoeuvre, and I saw him then trying to help him up, and this time push him properly while all the while apologising amidst sobs and lamentations. I imagine that particular *tifossi* didn't sleep too well that night.

"I feel terrorised by the supporter with his video or his photo camera, recording scenes for posterity; he puts himself right in front of the leading group to take the picture of his life. And he focuses the lenses on a specific point, then he loses perspective and that's when the trouble starts and when riders are brought down."

Like the famous 'photomaton' *gendarme* in the 1994 Tour, who, aiming to take a picture of the bunch sprint finish into the town of Armentières, stood in the way of Nelissen and Jalabert, and caused a terrible accident. The consequences were that two of the world's best sprinters and (especially in the case of Jalabert) serious candidates for the green jersey, were forced to abandon on the third stage with varying degrees of injuries.

But not all *gendarmes* are the same, nor are all the episodes linking rider and supporters quite so insane. There are admirable exceptions.

"In 1991 Fabian Fuchs, a Swiss rider and team mate in Banesto, was training with me in the area around Segovia. We were just about to come into a small village and he was surprised by the number of people in the streets waiting for us to pass through. Fuchs asked me if something had happened. Had there been an accident or something like that. I didn't explain things to him until we turned into the main street, because I didn't want him to think I was arrogant. There were people shouting, 'Perico! Perico! Perico!'

"Fabian was astonished and, more than anything, confused. And even more so when they started offering us Coca-colas, soft drinks, and some food too. They wanted us to stop and have a drink.

'Pedro, are these people crazy?'

'Not at all, we are in Spain. People are much more excitable here than anywhere else.'

'In my country, Switzerland, if drivers see a cyclist and can run over him they'll do so: one less cyclist. Here it's different, people cheer you even when you're out training, and they even invite you to have a drink. I'm amazed. I like your country.' He was living in Tarragona.

"I couldn't say the same about his country. Switzerland is the only country where I have been scared of riding a bicycle. I was not surprised to hear from Fabio that cyclists get run over in Switzerland. The mindset of Swiss people, with their laws, their seriousness, their perfect organisational skills, and their hard work does not match their lamentable attitude towards cycling races. Switzerland is very dangerous for cyclists.

"One of the times that I took part in the Tour of Switzerland, I mean as a professional, we were going through a little village on the edge of which there was a bridge. Underneath, a train was passing. The whole peloton was crossing it very rapidly, one after another, when suddenly I started to hear braking, one after another, and after that the crashing of iron. What was happening? I raised my head and I realised a driver had not obeyed the police signs to stop. 'I am here,' he was saying to himself. 'I have my rights and there is no reason I should stop if I drive on the right,' and he went straight ahead towards the race. And he was so calm! He was convinced he was absolutely in the right.

"I also got a good scare in one of the Zurich Grand Prix that I took part in. I was in a group of five escapees, which was not difficult to control, and with the police out in front of us, a car came headlong towards us and was about to run us over: he ignored the police motorcyclist who ordered him to wait at the crossroads and came straight out into the main road. He didn't even look. It was a miracle that he didn't run us over. They are like that in Switzerland. However, the foreign riders I have always got along with the best are the Swiss. They are responsible, trustworthy, pleasant and great team mates. The Swiss driver is a different matter altogether."

As was said at the beginning of cycle racing in our country, with regard to uncivilised behaviour on the road, when people saw the peloton, one cry would go up: 'Grab some stones; the cyclists are coming.' And the reason for that? Because the cyclists scared the sheep and the hens. Oh, for the good old days!

Chapter 13

1989

'There is no man more unfortunate than
he who has never known adversity.'

Demetrios

"In 1989 Echávarri had high hopes invested in Miguel Indurain; he'd won Paris–Nice and was at the height of his powers. He was the team's leader for the General Classification in the Vuelta. In order to help him I would play a more discreet role. I, being the centre of attention of our main rivals – they would be keeping an eye on me in any case – would act as a brake on any attacks the Colombians, or any other riders with GC ambitions, might make in the mountain stages. Coming second in the team time trial gave us a good early feeling.

"The race unfolded in a relatively relaxed way. Then, at the half-way point we faced the first mountain-top stage finish at the Celer ski-station. Half-way up the climb I couldn't help but be delighted with how my legs were responding. That 11th stage had been ridden at a fierce pace right from the start, with numerous men getting away, but on the false flat heading towards Benasque, where the puerto really starts, the BH troops of Javier Mínguez, practically annulled all the escapes.

"No sooner had the climb started when the peloton split. I allowed myself to be carried along by the leading group, while at the same time remaining watchful. Seven kilometres from the finish, Fabio Parra put in a strong attack and I followed him – he was a dangerous rival – and our leading group was whittled down to four Colombians (Parra, Vargas, Morales and Moncada) and me. Miguel was missing, so I preferred to sit on their wheels, despite the fact that I was feeling really strong. The Colombians launched a series of accelerations, but in the form I was in I had no great difficulty resisting them while keeping my eye firmly fixed on Parra. He was the man our Director feared the most, and I was to prevent him taking any time out of Miguel. That way the team continued to have two cards to play. At the finishing line I won the sprint to take the stage."

As the stages rolled by, one after the other, it became clear to Pedro that he was losing none of his strength. And so, with his morale sky-high, he went into the 23.5-kilometre hill climb at Valdezcaray.

"Like all time trials it was decisive. The time gaps would reveal who was who in the General Classification. Again I was the quickest, which left me second overall behind the race-leader, Martín Farfán. The following day a downpour on the Puerto de Alisas, some 40 kilometres from the finish, left the road surface extremely dangerous, and split the peloton into a number of groups. Farfán was dropped, which allowed me to take over the leader's jersey in Santoña. Almost without wanting it, I had found myself in yellow. Immediately afterwards came the fearful stage to the Lakes of Covadonga. Miguel fell while descending the previous puerto, the Mirador de Fito. Rain-soaked as it was, it proved to be perilous, and Indurain was not the only rider to come down; others, trying to get back to the front group, also suffered some heavy falls.

"All this created a certain confusion in the team: Echávarri was continuing to count on Miguel for the GC, so some of us stayed back, waiting for him. In the middle of that impasse Álvaro Pino took off, taking a number of riders with him. As he wasn't too dangerous in the overall standing, we let him go and maintained the gap while we waited for news of Miguel. On the flat road towards Los Lagos he managed to rejoin us. Pino rode a magnificent stage, winning at the top of that mythical climb, while I shed a few precious seconds to Parra. Everything had gone well up to that point, then suddenly the tables turned. I started to feel very different from how I had been feeling in the previous days, and began to find it difficult following the GC men. This climb has always been unpredictable for me – winning on it in '85; losing the yellow jersey on it the following year, and this time retaining it, but by a mere couple of seconds.

"The next day, another mountain stage, once more in the rain. Miguel had to abandon with a fracture to his left wrist. Of the team's two leaders, now only one remained – me. So I wouldn't need to hold back in the mountains, but the good feelings I'd had in my legs up till then vanished, and it became a real calvary. In Brañillín I held on to the overall lead by pure courage. Climbing the long and extremely difficult puerto de Pajares there was a series of attacks from the Colombians, with Parra at the head, and by the BH men led by Pino and Echave. I had to deal with that all by myself; in normal circumstances I would have responded, but I was feeling really bad. I tried to climb at my own speed, to give an impression of strength – it was a miracle that I ended up still with that two-second advantage over Parra. Once we were through the mountains I was waiting for the time trial at Medina del Campo, where I could recover the time I'd lost at Covadonga. I took 54 seconds out of my most serious danger, Parra."

Everything was seemingly moving in Pedro's favour. It looked as if he was going to end up winning the Vuelta for the second time, but he still needed to get through the mountainous stage through the sierra de Guadarrama, which finished in Segovia. He was on home soil.

"On that day I seemed to be feeling as confident as I'd felt in the first part of the Vuelta. Climbing La Morcuera, the first puerto of that penultimate day, I realised that my legs didn't feel as good as I had expected. I was struggling. On the second climb, the Cotos, I felt better; things seemed to be getting back to normal, and in spite of numerous attacks, I had everything under control.

"We went over the Abatos, then the Mina, and all that remained was the Navacerrada. It seemed that the day's battle was more for the stage win. On this last puerto Omar Hernández, a team mate of Parra, got away with another Colombian, Camargo, who was in the Postobon team. I wasn't very worried by that since I saw the attack as a move to win the stage. First mistake. Ten kilometres from the summit Fabio tested me, and I responded immediately. A little later he tried again, and again I went after him. But with his third attack, I preferred to let him go: I didn't want to cope with a climb full of these repeated attacks, since I discovered it was hurting me to respond to the constant fluctuations of rhythm. I though it better to climb at my own speed while maintaining the gap to Parra. Second mistake. He began pulling away from me, and I was losing sight of him. At first 20 seconds, a little later 30 seconds, then 40 seconds. I tried to keep calm, and to ride as hard as I could, but I could not hold the gap to him. In the final two kilometres of the Navacerrada, Ivanov began to pull for me, for no obvious reason because I hadn't asked anybody to collaborate with me. The following day I told myself that this was simply because he liked me, in spite of other interpretations there were that day. I kept calm, waiting for the descent – one that I knew very well – to pull back the time I'd lost. Up ahead the three Colombians were flying, but, as luck would have it, I found myself getting more help than Millar had in 1985, and nothing happened, other than me getting a real fright. I never had such an easy ride in the Vuelta. I won overall and took three stages. It all seemed to presage a fantastic year."

The Tour was yet to come. From the middle of May to July time flew by.

* * *

'I don't know why I have come here so soon: I could have stayed in Madrid.' That was Luis Gómez, a journalist for *El País* and a Tour addict. 'Making the journey to Luxembourg when nothing happens in the first week of the Tour. Oh, well!'

Pedro agreed with him. 'That's usually the case; the first days are sprint stages, time trials.'

'Nothing ever happens. The beginning of the Tour is always the same – sheer boredom. And this is going to be no exception.'

'I suppose not.'

'I would have done better to have got here once the mountains had started, like I've done in other years. But the editors insisted on it...'

The Spanish newspapers, even the general news ones, used to send one or two reporters to the Tour. The event merited it, especially since the last winner was a Spaniard. It was 1st July, 1989. That edition coincided with Banesto's entry as a team sponsor, and the following year they would take over from Reynolds. There was a presentation at the start in Luxembourg, with all the bank's top brass who had travelled there in the company's aeroplane. Headed by Arturo Romaní,

Mario Conde's right-hand man, and Martín Rivas, eventually, president and vice president respectively of the Banesto Sports group.

Three hours before the start of the prologue, Romaní and Rivas were greeting José Miguel Echávarri in the Hotel Pullman where the team was staying. Echávarri was doing the honours, and helping them to get a general idea about the world of cycling into which they were stepping. 'Cycling people are special. And if you get to know us you will see that we are out and out advocates for our sponsors. We are very faithful; but, let me make it clear, this world you are entering into is different. It has nothing whatsoever to do with banking. In a bank it is always possible to correct the situation if things are not to your liking, or not what you had expected. In cycling there is a multitude of things that determine a team's future or the outcome of a race: a banana skin; a drawing pin; any obstacle however small it might be, and all that planning goes down the pan...'

* * *

'Pedro! Where were you? They are calling for you. You should be off now! Come on, hurry up!' It was Carlos Vidales, the team mechanic

'I know, OK. Always in a hurry.'

"I was perfectly calm. Another of the team helpers tells me I need to start pedalling. And me – OK, everything's fine; nothing to worry about. Take it easy. I knew that I had a little time before the start and I rode directly to the starting ramp. I was listening to the shouts coming from everywhere."

The French television commentators were repeating over and over again that Perico Delgado had turned up late because he was drinking a cup of coffee. Pedro didn't realise what was happening.

'Go now! Go! Pedro, start straight away!' a distraught Echávarri was shouting at him.

"Echávarri's face told me more than all his shouting. I went up the ramp. I was about to set off flat out, then I realised somebody from the Tour's organisation had got hold of me. 'Thank God,'

I thought, 'I'm still in time.' But my Director, visibly frantic in front of the ramp, still carried on yelling at me: 'Pedro, get going! Start, now!'

"Again I try to get moving, but the official who was up there to help the riders had got a firm grip on me again. I looked at the analogue clock in front of me, and saw it indicate 40, 41, 42 seconds. I still thought I was in time. When I finished clipping in the pedals, the official gave me a push to start the time trial. Out of the corner of my eye I saw 46, 47 ... and only then did I fully take it in – I was starting late! Yet I didn't know if it was 46 seconds late, a minute and 46 seconds late, or two minutes and 46 seconds late. I rode the time trial flat out, without thinking too much about the late start, more about turning the pedals.

"Naturally enough, there were a lot of journalists waiting for me, and seeing all those faces I was about to confront, I didn't dare stop. I had no idea how much time I had lost; I preferred somebody from the team to tell me, without me having to give any explanations. So, I didn't stop riding until I got to where we were lodging. My time was 12-48; I had lost 2-54 to Breukink.

"The big question which people ask me nowadays is: 'But where had you got to?' The answer, being the most simple, continues to strike people as being implausible. There were all kinds of stories, coming from... I don't know where: that I was seen calmly drinking a cup of coffee; that I had been kidnapped; that I had been arrested by the police, or something similar. The reality was...

"Around two hours before my starting time I went out on the bike – pedalling gently at first, and then, as it got closer to my starting time, increasing my speed with some long stretches at a high rate. About half an hour before, I was already at the Start. I changed my sweaty vest for a dry one and put on my working clothes – the yellow jersey that distinguished the winner of the previous Tour. I didn't like the warming-up circuit that had been arranged for us, through the streets, with the public crossing every few metres. I did not like it one little bit. I wouldn't be able to ride fast for fear of crashing into some pedestrian or other and falling off. I wanted to start with my muscles ready to race, but I realised that all the warming-up process was being lost.

"On the circuit I met Thierry Marie, a team mate of Fignon. He was a very likeable rider and a specialist in this kind of short time trial.

'How did it go?'

'Fine, pretty good.'

'How's the course?'

'Eight kilometres; it's fairly short. You need to go flat out from the start; there is one steep gradient, so it's advisable to drop your gear a bit, or else it'll be a long way to the finish.'

'OK, Thierry, thank you.'

I look at my watch and I see that it's time. As I ride towards the Start I realise I have gone rather too far away.

"As I say, there are stories to suit everybody's taste. Maybe the most real was that I had been arrested by the police. In fact, that almost did happen, but it was somewhat earlier in the morning. After breakfast we went out to see the route of the prologue, as it was going to be closed for an hour, so that the riders could look over it. After giving it a turn and getting close to the finish, a policeman ordered us to stop and get off the circuit. This was just before the final kilometre.

'Where are you going?'

'I am a racing cyclist, from the Tour.'

'No, you can't go up here.'

'They've told us we can ride here.'

'Not now, you can't'

'Look – the bicycle, the jersey, the shorts; they said that we could ride here.'

'It is absolutely forbidden for anybody to ride along here.'

'But, look. I am one of the riders,' – we were speaking in French and we more or less understood each other.

'Along here it's only riders accompanied by cars who can go past. Anybody else, clear off!'

'Hey! Copper! That is Pedro Delgado. Perico! You let him go,' shouted some fan.

'I have said that nobody's going up here. Nobody is going past.'

"The one thing he neglected to say was 'over my dead body'. The situation was becoming tense and faced with my insistence about wanting to ride on the prologue circuit he grabbed hold of me to throw me off it. I wanted to see the final part of the course, and because I wasn't able to do so, I took myself off to look for some other point of access that was less closely guarded. A couple of hundred metres away there was another pedestrian walkway and I took advantage of that to slip through and finally look over the part that I still hadn't seen. But the policeman now knew my face, and when he saw me in the distance, back on the circuit, he called his companions on the radio and I found myself surrounded by policemen with furious expressions on their faces. I insisted that I was a rider in the Tour and all I wanted was to see the final part of the prologue course. Then even a patrol car turned up and they threatened to take me off to the police station for showing contempt for their authority. What a mess. I had no alternative other than to go back to the hotel."

* * *

'At five in the afternoon, what a glum set of faces we had on!' José Miguel Echávarri recalls. 'After all the explanations which I'd given that morning, there sat Arturo Romani and Martín Rivas – it was Rivas who said that the gypsies didn't love their children who behaved well.

'They kept a stiff upper lip, while for me it was an enormous embarrassment, bearing in mind what happened afterwards in the race. Pedro might have won three Tours: that of '87, '88 and '89, but he only won one.

'The lesson I learned is that cyclists are human, and they can end up losing heart completely. For two more days, until they reached Spa, Pedro found himself in the bottom three of the overall classification. I had to keep his spirits up. I saw him cry that night. There were a lot of stupid things said, yes threats from ETA, I know. When we left Luxembourg Pedro was next to last, and he was 9-57 down on the leader, Acácia da Silva, and 7-20 down on Fignon. Then he rode a quite magnificent Tour.

* * *

Close to 60 of us Spanish journalists were present at the unforgettable start from Luxembourg, without believing what we were seeing. I was worried about the fate of a compatriot and fed up seeing the facetious expressions on the faces of our French colleagues. The story of the little cup of coffee was doing the rounds of the gossip-mongers, even though it had been established that it was totally false. But Pedro still had something worse to deal with.

"This whole business made me more nervous than normal and that was my third really bad night in the Tour. On the two previous occasions I had more foresight and took a sleeping pill. This time I did without, and had cause to regret it. I went from being anxious to being irritable; I couldn't concentrate and my equilibrium was shattered. I couldn't sleep for nerves and I couldn't stop tossing and turning in bed. Yet, the time I had lost in the prologue was recoverable, and I couldn't wait to get back in the race.

"The following day was a split stage, with a massed-start race in the morning and the team time trial in the afternoon. In the morning, without feeling at peace with myself and without having slept, I began to attack towards the end of the stage, on a rather sinuous road. I gave no thought to the team event in the afternoon; I was trying – unsuccessfully – to claw back some seconds. In the afternoon I rode like a man possessed, in order to start pulling back some time on my rivals, if that were possible. But half-way over the course I couldn't follow the wheel of my team mates: I was completely empty, without any reserves. This was a *pájara* of major proportions. I came here determined to win the Tour, and here I was – last overall. If only I had taken the sleeping pill...! I believed I could have sorted the race out, but now..."

Some days before the start of the race, Pedro had expressed the thought that the Tour took years off your life. The Luxembourg business would certainly rob him of months at the very least.

"All of us who have ridden the Tour, which requires an enormous effort over the course of three weeks, say that sooner or later we have to pay for it; we recognise that we owe a debt

161

to our body. It is not merely a matter of climbing a puerto, then another and up to as many as 30; nor is it a matter of dealing with the temperature changes from cold to hot, nor of riding almost 4,000 kilometres at an average close to 40kph; nor is it just about coping with an incomparable tension throughout three weeks. It is about setting out to compete in the Tour year after year. Sport at the top level often ceases to be good for your health. The Tour is a continuing punishment on a cyclist's physical and psychological condition."

What is extraordinary is to see Tony Rominger win three consecutive Vueltas, climb the podium of the Tour, destroy everybody in the Giro, beat the hour-record with an out-of-this-world figure, while at the same time knocking on the door of 35 years.

"Many people wondered how Rominger, one year younger than me, was so strong when I was past it. Very simply, the efforts expended in the Tour have to be paid for; they take their toll. Rominger came late into professional cycling (at the age of 25), and where the body is punished is in the Grand Tours, the three-week tours. Every year from 1983 to 1993, inclusive, I rode two of the three – 77,000 kilometres full on. It was not often that Rominger rode two in a year, and many of the Grand Tours he did ride he didn't really challenge for overall victory: he'd lose time one day and then forget about the GC and only look for stage wins: fewer races at less intensity. As cyclists say, 'The race the greyhound doesn't run, stays in his body.' For that reason, Rominger at the age of 34 was able to challenge for the Giro or the Tour. Perhaps this is easier to understand if we compare it to a car. If you drive it 50,000 kilometres every year, and really cane it, it's obvious that it won't last as long as it would if you only did 25,000 kilometres and drove more gently."

The year when Pedro was at the very height of his form was 1989. So what happened at the prologue in Luxembourg, coupled with the time lost in the team time trial, was such a pity. Then there were yet more things he had to cope with.

"In those first days after the blunder there was a rumour going around that I was intending to pull out of the race. Faced with such an adverse situation and with no possibility of winning, I was going to return to Spain. I have no idea where that idea sprang from, but in the state of shock I was in I was quite incapable of making any decision. All I could do was let myself be dragged along by the routine of the race. In the peloton hardly anybody came near me; they left me alone in my own world. Although there was one who, from time to time, would come over and say a few words to me, Laurent Fignon:

'Encore içi?'

'Oui.

'Moi, a la casa.'

I answered with a shrug of the shoulders.

'Pedro. Dans votre situation, je serais a la casa [again spoken in a mixture of French and Spanish].'

My reply was more gestures of resignation than words.

"He would direct these friendly words to me every time he was going back to the tail of the peloton, either to his team car for something or other, or else because he wanted to have a pee.

"With all that insistence I cannot say that I hadn't thought about it, but I tried to picture myself, at home, watching the Tour de France on television. I realised that would be a huge mistake: it would make me even more depressed. So I remained in the Tour, realising that would be the best way of recovery.

"I had to set about restoring my morale during those first stages. I didn't stop hearing on Tour Radio that 'Perico Delgado was riding at the back of the peloton'. Again and again, a constant hammering. If I stopped to pee I'd be surrounded by a swarm of photographers who thought I was retiring. Everybody was of the opinion that I was going to abandon the race, but I'd made my decision, and I was waiting for the days to pass before we came to the next test – the 73-kilometre individual time trial. There I would recover not just some of the time I'd lost to my rivals, but, more importantly, my morale and the necessary optimism to deduce that this Tour of '89 was not over for me. I finished second in the time trial, only a short way behind the winner, Greg LeMond."

The storm clouds that Pedro could make out on the horizon as they departed from Luxembourg were dispersing. To finish second, behind LeMond, in a flat 73-kilometre time trial was something within reach of only a select few, the very best, the strongest of riders. Pedro was never a specialist at that kind of event, and yet here he was, dominating it, however discouraged he felt. Where would he be now, if it hadn't been for…?

"In a renewed frame of mind, I let the following days pass, waiting for the mountains. Now I was no longer riding at the back of the peloton; I was anticipating the Pyrenees, the first set of mountain stages in this edition of the Tour. On the first of these, at Cautarets, Indurain won his first Tour stage, and on that final climb I succeeded in pulling back almost half a minute on both Fignon and LeMond. But the day I had marked out as being the one where I would turn things round was the following day – a stage that ended at Superbagnères, after going over the summits of the Tourmalet, the Aspin and the Peyresourde.

"That day, when we were fully engaged on the Tourmalet, I instructed Julián Gorospe to set a strong pace. At the top of the climb we dropped Fignon and LeMond, but on the descent they got back to us. At the start of the Aspin, I was the one who, after three different skirmishes from the leading group, set out to give chase to Mottet and Millar, who had just gone off the front. And what a great trio we formed, as we combined perfectly, sharing the work and riding bit-and-bit to the finish. Behind us the PDM men were pulling, but all they managed to do was to save the bacon of the two leading protagonists: LeMond (riding for ADR) and Fignon (riding for Super-U). At the end of that day I was up to fourth overall, 2-53 down on race-leader Fignon. Everything was falling into place and, little by little, the imminent arrival of the Alps was inviting me to dream some not unrealistic dreams of what might be.

"The next important opportunity to recover time was the mountain time trial – 39 kilometres on Orcières Merlette. For a couple of days I had been suffering with a small callus on one of my toes; it was giving me agony whenever the road was uneven. I was hoping that it would ease off, but it didn't. In fact, at key moments in the race it distracted me whenever I made an effort. Although this is not an excuse, my time was not as good as I had expected it to be: I did pull back a bit, but only a bit.

LeMond was now race leader and I was still fourth, 2-48 behind the American.

"No sooner was the time trial finished, when I went over to the team mechanic to ask him for a pair of cutters. What with the disappointment of the result, I'd had enough of the pain from the callus. Wide-eyed in astonishment, he handed them to me without saying a word. The look on my face was enough. I don't know what he was imagining, but as he watched me making a great hole in the shoe to create some space for the painful area, I told him that I couldn't put up with any more of that agony. It was slowly killing me during the race, I told him.

"Free from the pain, I again found myself with illusions over the Brandon stage, with its climbs of the Vars and the Izoard. However, a strong head-wind, on that last climb put paid to any hope of dropping the others. The vital days for me were passing, and I wasn't able to take a decent bite out of the gap my rivals had on me, as I had been able to in the Pyrenees. The last chance would have to be the following day, on Alpe d'Huez. The team did a great job for me – making the race tough over the Galibier, then the Croix de Fer and the climb to Alpe d'Huez. Here my team mate, Abelardo Rondón, made the perfect climb for me, but in the end my legs would not respond. Even so, I did rise to third overall, 1-55 down on Fignon, who recovered the yellow jersey. That day I virtually gave up any hope for the General Classification: there were no more high mountain stages left; only the time trial remained – or a surprise attack.

"In fact, it was I who was surprised the very next day on the short, 92-kilometre stage to Villard de Lans. On the prolonged climb of Saint Nizier there were a number of different attacks, chiefly from PDM who were trying to drop me (to defend Theunisse's 4th place overall). When I made contact with the leading group, Fignon started to move off the front. I expected LeMond to react but, as if all this had nothing to do with him, he did nothing. So then I tried and almost got up to Fignon, but there was no collaboration; all Lemond did was to sit on my wheel,. So I moved aside. I had no intention of saving the race for him.

"A new slowdown. I see how the Frenchman is moving away once more. I jump again and at the summit we are around half a minute down on him. I presume that with scarcely 20 flat kilometres ahead of us, we will work together – the PDM men (Theunisse, Rooks, Alcalá and Kelly) and LeMond and me – and that we will reel him in with no difficulty. My disappointment was that now the only one to collaborate was LeMond, while the Frenchman took the stage win, and a few precious seconds with it. That day I saved the American's face. Furthermore, Fignon found a certain amount of help – from motorists. The fate of all of us seemed to be sealed. For me, the chances of repeating the previous year's victory were practically nil: all that was left was a medium mountain day and, somewhat as a last resort, I did attack on the first climb of the day, the Col de Porte, but there were no really steep slopes on which I could have got away alone. I tried again on the Cucheron with the same result and on the final climb, the Granier, I could already see I was beaten. All I achieved was that five of us came in together at the finish in Aix Les Bains.

"This year I proved what I had believed was impossible – that one can win a Tour without a team, purely by having the luck of the devil. I am talking about LeMond. First, there was the disastrous departure of one of the other *a priori* favourites; that's to say, me. After that came the involuntary collaboration, of different riders, according to how the race demanded it. At one time it was the PDM; at other times it was me, and for sure there were others on more occasions than I remember. The result was that on the final stage, an individual time trial over 25 kilometres into Paris and with Laurent Fignon in the yellow jersey, the American pulled off the impossible: in one fell swoop he won the time trial and the race overall. It was the only day that Greg LeMond merited winning that Tour de France."

Pedro, who in the end was third overall, started that last stage from Versailles 2-28 down on Fignon, with very little motivation because it was going to be impossible to gain or drop a position in the General Classification, other than by some misfortune or other. Were it not for the time he had forfeited in the prologue he would be the leader right now, but as he said, "I was trying in those last few days not to think about that, so as not to get furious with myself again for that disaster in Luxembourg. I was trying to find some peace of mind seeing myself on the podium."

It was a real misfortune not to come away with the yellow jersey of the *Grande Boucle* for the second year running. It would have been a magnificent year for him, after his victory in the Vuelta and his truly brilliant performance in the Tour.

Chapter 14

Alliances and Team-work

'There are no more legitimate unions than those
which at every moment are shaped by passion.'

Stendhal

'Daddy, why don't you win any races?' That was the question Jesús Rodríguez Magro once faced, from one of his own sons. Out of the mouths of children!

'Because I'm a very poor cyclist,' was the reply that came immediately to mind. He exaggerated. Magro was not a rider who often raised his arms in triumph as he crossed the finish line, although he did so on one occasion. His work was all about making sure that other, more gifted riders were able to raise their arms and squeeze their fists in that unmistakable victory salute. That was good enough for him. It was also good enough for Pedro Delgado, and for Miguel Indurain, two of his most distinguished team leaders whose lives he made that much easier.

"Not all races are cut from the same cloth. The way they play out is dependent on a whole heap of factors: some favour one type of rider; others a different kind. In my first Tour, in 1983, I went to the start line without having set myself any particular goals. I was there just to take part, yet as the race progressed I became convinced that I could win – until that one really bad day when I lost twenty-five minutes! That's what happens in races. The way you are, the way you race, the way others race – all that shapes how it finally works out. Cycling is not an individual sport; you need the support of a team. The team is primordial, not just for getting a good time in the team time trial; it is fundamental for ensuring that the team leader gets through without any nasty surprises, and for protecting him and keeping him fresh until it is time for him to make his move."

The *gregario*, the shield bearer, 'my good friend Sancho' is the leader's main ally, his squire, the one who gives whatever is necessary so his leader is untroubled until his moment arrives. And he is not only the good Samaritan; he is more than that because, when events demand that he help the leader, he gives his all. Not a quarter, not a half. Everything.

"In hotly-contested stages, those stages where the racing is hard and the peloton is lined out, the 'capitano', as they call him in Italy, doesn't even have to remind his team mates that he needs water; there's always one who goes back for fresh bidons and supplies him. The team is ever-ready to reel in an escape. If it has to pull, it pulls. And it does so *en masse*, to use the cycling term."

Delgado feels proud of the men he has had in his teams. With a few exceptions (LeMond in 1989, for example), individual victories invariably have their origin in a good team, or at least in the selfless contribution of those riders, good, bad or just average, whose actions go beyond those of even the 'Good Samaritan'.

"In the '88 Tour my team mates supported me enormously. Miguel Indurain, Ángel Arroyo, Jesús Rodríguez Magro, Omar Hernández – all of them worked themselves into the ground. How can I ever forget that sight of Herminio Díaz Zabala, a rider of limited capabilities in the mountains? He finished the Tour pretty much worn out from all he'd done, constantly working on the front and on those steep slopes that he couldn't stand. He used to control the group on the flat and as soon as the road went skywards, he'd lose contact. But, hard-pressed though he was, he'd climb what, for him, were simply walls, and then make up what he'd lost on the descent. And no sooner had he made contact, then he'd be at the very front of the peloton, pulling like the devil. Normally, dedication is like that – total, with nothing held in reserve."

The distinctive yellow jersey of the race leader has given rise to a legend: it is said to give wings to whoever wears it, and not only to the one who actually has it on his back. Results would suggest there is truth in it.

"When, through whatever circumstances, a small team gets the leadership, it transforms not only an average team leader, it

169

has the same effect on the whole team. You see men you could breeze past, or who could be dropped relatively easily on a climb, undergoing a radical change when they have a leader to defend or a race to win: they ride furiously; they're itching for a fight; they'll pull with extra motivation. At such moments they turn into a colossus, their limitations pass unnoticed. They are dropped, but they don't give up, because they have a special incentive – the yellow jersey of their team leader.

"A similar inclination lies behind many triumphs. In the 1989 Vuelta a España it was said that I didn't have a strong team. Perhaps there were better ones, but that was my problem, and I knew that as soon as I got the race leadership the team would respond and support me far more than appearances would lead you to believe. Time proved me right, and also proved me wrong, when I was the one who failed.

"The leader is always extremely grateful, or he should be. It starts to rain and they bring you a rain jacket; you're hungry or thirsty and they bring you food or a bidon. A puerto begins, you've just gone through the feeding station, and you find yourself without a drink, and there is the *gregario* who takes out his own bidon and hands it to you, his team-leader.

'What will you do when you're thirsty?' you might ask him.

'Let me sort that out. I'm in no rush, the finish can wait; you're the one who's going to have to deal with the attacks when they come. You carry on and don't worry about me.'

"There is a tacit agreement. We know how hard it is to win and how you can lose with the merest lack of attention. Everybody in the team knows that well enough. And there are other things that people don't see. In critical moments in the race, like at the feeding station, like when it starts to rain heavily, or when it's stiflingly hot – then it is essential that the leader be protected. And there is the crucial moment which can happen any day there is a sprint finish. A fall, a puncture, a split in the peloton for whatever reason, something which threatens the leader's position in the overall classification – all that is thought about beforehand. There is a particular tactic that is often used to deal with mishaps: if I am the team leader, it is customary that another rider of similar physical build to me forms part of our line-up for the Vuelta or the Tour, or for whatever race it is. He is somebody with the same measurements as me, who can make his bicycle available to me. In the vital moments of a sprint, or in the last ten or fifteen kilometres, when the Director's car is a long way back and we are travelling very fast, there he is, always tied to me, like my shadow. If I puncture, he gives me a wheel; if I come down he gives me a complete bike, so that I don't lose contact with the front of the race. There is great camaraderie there. With Miguel Indurain, for example: where he goes there goes his brother Prudence or Marino Alonso, two men with a very similar size of bike to his. With me, it was Rodríguez Magro or Roberto Lezáun."

There are even cases in which the presence of the 'look-alike' is carried to the ultimate extreme, so that the leader rides as comfortably as possible after a setback of some sort. "Jorg Muller, Tony Rominger's double used to raise his saddle a little higher than he needed, so that in the event of any mishap Rominger could take over on the spot. His bike had the same measurements as Rominger's, despite the fact that this meant a certain degree of discomfort for him. Things like that occur every day during a race, even in the most modest of races, so that the team-leader is protected at all times."

The only rider in his team that LeMond could get any help from, when he won the 1989 Tour, was John Lammerts. The other men who rode alongside him in the ADR team were an idle bunch whose main aim was to do nothing more than the bare minimum. So LeMond had to fend for himself. Often tucked in behind Lammerts, he took advantage of every opportunity that came his way and then finished off the job in Paris with a dream of a time trial. He was lucky to have so remarkable an ally; and Lady Luck provided him with other alliances when the need arose.

But when fortune is not on your side, you need to weigh up other possibilities, talk to the man riding next to you, make on the-spot-agreements, or non-aggression pacts for your mutual benefit. That's the way you get through so many races. Pedro has seen that often enough; sometimes he's lost out from such moments of cooperation; on other occasions he's been the prime beneficiary.

"Greg LeMond didn't have a strong team; they weren't able to give him much help; so he had to find opportune ways to improvise, and luck brought him external alliances, like PDM and me, for example, since we were doing our own thing and he profited from it. I, on the other hand, have also been known for having my own little alliances at various times. I have enjoyed them when they have gone my way and suffered when they have gone against me. It worked out in my favour, for example, on the Segovia stage in the Vuelta of 1989. Fabio Parra escaped and at first I let him go; it was a mistake. While Parra was disappearing further and further into the distance Ivan Ivanov began to work with me. I was delighted, although puzzled by it. I looked at him, surprised, and he gestured to me to get on his wheel. 'What a nice fellow. What a nice little present,' I thought as I settled in behind him. He set a constant rhythm that would prevent Parra's escape from getting anywhere.

"After the Navacerrada more riders come up to join in the work, like Suykerbuyck, a good rouleur, and Jon Unzaga, which meant that the lead which Fabio had established at the top of the Navacerrada, would be substantially reduced by the finish line. People at the time said I had bought Ivanov's services. Quite possibly in similar circumstances, I would have imagined the same, but the fact is that it had not been fixed. It was something which I often wondered about without ever being fully able to understand; I didn't know for sure why Ivanov did what he did. It was only years later, when I happened to be talking to him, he told me: 'For me, a Russian, riding with Perico Delgado who had just won the Tour de France, the best cyclist in the world at the time, was a satisfaction in itself. I was delighted to be riding alongside you and grateful because a few days before that,you had let me win the Brañilin stage.' Yes, I was second that day, and he paid me back on the Navacerrada."

The following day, there was a picture which went all round the world. In it you could clearly see Pedro Delgado handing an envelope to Ivan Ivanov before the start of the last stage.

"This was 'Perico's famous envelope', which my enemies used to gossip about me at the tops of their voices. For me it was a surprise and if it made me a bit infamous, they made me even more so – at least for a couple of days. I am still asked what was in the envelope. I enjoy keeping up the suspense, prolonging the uncertainty. What was I going to give him? My address. 'There you are, Ivanov, now you know where I live, and you can visit me whenever you like… and thank you'."

Well brought-up people do express their gratitude, and in the words of the proverb, 'what goes around comes around.'

"I wore the yellow jersey in the Vuelta a España in 1984, in Rasos de Peguera and I was convinced that the race was going well for me, that I could win it. Then it all went bad at the Lakes of Covadonga. Fortune smiled on Caritoux and Alberto Fernández, but not on me. Third overall, I still believed in my chances, especially in the stage before Segovia. The stages in my part of the country have brought me good luck; they have been generous to me."

And how they would the following year, in 1985, his year of Grace. Pedro, who knew every inch of his terrain, devised the plan and he set in motion an attack which he wanted to be decisive. 'He has always been recognised as being a magnificent strategist,' says José Luis Pascua Piqueras, his trainer, who can bear witness to that. He is spot on when he says: 'Ninety percent of the tactics he employed were his own. Drop back and then jump: that was so very typical of him. So, too, was another quality which he always had: being able not to put on weight. He could eat a stew with a stack of bacon in the middle of the season and it would not show. In November, the most he used to put on was a kilo; Marino Lejarreta, by contrast, would put on seven kilos in a month.'

"I didn't have to wait till 1985 to attack on the descent of the Navacerrada. I'd already done it in 1984 on the road towards Segovia, since my earlier efforts on La Morcuera and on Cotos had got me nowhere. Alberto Fernández, who was second overall, had immediately gone after me. But, as I always say, if you cannot get away on the climb, why not try it on the downhill?

"So I decided to gamble on the Siete Revueltas; I knew that Alberto was anxious when he was descending, especially if the road was wet, which it was that day. So I shot off and I managed to evade the close eye he had on me. I got up to Nico Emonds, who had already gone clear. The first time checks indicated about 30 seconds. I was delighted, absolutely delighted, because the gap which Caritoux, the race leader, and Fernández had on me at the start of that stage was less than a minute. 'Today I'm really stirring it up,' I said to myself, and that encouraged me even more. I knew that Alberto and Caritoux were on their own; they didn't have team mates around them. And even though there were two of them, I was sure they would be keeping a check on each other. They wouldn't be going all out to hunt me down; they would be holding something back, in case either one of them attacked the other. 'It's even possible,' I thought, 'that they will be reluctant to press hard for fear of giving the other a free ride, especially if they have tomorrow's time trial on their mind.'

"A new time-check: 40 seconds!

"In the end my disappointment, my real annoyance came because of the work of Moser and Masciarelli, both in the GIS-TUC team. Alberto and Caritoux had found some allies to put an end to my escape. It made me so angry I ended up asking Moser, a true Italian champion, what possible good it served for him to chase me down like that. With all the experience of his many years, he mocked me: 'Calm down, dear boy, take it easy.' That day I felt cheated, but I learned something about alliances in cycling."

That was not the only time that alliances were united against him. Something very similar happened in the 1987 Tour, when the rumours that Spanish MPs had suspended a session of Parliament so they could watch that stage on 23rd of July, which ended in Morzine, even reached Pedro's ears.

"Who doesn't remember the non-stop fight between Roche and me, which culminated on La Plagne. I was leading at that point, but with the Dijon time trial still to come, I was sure that I had to put more time into the Irishman. That stage was a huge challenge and I forced myself to do everything I could; I was convinced that I was going to crush him, especially on that last climb. When we reached it, I didn't have so much as a second thought: I attacked and away I went. I also tried to find somebody to collaborate with me. I spoke to Lucho Herrera to see if he would go with me. Lucho was always an expressionless rider, undemonstrative, never given to getting excited, or to initiating things on his own; he would always let things happen; and he would never take anybody's side until he was absolutely clear what the situation was. He held back. So I attacked alone at the foot of the col and gave it everything. 'Now it's in the hands of God.'

"Everybody reacted to my offensive. Roche had three *domestiques de luxe* at his disposal: Scheppers, his Carrera team mate, Loro from Del Tongo and the Peugeot rider, Roux, a Frenchman who just happened to be passing that way. Both Loro and Roux led for a good part of the climb – and not just on that day; they had worked for him some days earlier, and would do so again later. They did an important job in maintaining a strong pace without taking the Irishman beyond his limits.

"Scheppers and the allies, Loro and Roux, were setting the pace for Roche while ensuring that I didn't get too far ahead. Many fans told me that they saw Roche being pulled up the climb. I obviously didn't see it, nor do I know whether it was a momentary thing or something more. I am not going to get into that; there are race judges to deal with those things; even so, he must have done something because he was given a small fine, for a feeding offence.

"However, what did me most harm was the collaboration offered to him by riders from other teams. Because of them the time that I was so hoping to put into Roche almost went the other way. In the end I managed to take a miserable four seconds from him. That day, he won the Tour, in spite of the television images of him lying unconscious immediately after crossing the finish line.

"As a result of that he was able to disappear from sight at the finish. He was immediately whisked away by helicopter, thus avoiding the various media interviews. And while I was dealing with the journalists, he was already on the massage table. A good manoeuvre on Roche's part; as they often say in cycling, 'races are won in bed'.

"It was audacious to attack at the bottom of La Plagne, with its 15 kilometres of hard climbing, after we'd already gone over the

Galibier and La Madeleine. And I paid for it. I should have held back a bit, because three kilometres from the finish my strength began to fail me. The minute and a half I had on Roche evaporated so quickly that if the stage had been 500 metres longer he would have overtaken me. With the exhaustion I suffered in those final three kilometres I still had to deal with the press afterwards. In spite of the optimism of the Spanish supporters in the light of the Irishman's apparent fainting fit, I knew that it didn't really mean a thing."

Pedro was affected by his opponent's fainting even more than Stephen Roche himself was.

"That day's frustrating result affected me both physically and psychologically. To make such a brutal effort to gain...four seconds. With so few mountains remaining I knew that my only chance was the time trial, and there my rival was better than me. The die had been cast.

"Other tricks, which I find hard to understand – after all, we are all in the same profession – are those manoeuvres which some cyclists occasionally perform of deliberately blocking an opponent in the middle of a corner. I experienced it during the last stage of the 1985 Vuelta, and I suffered it again in this Tour, at the hands of the Belgian rider, Scheppers. It was on the descent of the Joux Plane, the day after the Morzine stage. Roche attacked on the way down and, while following him, his team mate set about impeding everybody in the corners, A couple of times he practically ran me off the road. The result of all this was that a gap opened up which I wasn't able to close by the finish of the stage."

The faithful squire had exhausted himself in the service of his lord, as cycling's lore demands, even at the risk of bringing about a crash.

Chapter 15

Foes of Mine

*'I have a Golden motto: never attack he who can't
defend himself, nor praise whoever I can't criticise.'*
Tomas Salvador

The more powerful the opponents you defeat, the more laudable
and rewarding are your victories. It is that which makes winning
a Tour so extraordinary. For a racing cyclist there is nothing
that can surpass it. To win the Vuelta or the Giro is a major
accomplishment, but the Tour is the equivalent of the Jules Rimet
cup. And why? Because only the best gather there. It is *la crème*
that the Tour attracts.

Pedro Delgado's years in *la Grande Boucle* coincided with the
most prominent stars of different generations. There he competed
with five-time champion Hinault, and Fignon, LeMond, Roche.
And then he come up against those who would succeed him,
fighting alongside Miguel Indurain against Bugno, Breukink,
Alcalá and Chiappucci. The sudden onset of his contemporary,
Rominger, surprised him, as it did many others. And in the
occasional race, he brushed up against some of those who were
to be the future stars: Berzin, Pantani, Olano, Zarrabeitia...

"I have ridden alongside cyclists who have achieved
everything in this sport. In chronological order, the first name
on the list is Bernard Hinault. The first time I met him was in the
Vuelta a España of '83, the very same Vuelta that forced him to
relinquish all thoughts of the Tour that year due to the extreme
efforts he made in Spain. Not only was he determined to win
it, the organising committee also wanted him to. And they gave
him their full and unconditional support to secure that victory so
as to enhance the international reputation of their race. Hinault
paid dearly for that victory against a generation of Spanish
cyclists who were to make a major impact in the peloton."

At the end of the Vuelta, Bernard Hinault had to undergo surgery on one of his knees which had been wrecked on the Spanish side of the Pyrenees. The Tour was out of the question; in fact he didn't fully recover until 1985.

"Hinault was an aggressive rider and a thorough non-conformist; he liked to organise the race and rule over it. He was a true patron of the peloton. What I most admired in him was his pride, his fight to become the leader, that particular way he had of making cycling more offensive, always on the quest for the epic, even when he was leading the race. On top of that, he was also generous with team mates and rivals, too, if he considered them to be worthy of it. On one occasion, I benefited from that generosity when we reached the finish line together.

"It happened at the end of the stage into Pau during the Tour of '86. He was a much better sprinter than me, but when we arrived together at the finish he decided not to contest the sprint. I can remember very clearly what had happened on that first mountain stage in the Pyrenees, with its 217 kilometres and the ascents of the Burdincurutcheta and the Bargargui in the first half, which significantly reduced the size of the peloton. At the head of the race, nobody wanted to challenge the mighty Hinault and his La Vie Claire team: they were so scared of them that nobody dared make a move in the 40 kilometres of more-or-less flat terrain with the extremely tough Col de Marie-Blanque still awaiting us.

"Such was their apathy that those riders who'd previously been dropped were re-joining the front group of the peloton. In the middle of all this I noticed Hinault gesturing to his promising team mate Jean-François Bernard to make a move just after going through the bonus sprint line. Jeff took off like a motorbike and I found it very hard to catch his wheel, but once I caught up with the group around him, he carried us at top speed towards the foot of the Marie-Blanque. I can imagine everyone at the back was caught off guard because the attack, 90 kilometres out from the finish line, didn't make sense.

"On the col, Hinault asked me to take the climb with a certain degree of caution, even though I was not considering an attack. In the first place, it was still a long way from the summit to Pau;

secondly, the Badger was a great rider, and ideal company to be with.

"We never exchanged a word during the escape, neither did we speak about who would take the stage victory. It was all about each of us having his turn on the front. I knew he was far better than me over this kind of terrain, so I thought it would be stupid if I were to ask him to let me win. It was better to keep my mouth shut. But, I did decide that I would, nevertheless, contest the sprint as soon as the finish line came in sight. 'And let's see what happens.' He proved to be a gentleman because he fought for it, but not with his usual competitiveness. Hinault was a good deal faster than me, and had an impressive track record of important victories, but on occasions he made concessions to riders in other teams. Such generosity is welcomed, especially when it comes from a great champion, and, of course, today's rival might be tomorrow's ally. And he had the reward of a five-minute lead over the other great contender in the General Classification, his team mate Greg LeMond. The American was deeply upset at the finish line: he felt he had been betrayed because he had not been warned of the attack, and then felt his hands were tied when it came to minimising his losses.

"The Badger's vision of cycling didn't fit with the exploits of that day; he wanted something more, more epic. So, on the next day, and now as race leader, he attacked again, on the descent of the Tourmalet. But this time there was a reaction from behind, as Millar, Zimmermann and Herrera all took up the challenge, and carried LeMond with them. Although it was not easy, they managed to give Hinault a hard time, neutralising him at the beginning of the climb to Super Bagnères. Hinault collapsed at the end of that stage, losing 4-39 to his rival LeMond, and for the rest of the Tour he was never able to get rid of him. In my view, on that day he lost what could have been his sixth Tour victory. A few days later, on the Alpe d'Huez stage, Bernard tried to spring another surprise coming down the Galibier, but Greg had learnt the lesson; he wouldn't lose the Frenchman's wheel; in fact, he became his shadow. Finally, Hinault had to be satisfied with second overall in Paris. He was neither selfish nor greedy; he was simply magnificent. But what he could not envisage was that his successor, at least temporarily, would come from his own team.

"There was another Frenchman among the great rivals of my generation. I confronted him for the first time in the 1983 Tour, while we were competing for the yellow jersey. He was one of the architects of Hinault's victory in that year's Vuelta when, on the Serranillos stage, between them they managed to wrest the lead from my own team mate Julián Gorospe. I am talking about Laurent Fignon.

"He won the Tour and yet I cannot stop thinking that either Arroyo or I could have beaten him. Had that Reynolds team been more ambitious, and more experienced, things would have been different. After that year, Fignon experienced a considerable transformation. He was a proud Parisian and, above all, he was presumptuous. He had his great year in 1984, when he took issue with the press, the public, and even with his own team mates. It's true that in that season he proved intractable and simply superior to the rest, but his comments were thoroughly inappropriate.

"I read an interview where he stated that he didn't know what Spaniards were doing in the race, because they never attacked, and were nothing but wheel suckers. I told him that if we didn't attack it was because we couldn't. So what else were we to do? And I even warned him that if we ever did have the slightest chance he would find out just what we could do. It's worth remembering Arroyo's victory in Morzine in the '84 Tour".

In Colombia they couldn't stand Fignon, because he once scorned Lucho Herrera, who was an idol there, with the words: 'When does this guy think he will win the Tour if he weighs 50 kilos?' Every time he opened his mouth he put his foot in it or made an enemy.

"Pride was the driving force behind his pedalling, but after his shining performance in 1984 came the injuries in 1985. He didn't take part in the famous stage of Super Bagnères in 1986, having retired the day before. But fate played a dirty trick on him, and 1989 would bring even more misery to him. An American would snatch the Tour from him in Paris, in his own town and in front of his own people. Many Frenchmen celebrated his defeat, which shows that he was capable of getting up everyone's nose, even his own fellow countrymen's.*

It was his pride that made him win races; that was his driving force. Had it not been for that temperament, he would have become the phenomenal rider he had been for a few years.

"What I liked about Fignon was his riding style, the way he attacked in the feeding stations, or when going through villages, in places where you would least expect an attack to be launched. Many times in a race he made his rivals feel insecure; he liked to ride in the echelons, even at the beginning of the race, and he liked to find allies with whom he could launch an attack on his fiercest rivals, at any time and any place in the race. If one of his rivals had a puncture, he made his team mates ride all out so as to frighten him and make him chase for a few kilometres until, upset and angry, he got back to them. That was why Fignon was feared so much."

Laurent Fignon's master of ceremonies was his director, Cyrille Guimard. Years later they would fall out, when they both forgot one of the key principles of cycling: the finishing line should have the last word; or, as folk wisdom has it, 'it ain't over till it's over.'

Pedro was witness to one of his most remembered and extraordinary days.

"Spanish fans will always remember Fignon spitting at a Spanish camera crew in 1989 when they were trying to interview him. Of course, even if he felt harassed, that action did him little service. And, at that moment, he hadn't yet lost the Tour! What's more, he was overconfident he would win it. That same day, on a Saturday, the day before the time trial, the whole peloton was travelling in the TGV high-speed train towards Paris. Apparently, with a 50-second advantage over LeMond, and with only 25 kilometers in the final time trial and the end of the race, Fignon had it in the bag. I and my team mates were sharing the same coach with the Super U. Guimard started to take out the champagne bottles and share a toast with everyone.

---

* LeMond overturned a 50-second deficit to win the Tour by 8 seconds, the closest result in the Tour's history.

He was wild. He wanted to celebrate Fignon's victory in the Tour with all his rivals who happened to be travelling in the same coach. We all looked at each other incredulously. 'He is being very bold! He's so sure Fignon will win the Tour.' He was such a hermit-like and introverted personality, especially when he had to greet a Spanish cyclist or director. We were constantly surprised during that unforgettable journey with his displays of cordiality. He spoke with everyone, he put his hands on your shoulder, he told jokes that only he understood because he was the only one who laughed. In short, he behaved as if we were all family. The race would not be decided until the last hour, yet he was so sure of the result. The man was half drunk and was inviting people all over the place, serving champagne left, right and centre, and toasting the victory of his rider. OK then, let's be happy! How happy would he be the day after? I guess he had stomach cramps! I cannot believe that, with all his experience in the world of cycling, he could be so inept. We cyclists always say that you can't call victory until the last finish line."

Another keen rival was Stephen Roche.

"He is Irish, like Kelly, but he had many bonds with France. His wife is Parisian and he spent his early career in French teams. Roche surprised me, as he did everybody in the world of cycling, in that magical year of 1987 when he won the Giro, the Tour and the World Championship. He was pushed by the Gods. He always had a tail wind, whereas the rest of us had it constantly in our face. What I especially liked about him was his ability to slip into escapes and what a headache that was for us. He was not much of an attacker: he just slipped so quietly into breaks.

"Until 1987 he was a rider who, like all good Irishmen, suffered enormously in hot weather: in July, unless there was a bit of bad weather he was a dead man. Whenever he faced a mountain stage and the temperature was high he would lose ten minutes. However, he was always ranked among the favourites at the beginning of every race. In that year, 1987, he survived July perfectly well, because the temperature was unusually mild.

"His strength was the time trial, and he is also remembered as one of the fastest and safest of descenders. He was a very likeable person, and the fact that the Irish sense of humour is said to be similar to the Spanish was probably the reason we got along so well".

Just like Fignon, LeMond took his first steps in professional cycling in the shadow of Hinault, and under the command of the unspeakable Cyrille Guimard whom, like the others, he would later abandon.

"The American, Greg LeMond, came to Europe, to ride in Belgium, just after turning 18. His first seasons foretold he would become a great champion: a fine rider, an excellent time trialist and a good climber, he was a rising star. He won the '86 Tour by coping with the mountains and with his own team mate Bernard Hinault. In the last week he never left his wheel, so as to avoid being taken by surprise.

"Later, after he was accidentally shot by his brother-in-law during a hunt, he would never be the same. The hunting accident affected him physically. He was the luckiest rider I have ever seen, always in the shadow, always reluctant to display the powers that a winner of three Tours de France is supposed to have. In the Tours of '89 and '90 the race circumstances allied with him because he was not physically superior at all. However, one must acknowledge he was always there, which is remarkable enough in that race. The only thing is that he never came to dominate; instead, he knew how to involve other riders, who inadvertently helped rescue him. By a series of happy coincidences, he found himself climbing up the leader board in 1989: one day he got the help of Fignon; the next day, in the Pyrenees, that of PDM; another day, it was me. He navigated all those situations until he reached Paris, where he won the time trial and, with it, the Tour.

"What I liked about LeMond was his regularity. He was not an attacking kind of rider, but with his wait-and-see approach, he always hung on in the mountains and got stronger in the time trial. I am sure the PDM team must have pulled their hair out at least twice, as all the leaders who left them ended up winning the Tour the following year. That is exactly what happened with me: I left the team in '87 and I won the Tour in '88. And the same happened with LeMond when he won the Tour in 1989, after leaving PDM the year before. Maybe Steven Rooks was aware of these coincidences, and that is why he, too, left the team in '89, following me and LeMond, and aiming to win the Tour in 1990 with Panasonic. But for him, the lucky charm was broken."

Also from the American continent, although further south, came another of Pedro's rivals, Fabio Parra, the best professional in Colombian cycling.

"He was a real headache for José Miguel Echávarri, my director, during many of my professional years. Parra was the Colombian who adjusted best to European cycling in those years and, like any good *escarabajo**, he was an excellent climber. He was also particularly intelligent when it came to coping with the echelons, the flat time trials, and for maintaining a consistency over three weeks against the highest level of competition. Quite a few times, during the Vuelta of 1989, he gave me a hard time. I admired his expertise and also his professionalism. He was serious yet pleasant, and extremely confident in his strength. I always had a great admiration for him and his riding style. If I may define him like that, Parra was a man who really knew how to suffer on the bicycle."

In any chapter on Pedro's old adversaries, Robert Millar is a must.

"Our rivalry, which lasted for many years and certainly had a frequent impact on the general classification, began in the Grand Prix of Liberation, in Rome in 1980. We were amateurs then, and I remember an Englishman (or so I thought) who was small and thin like me. He was a good climber, so on this flat, circuit type of race we were both always at the back, and having to make some fearful sprint so as not to get dropped.

"Our 'fights' can be traced back to 1983, when he won that stage in the Pyrenees. I was close to getting back to him. The year after, in the '84 Tour, I started to contest the mountain prize with him, and just when I was within a stone's throw of it, I broke my collar bone and that was that: he was the winner. In 1985 I snatched the Vuelta from him and in that same year, in

* *escarabajo* - literally 'beetle' - European nickname for Colombian cyclists.

the Tour, I did the same with second position in the mountain classification. And plenty of other times our paths have crossed, like in the Super Bagnères stage in the Tour of 1989, where we were away together for more than half of the stage, riding bit and bit. In the end he took the win. All in all, though, I believe I came out on top. I would understand it if he disliked me, especially after the Vuelta of 1985. He was a great climber; his Achilles heel was only the time trial. He was an atypical cyclist for our time, for being a vegetarian and wearing an earring. He was very consistent too, but there was always a day on which he seemed to lose his opportunity. Perhaps it was that he limited his aspirations to the mountain classification, or stage wins. I don't know. What I do know is that for many years he was a great rival of mine.

"As regards the Italians, one who really stood out was the mastermind behind Gewiss, and a fantastic strategist who wore the Giro's *maglia rosa* in the very year when he announced his retirement – Moreno Argentin. I'm not sure if it was ambition that he lacked, but he proved to be a better rider at the end of his career than at the beginning. He really focused on the classics and I'm convinced he played a crucial role in Eugeni Berzin's victory in the Giro of 1994.

"And Claudio Chiappucci…He was unpredictable; like Fignon he used every opportunity to attack, but I think he was too wild. He needed to be a bit more calculating. He was not an outstanding rider in his early years. He had to work very hard before he began to shine. I don't hold any resentment towards him, but I do have a score to settle with him. It was in the Giro of 1991, when all the *capos* – the team leaders – agreed to slow the pace down in view of the several falls there had been that day as the peloton went through unlit tunnels. Just before the finish of that stage we had to tackle the Terminillo, the major climb of the day. Bugno, Argentin and Chiappucci approached me beforehand and told me there would be no attacks; yes, we would ride to the finish of the stage, but we wouldn't compete for it. The whole of the peloton climbed the pass at a gentle pace: we had planned to launch an attack there, but we refrained from doing so to preserve the peloton's unity. Then it started to rain;

the weather got worse, and I stopped to put on the raincoat – a matter of 30 seconds.

"When I started riding again, I saw the peloton was really strung out. What's going on? Then I started the descent riding hard because I had a bad premonition. The race was split and I lost nearly 30 seconds to the other leaders. What had happened, I was told, was that Chiappucci, together with his team mates, had sprung an attack on the descent. Several of us were affected by this unsporting behaviour, among them LeMond, Jaskula and me, and, indeed others, who had been gullible enough to believe in a gentlemen's agreement. When I met Chiappucci I told him he was a piece of shit, and it was only by a miracle that I didn't go for his throat. He tried to excuse himself blaming his team mate, Poulnikov.

"That day I understood why his nickname was 'the gypsy'. This was the flaw in his character. But he had a positive side too – his absolute will to attack even when he was leading the race, like he did in the Pyrenean stage in 1990 that ended at Luz Ardiden. It was that impulsive streak of his that made him lose that Tour, because he had LeMond at a safe distance: the normal thing would have been simply to retain his advantage, thinking ahead to the last time trial. But instead of waiting for the final ascent of that day, there he was, attacking at the very first opportunity he had, on the Col d'Aspin.

"He was still in the lead on the Tourmalet, but on the final climb, his strength deserted him and he ended up losing two minutes to LeMond, which practically served the American victory on a silver platter. If someone is wondering where I was, well then, I was suffering at the time from a bout of gastroenteritis which left me feeling feeble stage after stage, and despairingly watching another Tour slip through my fingers.

"From that year onwards, Claudio underwent a great transformation and became an extremely self-reliant rider who would eventually compete with Indurain. The stage he won in Sestrieres in the Tour of '92, after more than 200 kilometres out on his own, will remain an indelible memory. At first, we in Banesto let him pursue his solo adventure; then we began to speed up when we saw the gap was continuing to grow, and that we weren't reeling him in. With the alarm bells ringing, we ended up riding flat out, with team mates dropping off in the process, in what looked like an impossible chase. Ultimately, Miguel had to intervene, after Bugno had launched a fierce attack. And just two kilometres from the finish, just when it seemed that the goal had been achieved, Indurain suddenly weakened and lost almost two minutes to the Italian. That evening, when we were all having dinner, Indurain admitted it had been the longest final kilometre of his life.

"After Chiappucci's restlessness, there was Gianni Bugno. He was such an unlucky rider: coming up against Indurain was a real misfortune. He was never an attacking type of rider, despite his exceptional physical qualities. He could win any type of race he wanted to. He could win a sprint finish, or climbing or a time trial; but there was Indurain always in his way. Bugno's strategy consisted in gaining some advantage in the time trial and defending it in the mountain stages. But when you meet another rider who does exactly the same, only his name is Miguel Indurain and he is better, then you need to change your strategy. Instead Bugno started to worry, and he was unable to find a weakness in Indurain or second-guess him, and he gave up. He was unable to take in the fact that in the first time trial Miguel would put 30 seconds or a minute into him. Instead of thinking about going on the attack at the start of the next day, or on a descent, he crumbled. After a few years, Indurain gained confidence whilst Bugno lost what little he did have. What I liked most about him was his physical power; he was an enviable rider. He always behaved very kindly with other riders, with assistants, with everyone. He was a very courteous person.

"I also had a few rivals among the Spaniards; these were rivals who, in all fairness, made an impression. Marino Lejarreta was a very consistent rider who stood out in the mountain stages and performed very well in time trials, too. I moved to Holland while he had previously moved to Italy. His move coincided with the worst time for transalpine cycling, which prevented him from displaying all the talent he had. Mountain stages barely figured in the Giro, and the races were so undemanding that they seemed to be designed for the Italian stars, Francesco

Moser and Giuseppe Saroni. In this context Marino felt a mixture of apathy and incredulity when confronting the bigger tours. He didn't believe he could really win, and he lost crucial time at key moments, either in the mountain stages or in time trials. What's more, like a proper Basque, he was badly affected by hot weather in the Tour. Those days took their toll on him. It wasn't until the end of his career that he could shine as a great rider. The only thing he didn't do was to confirm the victory he got by chance in the Vuelta of 1982.* In the Vuelta of '83 he was able to display his world class in the magnificent setting of the Lagos de Covadonga and in the Panticosa time trial. But then he would get stuck, and make no further progress. It was only when Manolo Saiz took him to the ONCE team that his riding talent would shine again. Manolo managed to build up his self-confidence and empower him with the necessary competitive spirit to cope with three-week races.

"A neighbour of Lejarreta was Julián Gorospe. He was not only a high-class, direct rival to me in our junior and amateur years, he also became more a friend than a foe as a professional. We spent quite a few seasons together in the Reynolds team. I had nothing but good things to say about him, although I did reproach him over one thing. Julián was a great rider. We belonged to the same generation, we had been together for most of our professional careers, practically since the beginning. He could win in time trials or when climbing a col. But his talent was hindered by obstacles that proved to be decisive, and cycling is merciless. His difficulties were in the echelons, and descending in the wet. And his rivals were unforgiving with these weaknesses; they made him suffer, so he eventually became even more vulnerable. The '83 Vuelta he lost on the slopes of Serranillos, following the attack launched initially by Fignon and then completed by his boss, Hinault. It left him with an inner handicap to the point where he couldn't even win other much easier races.

"That day on Serranillos he was left far behind, and he wanted to quit: the feeling of self-distrust lingered with him.

---

* Having finished second overall, Lejaretta was subsequently confirmed as the winner after Arroyo gave a positive in the final day's drug test, and received a ten-minute time penalty.

Psychologically, he threw away his hopes of winning any of the grand tours. Julián said that after that stage he would never be able to win a three-week race because he felt unable to maintain the physical and emotional stability for that length of time. And he repeated that to himself so many times that he became incapable of getting over it. He should have won the Vuelta of 1990, but he lost it to Giovanetti because of his lack of self-belief. That 'information virus' he seemed to have in his mind wreaked havoc on him, especially on the important days, those that he imagined were important, even if they weren't."

He had the ability to fight, which nobody would deny, but his real fight was within himself. He was once Pedro's rival even though they were in the same team. This was in 1984, and the third time Pedro had participated in the Vuelta a España. From the previous two he'd learned what he needed to know and the following year he managed to wear the yellow jersey in Rasos de Peguera.

"I held on to the lead for five or six days, then it was time to face that mythical ascent to the Lagos de Covadonga, the first perilous stage where I had to defend the yellow jersey. Before this unpredictable incline, we went over the Mirador del Fito, a hard puerto, capable of splitting the peloton. José Luis Laguía, Ángel Arroyo and Julián Gorospe set about the climb, riding hard on the front to discourage any attack; so hard in fact that they were towing me. We made it to the top, down the other side and continued flat out towards Covadonga. I wasn't able to recover, and we started the last and final climb to Los Lagos still at full throttle. But I couldn't stay with the pace of the leading riders and I fell behind: Julian was the only one left from my team. He dropped back to help me.

'Come on Pedro! Get on my wheel and I'll burn them off. I'm riding all out!'

'Wait, Julian. Wait for me!'

I had just collapsed, so how on earth could I follow him? I needed to take some air, but even so I managed to stay with him.

'Are we together, now? Let's go then.'

'Julián, take it easy. Hold on a bit more.'

But, as he'd said, he was riding all out, and when he pushed I fell behind. But again he waited for me.

'Come on Pedro! Just one more time! On my wheel and I'll catch them!'

'Juliaaan!'

Then the same thing again: he, in front, going like a motorbike; me, behind and falling further back. I was almost suffocating and he, willing to help me, only contributed to my suffocation.

'Not so fast, please.'

'You see? Here I am again. Stay on my wheel.'.

'It's too fast, Julian. You're going too fast.'

It was no use. It was impossible to reason with him. He didn't understand that I had no strength left and he didn't seem able to set a pace in accordance with my dwindling forces. So in the end I decided to ignore him.

'Hey man, do whatever you want,' I shouted to him.

"Here was my own team mate finishing me off. When I crossed the finish line I wanted to go for him, but I was so tired. If it had been anybody else …perhaps. But no, it was him. It was Gorospe, generous with the efforts, generous enough to help a team mate, and on this occasion generous enough to help me dig my own grave.

"Years later, something similar happened to Tony Rominger with his team mate Fabio Rodríguez: he felt so strong that he started to pull, exposing the weakness of the leader, which eventually made him fall behind.

"Gorospe was an exceptional rider; 'Juliancho' we used to call him in the Banesto team. With a bit more cunning and more self-confidence he would certainly have filled his *palmarès* with more great victories for Spanish cycling. I remember thinking in those days, that he was one of those riders who never performed so well after they'd crossed the Pyrenees."

Another Basque rider who rode for a season with Pedro in the Seat-Orbea team was Pello Ruiz Cabestany.

"Pello was another of those great cyclists that the Basque country produces. He was a friend of mine and I never considered him an enemy. He has more reasons to bear a grudge against me, than I against him. I even snatched away his place on the podium in the Vuelta in 1990. I always liked his riding style; just like Roche, he knew how to slip into an escape group, and that allowed him to win some important races. He was at his best in time trials and he could descend very well, but above all he was a very cunning rider, a sly old fox. Furthermore, he coped very well in the mountain stages. Within the peloton he provoked a certain antipathy due to his personality, but, all in all, he was a great contributor to Spanish cycling and he is a friend I'd like to remember.

"And, as with Pello, I was also fond of that Castilian rider, Ángel Arroyo, whom I happened to spend some time with in my early career. I liked the way he rode. He had the fierceness that Gorospe lacked. After finishing first in the '82 Vuelta, he used to say something that gave away his rebellious nature: 'Kill the enemy'. He repeated that phrase time and time again even if he was shattered. He was a very consistent rider in all areas but, above all, he was a natural-born fighter, who wouldn't give up easily. It was so sad that the debilitating Malta fever brought his career to an early end."

Among Pedro's other rivals, surprise has a name and a face: Tony Rominger. The Swiss was a year younger than Pedro and seemingly full of energy.

"I always got along well with Swiss cyclists, and Rominger was no exception. As was the case with Julián Gorospe, his only problem was that three-week races dragged for him. He used to go after a stage victory in order to justify his presence in the race, after which he would even think of quitting. Fortunately for him, but not for Montoya and me, he didn't quit the Vuelta in 1992. He had a really black day in the time trial in Benicassim, performing so badly that I think he did consider retiring from the race. Then, in the Baqueira-Beret stage he complained that he felt a bit sore all over after he'd fallen – the implication being that he was thinking of going home. His Director, Juan Fernández, didn't pay too much attention to any of that, however, and encouraged him to continue: he was, after all, together with Echave, the team's trump card. So, in a poorly disguised eleventh hour, he got over the Boanigua pass and was able to confront the end of the stage with a certain degree of optimism.

"The following day, on the Luz Ardiden stage, Lale Cubino, from Amaya team and a team mate of Montoya, the race leader, escaped. On the ascent to the Tourmalet and all the way to the finish line in Luz Ardiden, Rominger was the only one who offered me any assistance; everybody else simply sat on my wheel. I had so much pressure on me, especially from Montoya, that I let the Swiss go a few metres clear towards the end of the stage, so as to break their siege on me, and help put another man in the General Classification who could potentially become an ally later on. With the time he pulled back on that stage he became a different rider. I cannot imagine what went through his mind over the course of those two days, but the rider who wanted to quit turned into a rider with a realistic chance of winning the Vuelta. And win it, he did! And then he won the next two! And to think that he couldn't cope with a three-week long race!

"With the support of his renowned doctor and trainer, Michele Ferrari, Rominger even managed to beat the hour record and to become the most serious rival to Indurain in the Tour of 1993. He had always been a very good time trialist, and he climbed well, too. The problem was that he wasn't consistent enough over three weeks. But when he succeeded in overcoming that obstacle, and that one crucial day which all cyclists have to go through (however much a champion they might be), he revealed himself as the great rider that everyone imagined he would be."

Then there were those who were not even remotely Pedro's enemies. They were the ones who demonstrated nothing other than loyalty, team-spirit and know-how, and who make this sport great – the inappropriately-named *domestiques*, Pericro's friends for life.

"Anastasio Greciano, Jesús Rodríguez Magro, Juan Martínez Oliver, Abelardo Rondón…, the best companions I ever met. They were the best of professionals, always ready to give everything for a team mate without concern for themselves. Always for the team, whether I was there or not, they spared no effort, and I will forever take my hat off to them, for their courage and sense of honour. They have my deepest respect for the personal and professional journey they have followed throughout these years."

Chapter 16

A Blank Year; A Black Year

*'The only thing one really knows about human
nature is that it changes.'*

In 1991, the peloton breathed a little more easily; for some reason
Pedro Delgado had undergone a striking change. The winner of
two Vueltas, the Tour in 1988, and the man who had provided
such an extraordinary three-week exhibition in the '89 Tour was
not the man he was. He seemed to have become completely
jaded.

"I too had a transition year, like in politics. And it was not
a sabbatical, because I didn't stop riding. It was a blank year,
or to put it another way, a black year. In 1989, in spite of the
lapse in Luxembourg, I won the Vuelta and I was bursting with
energy throughout that season; I was at my peak, and riding so
easily. Then, in 1990, I came up against problems, both in the
Vuelta and in the Tour, but that didn't stop me knowing what
I was capable of. The real trouble came in '91, when I lost some
of my confidence; I wasn't where I expected to be, and I decided
to adopt a different kind of training in an attempt to change and
to improve. What a year that turned out to be – the worst I ever
had."

His coach, José Luis Pascua Piqueras provides a perfectly
simple explanation for that change in Pedro. 'In 1991 we had to
face up to the effects of his ageing. So, we refined his training
programme: instead of quantity, we put the emphasis on
quality. This was not the most drastic transformation we ever
decided on; it was not like in 1984, for instance. What we did
then was to alter his training with the specific aim of improving
his time trialing. We were sure that either we would make
improvements in that speciality, or that there was nothing that
could be done. Pedro began training with the aim of getting

among the top ten in any time trial. We reduced his climbing ability, but we increased his performance against the clock. In 1991 the aim was different, and that made for other changes in Pedro's working routine.'

"As the two previous Tours had not gone well for me, we decided that I should go back to Italy to ride the Giro again, just as I did in 1988, while still keeping ourselves focused on France. I believed I could have won the Tour in the previous two years, if it hadn't been for the business in Luxembourg and then the gastroenteritis I picked up mid-way through the race the following year. The effects of that experience in Italy had, therefore, been excellent, in spite of the Gavia, and I fancied the idea of repeating it. I turned up for the '91 Giro with greater ambition, aiming to make it to the podium, even winning it, if that turned out to be within reach. At the same time, however, we wouldn't lose sight of my principal objective – the Tour. But as the days went by I felt that my legs were not responding. Things were not going well in Italy; so, instead of getting myself worked up about it, I resolved to take it easy and to prepare for the Tour in the best way possible. Putting in the kilometres – that would get me in shape."

But as the Giro progressed, Pedro saw for himself that things felt different from previous years: even putting all those kilometres in his legs was not doing him any good. Was he becoming disillusioned? Had he had enough of cycling? Was he overburdened by racing?

"What struck me in 1991 was that I was racing too much. Personally, I liked training at home, going to team get-togethers, then racing; but in those days it was fashionable to train by racing, and so the team put me into one race after another. Yes, I definitely wanted to race, but afterwards I needed to rest, in order to absorb the work I'd done and thereby raise my level of performance."

When the Latvian, Piotr Ugrumov, surprised everyone by finishing second behind Miguel Indurain in the 1993 Giro, he had no difficulty explaining why there had been such a radical improvement in what he was capable of: 'When I was at Seur,' he said, 'it was race, race, race – more and more kilometres in competition, always flat out. Here, in Italy, they allow you the time to prepare for the races.'

In Banesto, as in so many other European teams, from what Pedro says, it was very much the same.

"I don't know why, but at that time it was racing, racing, racing that was all the rage as far as cyclists' training was concerned. If you were not on form, get out and race, and that would help you to find your form; that was the typical response in those days. The fact is that when I got to the Giro I was pretty well stuffed full of kilometres. I had ridden in the Tour of Romandie, the Tour of Trentino as well as a number of one-day races. I was racing as if I were in the Vuelta: here, there and everywhere. Then the Giro. After that there'd be some other race that would stop me going to the usual team altitude training camp, which I'd been doing for years prior to setting off for the Tour.

"When I arrived in France I was conscious of my change of preparation at every level. I didn't have any spark. I could see I wasn't going well, even though I did well enough in the first time trial. Miguel Indurain won it and I was eighth, which made me feel a bit more optimistic. But inside, I still sensed things were not good; my legs felt heavy and I was pedalling without any joy. All that made me feel rather insecure. I tried not to let it get me down, nor to think too much about it, but rather that everything would change once we got into the mountains, which I was waiting for with a certain degree of anxiety. Furthermore, I had always come good later in the race, and perhaps once we had passed the half-way mark and were on my kind of terrain it would be better.

"The first mountainous day of the Tour would take us into Spain, through the Pyrenees to Jaca; it was not a very demanding day. Mid-way through the stage a dangerous escape formed, led by Luc Leblanc, Pascal Richard and Charly Mottet. It was a situation which once again tested the race leader, Greg LeMond. His team, the French team 'Z', didn't want to make too much of an effort controlling the escape, and the gap simply grew: five minutes, six, seven until they were more than ten minutes up. After the American's last two Tour victories, we in Reynolds were fed up watching others saving his skin; we decided we'd just wait and see. In the end, from the summit of the Somport down to the finish, we did start to ride – we almost felt forced to, because the situation was becoming quite surreal. Whenever the Tour crosses into Spain, that Hispanic shrug of the shoulders makes us feel stressed, over and above whatever the demands of the race might be."

That evening, Javier Gómez Navarro, then Secretary of State for Sport, went to have dinner with Banesto at their hotel in Jaca. It was a day when all manner of criticism rained down on the Spanish team. People were expecting a Banesto bean-feast, and what happened? Mottet won the stage, leading in a group that had simply been allowed to escape at their leasure. Navarro spoke to Echávarri. 'I am alarmed by these criticisms. How is the situation?'

José Miguel was of the opinion that the politicians profited from Spanish successes in Paris and that Gómez Navarro saw himself losing out on that. Arrantxa Sánchez Vicario's triumph at Roland Garros and Pedro's win in the 1988 Tour encouraged him to think there would be an avalanche of such victories.

'And how is Pedro, then? How is Pedro?,' the Secretary of State wanted to know. Miguel's name apparently didn't come to mind.

'Look, Javier,' Echávarri replied, 'Wait till tomorrow.' He was alluding to the Tourmalet stage.

'Yes, alright, but how is Pedro?'

'Pedro is fine; but Miguel is doing very well.'

* * *

If Pedro Delgado had been allowed to design a stage of the Tour and crown it with the hot July sun, he would have drawn the very one that went from Jaca to Val Louron. Plenty of kilometres, laced with some difficult puertos of the precise length to do damage, and heat, plenty of heat, to punish the enemy. That would have been his archetypal stage, the stage he always imagined. And yet...

"For me it turned out to be a dreadful day, in spite of that dazzling sun and the cloudless sky; it confirmed that I was not going well. It was horrible; it wasn't that I couldn't attack; I couldn't even hang on. I felt I was so limited, and there I was in the middle of a sea of doubts. After the Portalet – the first climb of the day – came the Aubisque. I didn't make an ascent that would have set the world on fire, but I climbed it well enough: there was a selection of 15 riders and I was among them. That instilled some confidence in me, in spite of not being able to get rid of that feeling of heaviness in my pedalling. After that, was the Tourmalet.

"Between those two cols the race became animated, and after leaving Argelès-Gazost the road rises for about three kilometres at a steady gradient of between 4% and 5%. You have to suffer during that stretch, and I realised then that at the fierce pace that was being set, this would be a day for maintaining concentration. In a peloton now of some 50 to 60 riders I could see I was among the tail-enders, and on the point of getting dropped. I have ridden that stretch often enough to know that a little later the gradient eases off, and you get to a level stretch, but I didn't want to think about what came after that – the dreaded Tourmalet. From the bottom of the col the pace was lively – not too demanding, but we weren't hanging about either – and yet I couldn't follow it. I was dropped. I was exhausted.

"There were still some 40 riders at the head of the peloton – a huge number, bearing in mind that we were on my favoured terrain, and I was no longer among them. This was bad, really bad. I was not used to finding myself in this kind of situation, except when I was ill."

Ronan Pensec from the Amaya team attacked and thereby war was declared. He was absorbed back into the group. Then it was LeMond who tried to get away, and it was Indurain who caught up with him. Echávarri's car overtook the Amaya team car of Javier Mínguez, who shouted, 'Miguel is going balls out! I've seen Pedro and he's buggered.'

Echávarri knew only too well what was happening: 'Pedro was foundering on his own battleground, which was like Miguel failing in the time trial. The Tour was over for Pedro; he was finished. Inside, the man was going through torture. He said he was OK, but I knew he wasn't.'

"Fortunately that day Miguel came through. Chiappucci had escaped, Miguel attacked on the descent of the Tourmalet and took the leader's jersey in Val Louron. That covered up what for me was a truly black day."

Echávarri was aware of Pedro's problems: 'He was suffering and I needed to stay with him; Miguel was going fine, and it was there, in Val Louron, that the change of leadership in the team took place. Out of respect we hid our feelings. Pedro knows that nothing was being taken away from him. He was highly decorated, and had been the standard bearer of an entire nation during 1987, 1988 and 1989. In 1990 there were a good few people who were critical of me for not taking the leadership away from him. But why should I have done? Miguel still wasn't ready, although it was clear that he could make it to the podium. From then on you could see the unstoppable approach of the Indurain hurricane. I must express my gratitude to both of them, to Pedro and to Miguel, for how much they respected each other. They provided an impressive example.'

For Pedro, his form remained a problem.

"I still don't know with any real certainty what happened to me. The winter and the start of the season had been just like any other, but then later in this year, 1991, I was not going at all well. Just after the Tour I did begin to improve a little. What I needed, I think, was some rest. That day on the Tourmalet I went downhill physically and my spirit sank when I saw there were still 40-odd riders there, and I couldn't stay with them. I had no excuse; no stomach problems, no *pájara*, nothing. I just lost heart. It was me, and my legs which couldn't carry on. It was among the hardest days in my entire cycling career; you have prepared all year long for the Tour and at the crucial moment, you fail. I was oblivious as to what was taking place at the head of the race; initially I was just fighting to lose as little time as possible. But on the upper slopes of the Tourmalet you have a perfect view of the final kilometres. What I saw there were cyclists, far off in the distance, like ants on the winding road, practically at the summit and me, two kilometres further back, a world away for a rider who has any aspiration towards winning the Tour.

"On the descent I disconnected my mind completely from the race. 'Now just get to the finish,' I was thinking. Although you find yourself mixed in with other riders, I preferred to be by myself during those last kilometres. Some Spanish fan whom I came across on the Aspin gave me a time check. 'Ten minutes to the leaders!' In a different league. And there was still Val Louron to come.

"During the last few kilometres of that extraordinarily hard 232-kilometre stage, I was mentally preparing myself for the meeting I'd have with the Spanish journalists as soon as I crossed the line, and wondering what I would tell them. 'Take it easy, Pedro,' I said to myself. 'No need for excuses; when the legs don't work, they don't work. If they ask you something you don't like, stay calm; they are here to see you fight for the victory, so it's only natural that they should want to know.' I was going over all this in my mind so as to deal with this ghastly day. No sooner had I crossed the line, there were the journalists, crowded there – 'Take it easy, Pedro. Your time has come.'

'Well then, are you happy?' was the first thing I heard. I didn't dare to look into the face of the journalist who had asked me that.

'Happy? Am I happy? Good God, man, I don't know what you mean.'

'Well, aren't you happy that Miguel has got the yellow jersey?'

'How could I not be happy? That is fabulous.'

I had been so wrapped up in my own world that I hadn't found out that my team mate had become race leader. I didn't know at all.

"For me that was a liberation: nobody was asking what had happened to me; it was happiness everywhere because of the wonderful exploit of another Spaniard. The very fact of not having to provide explanations helped me to find some peace of mind after what, for me, had been a day to forget."

With the coming of the so-called 'Indurain hurricane' there was a sea change, not only within Spanish cycling, but on the world stage. And the changeover – and this is the good thing about it – happened without any traumas: the batton passed from Pedro to Miguel without any anger.

"It was fine by me because I began to enjoy cycling in a much more relaxed way, and with far less tension. Throughout the following three years, I rediscovered the form that I lost in 1991, and I went back to training in the way Pascua and I had always done – racing followed by resting. And Miguel Indurain was steadily coming to dominate the Grand Tours, and most especially the Tour de France, where he didn't stop providing triumphs for the fans to celebrate."

Pedro still has some indelible memories of Indurain.

"He was always the favoured son, the adopted son of José Miguel Echávarri, who worried so conscientiously about preparing him. In his first year as a professional, in the Vuelta a España of 1985, he managed to take the race leadership. I then took the jersey away from him on the Lagos de Covadonga stage. That was hardly surprising: he was very young, 20 years old, the youngest leader there had ever been in the Vuelta, and he didn't stand out principally because of his talent as a climber. He was a big rider, heavy, who needed to develop, which is precisely what he did. With Miguel, Echávarri corrected the mistakes he'd made with his other cycling 'son', Julián Gorospe.

"When I went back to Reynolds from PDM I sensed that Indurain enjoyed favourite status, and I don't mean he didn't deserve it. Quite the contrary. What's more he was also a very decent, unassuming man and a good team mate, and for that very reason he didn't provoke any jealousy within the team. Naturally, everyone has his soft spot and Indurain was Echávarri's. In the '89 Vuelta, and also in that of '90 and '91 Indurain occupied a preferential place when it came to planning for the race. Echávarri repeatedly said, 'I would like Miguel to win a Vuelta.' He really wanted that."

Echávarri took Miguel off to Italy so that he could meet Doctor Conconi, the pre-eminent man in sports medicine at the time and, along with Michele Ferrari, one of the architects of Francesco Moser's hour record. After assessing the exceptional qualities of the cyclist he had in front of him, he recommended that he should lose some weight, but he saw in him a man for the Classics, not for the Grand Tours.

When Delgado won the Tour in 1988, Miguel said to him on a number of occasions, 'I'll never be capable of winning that race: the mountains are so hard; it goes on so long; I'll never be able to cope with that.'

'No, not at all, Miguel. It's like everything else,' Pedro explained to him. 'You have to grow into it; you're still very young, and you need to continue absorbing the work gradually, bit by bit.' But Miguel refused to accept that he would be capable of winning a Tour himself, despite of all he had done for Pedro.

"That year he helped me enormously, especially in the high mountain stages, like the one Lale Cubino won at Luz Ardiden. Climbing the Peyresourde, Miguel went to the front and set the pace. We began with about 100 in the group, and the pace felt comfortable. Half way up the climb and we were down to something like 40; the rhythm was constant, and it never slackened. As we continued climbing, more and more were slipping off the back. I came up alongside him and said, 'Take your foot off the pedal a bit,' because if he carried on like that he was going to find himself out on his own and still with the Tourmalet and Luz Ardiden to climb. I don't know whether or not he was on the limit; I was not able to discern that since the expression on his face gave nothing away; he simply gave a nod, and to the relief of the few still left, he slackened the pace a little. Even when he did so nobody dared attack, which was an indication of the strain he was inflicting on us during that ascent. That day I really became aware of the rider he was developing into. Extremely strong in the time trial and capable of climbing at speed; he was a great climber and it was only a matter of time before we'd see him win something big.

"I kept telling him: 'Do you understand, Miguel? Do you realise what you could do? With your quality you have to ride everything – everything. You're quite capable of winning the Tour.'

'Oh, I don't know,' Miguel would say, and he'd go on and on, 'I don't see it as clearly as that.'

"Indurain admired me, but he continued carrying that doubt about himself in his own mind. Mind you, it didn't stop him working. He'd always work a little bit harder, and in spite of his doubts, he forced himself to improve year by year. That commitment bore fruit. There are a number of things I can think of now, things I used to say to him before he was the rider he later became. His problem, the one defect I saw in him, was in getting to be race leader, because once he was, it was then all downhill. Once he was wearing the yellow jersey there was nobody who was going to take it off him. But first he needed to get hold of it.

"He won the Volta a Catalunya in '88, Paris-Nice in '89 and '90 and a number of other races which I had been leading. I could see that he was not an attacking kind of rider, and he often used to say that he would never have that inclination to attack which characterised me whenever we were climbing. He insisted that he could not jump away out of the peloton in that way. There was nothing I could say to him about that, because everyone has his own way of riding. But once he got to be race leader, he was not going to lose his grip on it. Being leader gave him great confidence and strength. His rivals would be beating against a brick wall, regardless of the terrain on which they chose to attack him – climbing, descending, in the echelons."

With hours of training and many sacrifices aimed at defeating his own body before anybody else's, Indurain developed and Pedro bore witness to it.

"His coolness when he was racing was admirable – how he examined the lie of the land and the situation. As for my theory about the yellow jersey, he confirmed that when he took it for the first time in the Tour. There was still a certain degree of uncertainty about him, some lingering doubt as to whether he really could win the Tour, in spite of the fact that during the previous year he'd come to be viewed as one of the favourites. My own thought, though, when he put on that first yellow jersey at Val Louron, was that the others were going to have to do an awful lot if they wanted to strip it off him. In normal circumstances, free of any illness and with the leadership in his pocket, there wasn't a rider around who could do him serious harm.

"Analysing my own chances in the '91 Tour convinced me that I had no option other than throw myself into the task of assisting Miguel. My presence and my experience could help to control the race. One day, towards the end of the Tour, on a medium mountain stage where the climbs were not too severe, and where Konyshev won in a ten-man sprint, there were attacks from the word go. No escape was able to get away and stay away. It was leg-breaking country with one 3rd-category col and a 4th-category. We were really clearing the decks for action – climbing on the big ring and in the 19 sprocket, keeping up a high speed with each doing his turn on the front. The peloton would quickly split into pieces, then with a great effort come back together again. People were constantly being shelled out of the back and everything was getting increasingly out of control.

"During one of these accelerations a group was formed which was infiltrated first by Bugno, then by Chiappucci. I went after them. And Miguel? Miguel, where is he? I look behind and I see him, twentieth or thirtieth place in the peloton. I drop back to him. 'Miguel, please, move up. Don't you see that if that group gets away with Bugno or Chiappucci, or the pair of them in it, we're going to have problems?'

"In the end we were able to let a group slip away, but it was a group that didn't contain any dangerous men, and after that the stage calmed down. So we managed to save the day when the legs of the leader, Miguel, were not responding as well as they needed to. We were able to control Bugno, Chiappucci and Mottet without them being aware of the yellow jersey's problems. If others wanted to escape? Fine – let them go. But we stick with Miguel, the one they say doesn't suffer. Doesn't suffer? He suffers, alright, just like everybody else. The difference is that when he's having a bad day, as everybody does, he doesn't let it show. He knows only too well that he's going through a bad time, but he knows how to deal with it, and what's more, how to conceal it. For me, on that day he became even more of a champion than he had already shown himself to be, even though we had to push him a couple of times to get him back into the group of his main rivals. Let me finish this off with a phrase I remember Javier Mínguez using about Miguel: 'Indurain is a slave to the bicycle.'

"Just like I went through my *via crucis* in the Tour of 1991, Indurain experienced something very similar in what Spaniards refer to as 'the Tour that Miguel didn't win'. I am talking about the edition of 1996. That year he found his legs not responding as well as in other years, and he was overtaken by rivals he had previously beaten. It was said that the 'Indurain era' had reached its conclusion. I was not fully in agreement with that view which everybody was giving voice to.

"First of all, 1995 had been a year loaded with more days of competition than normal. On top of that, the season was extended, with the World Championships in Colombia taking place in October, whereas they usually occurred in August. Nor was Miguel one to hold anything back; if he could win, he would do so. It was gold in the time trial and silver in the road race. Then, in addition to that, it was in 1995 that he wanted to leave his mark, as other great cycling champions have done, with the hour record. He beat it in Bordeaux, even though he wasn't a regular on the track. Once again, his strength allowed him to achieve it. In short, it was a very long year, and it had been full of racing.

"I mention this because in 1996 he was again confronted by a very heavy racing calendar. He didn't want to go to the Giro because of the wear and tear that entailed. Instead, he went to race in other places and, as his victories testify, faced other rivals in the Volta a Alentejo, the Vuelta a Asturias, the Dauphiné Libéré and the Bicicleta Vasca. Bearing in mind the effort that all this took, the Giro would have been a better option: it would have meant fewer days of racing; the same rivals; everybody more or less equally tired; less travelling and a more orderly life. At that time when, on average, you raced more than 100 days a year, and the top men as many as 130 days, it was very important if you were already the other side of 30 to have some periods of rest. You needed that to keep the freshness in your legs. It was a pity that Miguel brought the curtain down on his racing career that year, because I am convinced that his physical capabilities were still intact. It was only that his season was so badly planned."

Chapter 17

Good Morning, Sadness

'He who grieves prematurely, grieves more than is necessary.'
Seneca

'How are you doing, Dominique? What did you make of the Tour this year?'

'Same as every year, Pedro. It was very hard.'

'But it won't be the last.'

'I won't be doing any more!'

The 1990 Tour was over. The paraphernalia of the biggest bike race disappeared as if by magic. All that was left were bits of paper, advertising scraps and damaged cardboard visors, all of which the garbage collectors would remove. And the next day, Monday, there would be nothing. Paris would return to its usual appearance, and its relative tranquility, in its streets and on its terraces with their red awnings trimmed with purple. Without much fuss, one more Tour would go into the record book of the City of Light, just as it has done every year since 1903.

For the cyclists, however, it would leave a much deeper impression: happiness, for having got to the finish; fatigue, for the thousands of kilometres they'd ridden; and a sinking feeling for the victory that proved to be beyond them. Yet these mixed emotions could not prevent them looking into the future.

"When we reach the finish of the Tour, on the last moments of that stage, we became aware of just how tired we are, but also there's a great sense of peace that comes over us. After twenty-odd days of fighting with no quarter asked or given, we arrive in Paris and throughout the first kilometres of that day we do nothing but chat with others, regardless of whether they are in the same team or not. There was Dominique Arnaud, team mate and room mate, telling me he wouldn't be riding it anymore; he, a French cyclist, and as tough as old boots, didn't want to fight any more battles on that front.

"But I knew him only too well. He was deceiving himself, saying one thing and thinking the other. I was convinced that the following year, when the time came for the riders to be selected for the Tour, he would do everything he possibly could to get José Miguel to take him. The truth is that lately he was not thinking straight. He'd had a hard time keeping up and working with the team during the difficult moments. I found it funny him saying this was his last Tour, when, deep down, he was thinking just the opposite. Cycling lets you know when the end has come. But in my case, I wasn't even contemplating it. I had always thought that I would quit when I was 32 years old. At that point I was 30 and it seemed far too soon to be thinking of finishing with all this. Time then passed very quickly. I had already turned 34, and I'd thought my time would come even later…"

Miguel Indurain's victory in the Tour of 1991 announced the emergence of a new crop of cyclists. The generation of '60 was ending, and that of '64 was coming to the fore, full of strength and ambition. "Everyone was talking about Alcalá, Bugno, Indurain, Breukink, young men who were elbowing their way through the likes of Fignon, LeMond, Roche, and me. And the Tour was becoming more and more difficult for me, and the only satisfaction to be had from it was being able to help Miguel win another."

Yet, even in the '92 Tour Pedro came very close to a stage win. "Working alongside Miguel, and working for him, I knew that I would enjoy some opportunities, even to do well in the GC. Both LeMond and Fignon, and Roche too, although he was a bit stronger, spoke of their difficulties when they were up against the new men; and the style of racing was also different.

"On the 12th stage, I had the chance to slip into a break which Roche also latched on to. The absence of Miguel in this group meant I didn't have to take any turns on the front. As the finish approached, my chances of victory increased, or at least, that's how it seemed to me. According to the profile in the route map, the stage was ending on a second-category climb, but I found it much more gentle – just a steady climb without any gradients worth mentioning. It could have been a third-category, but even then only by virtue of its length. After several attacks, I had to resort to a bit of play-acting to surprise the others in the group. I got rid of them, except for Jaermann, a Swiss rider; I couldn't shake him off my wheel and he finally beat me in the sprint. This was the Tour in which Chiappucci won in Sestrières. It was an unparalleled stage victory, and he showed exceptional form. Nevertheless, it wasn't enough to unseat Miguel, the overall winner."

Pedro's inclination to take on the Vuelta that year had been different – more ambitious and daring, very much more the Pedro Delgado of his younger days. It gave him the opportunity to redeem himself after the lean year of 1991.

"Riding 'at home' always makes it more enjoyable, and this year, with Miguel off to Italy to try his luck in the Giro, I started as the team's sole leader. The first week of the race developed calmly, and Jesús Montoya appeared on the scene, overjoyed after the Benicasim time trial, and in the lead. Rominger, a specialist in time trials, had ridden a disaster; I was fine. Some days later, we reached the first day in the mountains, at Baqueira Beret. There I got to scratch a few seconds away from the Murcian in the General Classification.

"The next day we moved on to French soil with the cols of Portillon, Peyresourde, Aspin, Tourmalet and Luz Ardiden. I was feeling quite good that day and I decided to attack in the feeding zone, although we didn't manage to surprise Montoya, who'd become my shadow. On the Tourmalet, his team mate, Cubino, took off, and the whole weight of the race fell on my shoulders, and it did so to a degree that I could hardly have anticipated.

"As we set about climbing the Tourmalet, Mínguez, his Director, shouted, 'Montoyita, now you know what I told you!' Montoya nodded, to make it clear to his Director that he had understood.

Shortly after that Mínguez was at it again, 'Montoya, didn't I tell you to get on Perico's wheel!' he exclaimed, with no sense of discretion, leaning half out of the car and banging on the door.

"I was amused by all this and a playful streak rose up in me: I decided to drop back deliberately, little by little, to see how

Montoya would react. It got to the point where we were losing contact with the escape group, and when the gap reached 100 meters, he set off after them. I reacted immediately behind him. Then, as we got back to the front group, I launched a vicious attack. The little group disintegrated even more, but, seeing that I could not drop the yellow jersey, I decided to give up.

"Mínguez returned to the fray again, only this time more intimidatingly. 'I told you – on his wheel!'

"Montoya gave him a look to make him understand that if I dropped back, he was not going to stay with me; after all, he was the leader of the race.

'On his wheel, Montoya! On his wheel. Even if he stops,' the Director ended up ordering the now frightened Jesús.

"As I was feeling mischievous, I decide to provoke him once more. I begin to drop back again, with him behind me. I slow down and he's still following my wheel. I carry on going slowly and he sticks to me. The group we have been riding with is now some distance ahead, but Montoya is obeying his orders; he only has eyes for me. We are now going so slowly, that finally I brake and, as bold as brass, I put my foot on the ground. 'OK, that's it!' I indicate to him with a gesture of my arm. 'Now what?'

"Montoya looks imploringly at Mínguez, begging permission to get away from my wheel, but his Director, didn't even want to acknowledge what he was seeing in front of him. There are some moments of hesitation, until Montoya sets off after the group. Then it's me following him. As I get back to him, I attack again. 'We're behaving just like little children,' I think to myself."

Meanwhile, up ahead, Cubino continued with his adventure, oblivious to everything that was happening in the group behind.

"We held the gap thanks to the relays that Rominger gave me. From the others, there was nothing. Tired of this situation, and in order to provoke a different reaction in our group, I let the Swiss go to see what would happen in the final part of the stage. Not one man went after him, not even Montoya, the race leader. They were all waiting for me to go – yet again. Everybody stayed on my wheel. I was annoyed by this fixation they had with me. They didn't want me to win the Vuelta, but they didn't seem to realise that with that attitude they were not going to win either, except maybe the Swiss.

"Some days later, at Lagos de Covadonga, the Colombian Fabio Rodríguez rode so hard on the climb, that he dropped Rominger, his own team leader. I had no team mates to help me in the mountain, so I kept waiting. This climb has always had some surprise or other in store for me and I didn't want to take the initiative. Fortunately, this time I was feeling good, but still I continued to bide my time until we were through the area of La Huesera. That endless, 500-metre section with its interminable 14-15% gradient always told me how my legs were doing. I attacked shortly after that, at El Mirador de La Reina, and managed to win the stage, as well as pulling a few seconds back on Jesús and Rominger. There were no more summit finishes, so the race was between the three of us, but less than one minute covered us. Favourite was the Swiss, because of his time trialing ability and the 37 kilometres against the clock on the day before the penultimate stage. On the eve of that crucial day, I tried to surprise them in the mountain stage of Ávila, but Montoya's team did a great job and ended up neutralising me. Even so, I had another little scare in store for them on the cobblestoned entry into Ávila, and finished with a three-second reward."

The psychological war between Pedro Delgado and Jesús Montoya and his Director, Javier Mínguez, had not ended on the Tourmalet; it dragged on and on.

"Montoya and Mínguez were still obsessed with me. They wouldn't allow me out of their sight for one moment. So, when we arrived at the feeding station during the Ávila stage I let myself drop back out of the group to pee, with Marino Alonso pushing me. For those moments, my 'shadow' relaxed. I was peeing and we were calmly passing through the feeding zone. When I finished with my needs, I told Marino to forget about the food, and to attack. We warned another team mate, Paco San Roma.

"What happened was that Paco jumped, with us on his wheel, while Montoya was collecting his musette. I do not know what went on behind me, but I'm sure that when Radio-Vuelta broke the news of my escape, Mínguez started hurling abuse in all directions, because, for the second time, there they were, bent double in pursuit. We seemed to be on the point of emulating what had happened in Serranillos in the Vuelta of 1983 with Fignon and Hinault, but in the end, nothing came of it. The whole Amaya team eventually caught up with me – some 25 kilometres later. It did not work out quite as I had anticipated, and at that point I realised that my chances of winning this Vuelta, if I ever had any chances of winning it, had evaporated. In the time trial I had to bow to the evidence, after Rominger's exceptional ride. He unseated Montoya and me at a single stroke, and the race was his. I accepted the third spot in the overall as good, bearing in mind what had happened in those three weeks."

The visit to the podium of a major stage race encouraged him. Although in the Tour it was clear that he was no longer in the running, the Vuelta was a different matter. Here he showed that his prospects, if not as bright as they had once been, were still good enough for him to be somebody to be reckoned with. What's more, his team understood that.

"In 1993, Banesto made me bring forward my preparation so that I would be fit for the Vuelta. I won the Catalan Week, a sign that everything was going well. The bad thing was that in the Tour of Aragón I caught a cold and had to abandon. At the start of the Vuelta, in La Coruña, I felt good. In spite of the mechanical difficulties I had in the prologue, I ended up feeling satisfied. The first leader was Zülle. My problems started when the weather turned for the worse, and the aftermath of the last bout of flu resurfaced. I hoped to get rid of it in Castile. But the weather was still against us, and in the decisive hill-climb of Navacerrada, I knew that I was not breathing well, as I couldn't raise my heart rate, I had no 'spark' at all. Zülle took 2'-36" out of me. All was not lost, and yet...

"The next day at the Castellana circuit, everybody had a scare; there was a fall in which Montoya and Rincón, Amaya's two leaders, were involved, and the peloton was split. The men from ONCE and Clas accelerated and gained more than a minute on them. It was not very sporting behaviour, but in the reverse situation, if it had been Rominger or Zülle who had fallen, the Amayas would have done the same. All 'gifts' are welcome. I wasn't feeling good, nor did I have any strength. The fact is that the outcome of the race was already determined: Rominger and Zülle for the victory, and Cubino filling out the podium. And I, like those little ants... accumulating more losses of time in the key moments of the race. Now I was no more than a witness in the front row of a no-holds-barred fight between the Swiss. It was an edition of the Vuelta in which riders tried to gain from any misfortune that their competitors experienced, so they could grab an advantage for themselves.

"On Stage 19, Zülle fell while coming down La Cobertoria, 50 kilometres from the finish at the top of the Naranco. Rominger immediately sought to profit from this, launching himself like a madman, down a descent that was always dangerous. It enabled him to extend his lead over his compatriot by 44 seconds, so that he would go into the last stage, a 44.6-kilometre individual time trial, with a 1-17 lead overall. His second victory in the Vuelta seemed assured. The end, however, turned out to be heart stopping, with Rominger apparently on the verge of losing the race to Zülle in the time trial. As the time gaps between them were being relayed back, the image of a desolate Fignon when he lost the 1989 Tour in Paris against LeMond came to many people's mind. It came close to happening, but in the end Rominger did manage to hold on to win by 29 seconds. And me? Sixth in the General, and in the time trial I came in fourth. At least I came out of the Vuelta with my morale high."

But in France Pedro was feeling his age.

"My sense of helplessness increased, and there came a moment, in the '93 Tour, when I couldn't even work with Miguel at the critical moments. Simply in order to try, I had to sneak into some escape before the climb and get a bit of a lead, so that I could be at his side when the heat was on. I did that on the Serre Chevalier stage, and I repeated the manoeuvre in the *etapa reina*, which finished at Isola 2000, after going over four brutal cols, including the Izoard and Restefond. I was climbing well enough, but I was limited. It crossed my mind that when Rominger – who was Indurain's most dangerous enemy – escaped, I should be doing something more than just helping to maintain the speed of the chase. Yet even with the little I was doing, I could hardly hang on to the group of favourites! 'If I had gone to pull at the front, I'm sure I would have slowed the chase down, and the escape group would have taken even more time out of us. What a situation to be in!' I thought, laughing at myself.

"I had been over-optimistic on the Serre Chevalier's stage, when I managed to get into a break before facing the most feared climb of that Tour, the Galibier. This is the hardest col I have ever climbed: you approach it via the slopes of the Télégraphe – two passes in one and 35 kilometres of hard climbing – minus four kilometres of gentle descent. Everything went down the drain when Indurain and Rominger reached me and went past like motorbikes, with the Swiss in full cry attacking my team mate. I tried in vain to hang on to them when they reached me, but Rominger had decided to cut loose. After a couple of kilometres of chasing them and seeing them move farther and farther away, I realised that this was going to be mission impossible. I was so disappointed, 'I couldn't even be of any use on my own terrain.' I carried on, saving my strength for another high mountain stage the next day."

Pedro overcame that collapse of mental strength and once more drew upon the experience that had come from all those previous Tours and ended with his head up.

"Making use of my seniority, I took advantage of the flat terrain to get away, to be ahead at the key moment. That day of Isola 2000, I found myself escaping with my old fellow sufferer from earlier seasons, Robert Millar. His mission was to add to his tally of mountain points and hope for a stage win; mine was to stay at the head of the race to be close to Miguel, so at least he'd have a team mate when the battle was raging. Climbing Restefond, the highest pass in France with its altitude of 2,802 meters, the hardest one that day, I let the Scotsman set the pace and waited to see what was happening among the roosters. Clas, Rominger's team, made the climb harder and nearing the top I dropped back to the Indurain group, because he no longer had any team mates left. At least this day I was able to be with him until the final climb. Then, as usual, Miguel would take charge of controlling Chiappucci and Rominger.

"In this Tour of '93, in which Rominger revealed himself, I came to realise that, for me, cycling was coming to an end. During the first week, on the flat stages, I was not firing on all cylinders, and it took a great effort to follow the peloton. When the mountains came, I was a little better, but there were many riders – not half a dozen as before, now 20, or more – who were stronger than me in what had once been my territory. Thinking about it during those days I reached a decision: 'I am 33 years old, I can still do more in cycling, but not in the Tour. I should not have come here, and furthermore, I am occupying a place that someone else in the team could have had. I'll ride one more year, then hang up the bicycle. Competitive cycling is over for me'."

He was not a man for forming grupettos just to get through the stages somehow or another. After almost fifteen years of professional cycling, lest anyone forgets it, Pedro is a man for the supporters. It was their shouts of encouragement at critical times that pushed him upwards and carried him over the finishing line, when his strength was exhausted and his inspiration at rock bottom.

"They gave me so much encouragement in the '93 Tour that I decided to prepare a worthy farewell as a tribute to what the fans had done for me. That was the very best thing for me in my last two years as a rider. The law of nature decreed that I would be leaving professional cycling, but I'd be doing so with my head held high. I ignored some who advised me to retire in 1993, and I decided to face 1994 with renewed hope.

"In Banesto there were some important changes after the absorption of the former Amaya team, with its leaders, Jesús Montoya, Antonio Martín and Mikel Zarrabeitia. The squad was very extensive and it had serious aspirations, despite the setback for the team and for the world of sport, caused by the death of Martín*. With such important acquisitions, the beginning of the season was quieter for me and I put myself into the hands of my life-long trainer, José Luis Pascua. I did not want to bow out

* Not yet 24, Martín was killed in a road accident while out training soon after signing for Banesto. The previous year, riding for Amaya, he had finished 12th overall in the Tour de France, winning the young riders classification.

by just riding the Vuelta; what I really wanted was to be among the leaders, to say goodbye to cycling in the grand manner. The prologue at Valladolid marked out Tony Rominger as the strongest from the very beginning. Soon, in the Sierra Nevada, he would want to show who was the boss of the race. It was him, of course.

"I was not going badly, but perhaps I lacked a little bit of confidence. I recognised the superiority of the Swiss and I told myself that I would have to ration my strength if I wanted to get on the podium. I would need to calculate the moves in my mind to get a positive result in Madrid."

Rominger dominated the race at will, leading from first day to last. There was never a day when he was put on the spot. His compatriot, Alex Zülle, who had made things difficult for him the previous year, was well below his best, as was obvious in the Benidorm time trial. The only team that could stand in Rominger's way in his pursuit of the title was Banesto, where Zarrabeitia and Delgado appeared able to respond to him, while the other Swiss, Zülle, was yo-yo-ing up and down the top end of the General Classification.

"My place on the podium was teetering on the penultimate day. A 53-kilometre time trial with Zülle, a specialist, only 17 seconds behind, made me fear the worst. My home ground, Segovia, again brought me all the luck that was denied to the Swiss, although it was very windy and that benefited him more than me. Naturally enough, I was thoroughly familiar with the route, which included some very technical parts. Knowing which sections to ride flat out, and where to recover, I came out on top. The key was to go out very strongly through the first 15 kilometres and then to apply my effort more steadily. The first time checks were very good, more or less on a par with Alex. Then misfortune began to descend on him: four times he had to change his bike. He told me that in the end he was not comfortable on any of them, and that the last two changes had been unnecessary. I beat him by a minute and one second. My dream of getting on the podium in my farewell Vuelta became a reality."

Joop Zoetemelk won the World Championship at the age of 39; it was his penultimate season as a professional cyclist. The following year his presence in the peloton would have gone completely unnoticed, had it not been for the rainbow jersey that made him stand out. A place on the podium of a great stage race is not within everyone's reach, and anyone who does achieve that can hardly be said to have reached the end of the road. This third place overall caused many to dream… Pedro, on the other hand, knew what he was doing. He had made his decision and did not plan to revisit it: 1994 was his farewell year. But still some insisted.

"I received pressure from within the team to go to the Tour; there were also offers from other teams for me to continue riding, not only during 1995, but also into the '96 season. I do not know if it was right or wrong for me to retire then, but that was the decision I'd made, and I am convinced that you have to face reality, especially if that reality is you, yourself.

"During my career I did not win more than two Vueltas and one Tour; it could have been more. In the end, it was important for me to leave with both me and my fans feeling good about it. I wanted to retire with my head up and my dignity intact. I hope I have succeeded in the latter.

"By the way, do you know why greyhounds run so fast? Because they are perricos delgados."*

* 'perricos delgados' translates literally as 'thin little dogs'

Epilogue

THE BEST MEMORIES

1982

VUELTA A ESPAÑA:

19 stages and 3,456 kms.
Podium: Marino Lejarreta; M. Pollentier; S. A. Nilsson.

"This year I was struck by a dreadful *pájara* on the stage from Zaragoza to Sabiñanigo, where I came to think this sport was just not for me. On top of that, there were days and days working for our team leader, Ángel Arroyo. I finished 30th overall, utterly exhausted."

1983

VUELTA A ESPAÑA:

19 stages and 3,398 kms.
Podium: Bernard Hinault; Marino Lejarreta; Alberto Fernández.

"I finished 15th. Once again in Sabiñanigo, I got to understand the limits of how far you can get if you don't look after your health for just one day. I caught the worst cold in my entire racing career. And there is the memory of Bernard Hinault, attacked on all sides throughout the whole of the Vuelta, and coming back from the dead on that one day in Serranillos, where he won the race."

TOUR DE FRANCE:

22 stages and 3,809 kms.   140 starters and 88 finishers.

Podium: Laurent Fignon; Ángel Arroyo; Peter Winnen.

"I finished 15th overall. I believed that this year I could have won the Tour, if we'd had a little more experience and ambition in the team. It's worth remembering the *pavé* stage on 4 July where we covered what is the final section of Paris-Roubaix, and I blame our inexperience for losing 9-48 to the leader. Also there was Alpe d'Huez where I ended up being 2nd overall at 1-08. Inevitably, I remember coming down the Peyresourde in the position I adopted for the descent. And my stomach problem due to drinking a milk shake that had gone off, which deprived me of a place on the podium."

1984

VUELTA A ESPAÑA:

19 stages and 3,593 kms.
Podium: Eric Caritoux; Alberto Fernández; Raymond Dietzen.

"I finally claimed a leader's jersey on the Rasos de Peguera stage, although I lost it five days later, at the Lagos de Covadonga. I held on to a good chance of winning overall right up to the end, but I think the alliance between Moser and Mascciareli on the road to Segovia, coupled with a fall in the final time trial at Ávila, meant I had to make do with 4th overall."

TOUR DE FRANCE:

23 stages and 4,021 kms.   170 starters and 124 finishers.
Podium: Laurent Fignon; Bernard Hinault; Greg LeMond.

"We found ourselves up against Fignon in his pomp, and he was unbeatable. On Alpe d'Huez I lost all chances in the GC. I reckon I would have been 4th overall and won the KoM prize (both went to Robert Millar), but then I crashed against a concrete parapet while descending Joux Plane and broke my collar bone, so I didn't manage to finish."

1985

VUELTA A ESPAÑA:

19 stages and 3,474 kms.
Podium: Pedro Delgado; Robert Millar; Francisco Rodríguez.

"Nobody gave me the remotest chance of winning; not even me. The win at Los Lagos put me in first place overall, but I lost it the next day – a bad day, which put all thoughts of winning out of my mind. Luckily for me the negligence of Robert Millar's Director allowed me to turn my dream of winning a Grand Tour into a reality – and on the penultimate day riding into Segovia!"

TOUR DE FRANCE:

22 stages and 4,109 kms.   180 starters and 144 finishers.
Podium: Bernard Hinault; Greg LeMond; Stephen Roche.

"The key moment of the race came on the Morcine stage, where Herrera and Hinault escaped by themselves. I stayed back, expecting a reaction from the other favourites and those well up in the GC. On top of that I lost a good deal of time in the time trial. That, together with a cold I caught in the middle of the race, pretty much spoilt my chances. My 6th place overall, plus winning the *etapa reina*, at Luz Ardiden, I reckoned was about right."

1986

VUELTA A ESPAÑA:

21 stages and 3,666 kms
Podium: Álvaro Pino; Robert Millar; Sean Kelly.

"I wanted to repeat my previous victory, but from the middle of the race onwards, in the mountain stages around Segovia, the way I was feeling was not very encouraging. I was more confident for the Sierra Nevada, but a heavy cold in the days before ruined my chances in the race. I finished 10th overall. We rely so much on our health!"

TOUR DE FRANCE:

23 stages and 4,094 kms.   210 starters and 132 finishers.
Podium: Greg LeMond; Bernard Hinault; Urs Zimmerman.

"It seemed that the Tour has a jinx on me. After winning the stage into Pau together with Bernard Hinault, my health was good, my form was good. Now, with this win, I was becoming very hopeful for the podium, but the sudden death of my mother, the day before the Alpe d'Huez stage, broke my spirit and I didn't have the strength to carry on."

1987

VUELTA A ESPAÑA:

22 stages and 3,921 kms.

Podium: Luis Herrera; Raimond Dietzen; Laurent Fignon.

"In the Dutch PDM team there was not a lot of interest in the Vuelta this year. These were the glory years of Colombian cycling. What comes to mind was the day after Andorra, where a group of 10 riders was formed on the ascent of the Puerto del Cantó. Only Fignon seemed able to cope with the fierce pace they were setting. The rest of us watched incredulously at what seemed to be a race among Colombians. On the descents we pitched in a bit, but it was clear that they were going to win the race. For my part I didn't improve on my 4th place through the time bonuses. Nor did it make much difference once Kelly had withdrawn in Ávila because of a saddle boil; his lead simply passed to the second overall, Lucho Herrera."

TOUR DE FRANCE:

25 stages and 4,231 kms.   207 starters and 135 finishers.

Podium: Stephen Roche; Pedro Delgado; Jean François Bernard.

"The 41seconds we lost in the team time trial to Carrera, Roche's team, cost us dear (I lost the Tour by 40 seconds). The best thing of all was getting the lead on Alpe d'Huez, and risking the all or nothing attack 10 kilometres from La Plagne. This year I realised that I didn't need any 'gifts' to be capable of winning this race. The dream I had in 1983 that one day I would win it came back to me as brightly as before."

1988

GIRO D'ITALIA:

21 stages and 3,597 kms.   180 starters and 125 finishers.

Podium: Andrew Hampsten; Erik Breukink; Urs Zimmerman.

"I finished 7th overall. I came to the Giro with a controversy raging about me not taking part in the Vuelta. What was unforgetable was the stage of snow and icy weather on the Gavia. It was certainly the *etapa reina* as far as the cold was concerned. The most positive result was just a second place on the mountainous stage 12."

TOUR DE FRANCE:

22 stages and 3,286 kms. 198 starters and 151 finishers.
Podium: Pedro Delgado; Steven Rooks; Fabio Parra.

"In the Tour I experienced the love/hate relationship that I had throughout my racing career with this race. Physically I was better than my rivals and just when I thought everything was decided on the way to Paris, I received the news of my dope test 'positive'. They made me doubt everything, even myself. Fortunately, everything was cleared up and I was able to vouch for my innocence of something which never needed to have happened."

1989

VUELTA A ESPAÑA:

22 stages and 3,683 kms.
Podium: Pedro Delgado; Fabio Parra; Oscar Vargas.

"My three stage wins in Cerler, in Valdezcaray and in Medina de Campo, made it abundantly clear that nobody was going to take this Vuelta away from me, although Fabio Parra tried non-stop to do so."

TOUR DE FRANCE:

22 stages and 3,285 kms. 198 starters and 138 finishers.
Podium: Greg LeMond; Laurent Fignon; Pedro Delgado.

"This was the year when I felt I was at my strongest ever. The start of the prologue in Luxembourg, possibly the biggest mistake in my entire career, cost me my second Tour without a shadow of a doubt. It took a huge effort to recover, not just the time I'd lost but most especially my morale. Coming out of the Pyrenees I began to dream of the 'yellow'."

1990

VUELTA A ESPAÑA:

22 stages and 3,711 kms.

Podium: Marco Giovannetti; Pedro Delgado; Anselmo Fuerte.

"José Miguel Echávarri was committed to giving Miguel Indurain all the support necessary for him to win the Vuelta. However, slipping into the escape group on the road to Ubrique, where our team mate, Gorospe took the overall lead, was the Italian, Giovannetti. He put paid to our aspirations in Madrid."

TOUR DE FRANCE:

21 stages and 3,504 kms.   198 starters and 156 finishers.

Podium: Greg LeMond; Claudio Chiappucci; Erik Breukink.

"After the Tour of '89 I began this one a little bit unsettled; the last important days didn't go as I wanted, since with Chiappucci's escape on the first day, and the gastroenteritis I picked up in Millau, I could see how LeMond was taking control of another Tour. I am convinced that if my health had held up, the result would have been different from the 4th place I ended up with."

1991

GIRO D'ITALIA:

21 stages and 3,715 kms.   180 starters and 133 finishers.

Podium: Franco Chioccioli; Claudio Chiappucci; Massimiliano Lelli.

"Looking for good memories from the past I come to this Giro, which gave me more pain than glory. There was nothing good about the experience and I had to concentrate on getting ready for the Tour. I finished 15th."

TOUR DE FRANCE:

22 stages and 3,914 kms.   198 starters and 158 finishers.

Podium: Miguel Indurain; Gianni Bugno; Claudio Chiappucci.

"The experience I had in the Giro was repeated here. I was never at ease. Climbing the Tourmalet, I could not follow the pace of the group and my moral went to rock-bottom. As a counter-point to this, Indurain took over the race leadership, and defending it livened me up sufficiently to recover my spirit. I have always thought that an over-load of races and the added tension of having to win got to me that day in the Pyrenees. I finished 9th in Paris."

1992

VUELTA A ESPAÑA:

21 stages and 3,395 kms.
Podium: Tony Rominger; Jesús Montoya; Pedro Delgado.

"I believe this was the most competitive Vuelta I ever rode; the memory of the Luz Ardiden stage, where I would describe as 'hard' the way I was so heavily policed by my opponents to ensure I did not win the race. What stands out most is my stage victory at the Lagos de Covadonga. And a few days later, my surprise attack at the feeding station on the Ávila stage, where I made the Amaya team swallow their food. And not only the riders, but their Director, too, I'm sure."

TOUR DE FRANCE:

21 stages and 3,914 kms.   198 starters and 130 finishers.
Podium: Miguel Indurain; Claudio Chiappucci; Gianni Bugno.

"Although I was not the protagonist, I cannot avoid mentioning the Luxembourg stage, where Indurain gave such a demonstration of power; nor the Sestrieres stage, where Chiappucci, with an escape of more than 200 kilometres in the high mountains, got the win, when we, in Banesto, were expecting to see him weaving from one side of the road to the other. A second place at Saint Gervais was my best effort; I tried some theatricals in the final kilometres to fool Jaerman, but the Swiss didn't take his eyes off me for one moment, and I simply couldn't catch him by surprise. Overall, I finished 6th."

1993

VUELTA A ESPAÑA:

21 stages and 3,605 kms.
Podium: Tony Rominger; Alex Zülle; Laudelino Cubino.

"My memory is of the uphill time trial on Navacerrada which convinced me that I was not going very well this year, and the images of the climb to Los Lagos, where I was dropped and chased the leading group, as they attacked or slowed down, is a faithful picture of 'wanting to but not being able to' in this Vuelta. The best thing was the wonderful behaviour of the fans and the encouragement I received from them throughout the race. And that was in spite my mediocre performance, without any stage wins, or anything heroic. The fact is they were the real driving force in my legs in these final stages of the Vuelta. I finished 6th overall."

TOUR DE FRANCE:

20 stages and 3,714 kms.   180 starters and 136 finishers.
Podium: Miguel Indurain; Tony Rominger; Zenon Jaskula.

"I took the decision in the course of this Tour to quit cycling; my legs were no longer what they had been in the mountains and I didn't want to end up grovelling. I remember the sixth stage being a nightmare: ridden at 50 kms/hour over undulating terrain and 160 kilometres at the back of the peloton and on the point of being dropped during the second half. I did occasionally attack, as on the Serre Chevalier stage and the Isola 2,000 stage, but these were acts of treason – attacking in the valleys so as to scrape into an escape group and to be up ahead, waiting for the arrival of the 'capos'. That way I could be alongside Miguel and able to lend him a hand. My final 9th place overall was a joy to me."

1994

VUELTA A ESPAÑA:

21 stages and 3,631 kms.

Podium: Tony Rominger; Mikel Zarrabeitia; Pedro Delgado.

"I wanted to say goodbye with a good taste in my mouth and I think I managed that. I didn't go in for any flashy display of strength, because Rominger wouldn't allow it, so I concentrated on maintaining the most consistent position I could. Going through my mind was the expression, 'riding with a calculator' to measure out my efforts and fulfil my dreams. At the end, in the time trial at Segovia, I was able to hold on to my podium position, ahead of a not very inspired Zulle. The batteries held out."

1995

'Hi, there, Pedro. My name is Luis Miguel de Dios, and I'm Deputy Director of Sport at Spanish Television. How are you, today?

'I'm fine; I've had an easy day, trying to reserve my strength for tomorrow's stage; it's a mountain stage on Boi Taüll. It'll be hard, and decisive.'

'Is it true that you're leaving cycling? You're hanging up the bike?'

'Yes.'

'The fans are going to miss you. Have you thought about what you're going to do?'

'I've no idea. Right now what I want to do is switch off. Do other things.'

'Do you have a business?'

'No. At the moment what I want is to get away from all the demands and the stress of these years. But I have nothing in mind.'

'And it wouldn't appeal to you to commentate on races, like

Ángel Nieto does for the motor bikes? At TVE we're looking for someone like you to get involved in the many cycling broadcasts we put out. The truth is that having you with us would be ideal. You'd be perfect for us.'

We stepped out of the lift where we were having this conversation; it was going on usually long and this didn't seem the most appropriate place to continue it. The offer was as unexpected as it was attractive, but I left it for the moment. The race had priority, and there would be time later to talk about it.

This occurred in the hotel Hesperia Sant Joan, after the third stage of the Volta a Catalunya in 1994, which finished in Barcelona. In those days the race took place in September, and was practically the last international event in the road racing calendar*. It was a meeting that was to change my life.

The proposal from Televisión Española seemed very interesting to me, and I was due to appear on the daily programme, *El Día Después* [The Day After]. A few days later I met the people in charge of sport at TVE and we reached an agreement for 1995. Ever since then I have been talking about the major cycling races for RTVE

Collaborating with the media was not a complete unknown for me, because, since 1988, I had been doing it with Cadena SER, the radio channel with the largest number of listeners in Spain. I have continued to do that throughout these years.

* Pedro finished second the following day on Boi Taüll, behind Chiappucci, and third overall four days later in Barcelona.